This is the Key of the Kingdom:
   in that Kingdom there is a City
   in that City there is a Town
   in that Town there is a Street
   in that Street there is a Lane
   in that Lane there is a Yard
   in that Yard there is a House
   in that House there is a Room
   in that Room there is a Bed
   on that Bed there is a Basket
In that Basket there are some Flowers:

   Flowers in a Basket
   Basket on the Bed
   Bed in the Room
   Room in the House
   House in the Yard
   Yard in the Lane
   Lane in the Street
   Street in the Town
   Town in the City
   City in the Kingdom:
Of the Kingdom this is the Key

A seventeenth-century nursery rhyme

Humphrey Carver

Compassionate Landscape

UNIVERSITY OF TORONTO PRESS

TORONTO AND BUFFALO

© University of Toronto Press 1975
Toronto and Buffalo
Printed in Canada

Library of Congress Cataloging in Publication Data

Carver, Humphrey.
    Compassionate landscape.

    Includes index.
    I. Carver, Humphrey. I. Title.
    HT166.C32A33   712'.092'4 [B]   75-22280
    ISBN 0-8020-2186-7
    ISBN 0-8020-6269-5 pbk.

This book has been published with the assistance of grants
from the Canada Council and the Ontario Arts Council.

To Anne with love
and to
Debby & Jenny
Peter & Penny
S and K

Perceptions

In waking moments, even before my eyes are open, I hear sounds that remind me where I am, who I am, and where I came from. That undertone of sound is the morning traffic moving obediently along the streets of the city. The rising and retreating hum of a plane reminds me that a journey has to be arranged to a distant part of Canada. The place is astir; things are to be done, some compelling and awkward situations to be met, some happy events to be contemplated with lingering pleasure. Within the familiar shapes and shadows of my own room, my own house, I am aware of the exterior environment that looms over me and demands that I respond.

When through my open window I first hear the voice of the crow in the tops of the elms, I know that it is spring, and this transports me to two other places. The first is a Sunday morning in 1937, to the place where I lived near the shore of Lake Ontario. The winter's over and the sun brings a delicious trickle of clear water out of the snow patches and down the stream into the lake. I have come to live in Canada. I have a wife and child. This is the place I have chosen.

The other layer of memory is many years further away. I'm looking across an English Cotswold valley, the rooks are calling to one another with their sad, nostalgic voices as I gaze across the woods to the hillside beyond. It's one of those first stirring childhood moments of self-realization. Here I am, with all the world before me: I wonder where I'm going to go and what I'm going to do.

For each of us, the environment we live in is a very private affair. We are surrounded by sights and sounds that evoke memories and stir responses. No one else receives quite the same impressions and messages. No one else in the whole world could know what sequences of recollection are stimulated. We are each very much alone in the landscape, in our private environment.

And yet there is also a shared environment . . .

Collectively, people are aware of the environment in which we live, perceiving that we ourselves and the landscape around us are all part of the created universe. Collectively, we leave our mark upon the landscape, adapting it to our lives and then reacting to what we have done to it, with pleasure or with horror.

During my allotted three score years and ten, the public perception of the created and adapted landscape has changed. I look back and see how I have taken part in this change. At first there was compassion for those who suffered most from the damage done to the landscape by the dirty and destructive growth of industry. Stirred by that strong nineteenth-century conscience and sense of guilt, society acknowledged its responsibility and sought to rescue the victims of slums and poverty. Then there was a realization that industry was simply an extension of our own hands and minds and that, as we are ourselves part of the created universe, so what we create can have the same beauty as the landscape itself. In our creative hands and minds the steel and glass of cities can be made beautiful, the infinite power and resources of the physical world around us can be made even more glorious, by us collectively.

But in the latter part of my time, it has been further perceived that the power and the resources of the earth are not, in fact, infinite, and that the impact we collectively make upon our own environment threatens the very continuity in the chain of life of which we are a part.

I think these have been the principal experiences of my generation, as perceptions of the human environment have changed and deepened. Though my own participation in these changes is entirely insignificant, it may be of some interest to catch a glimpse of this great social reorientation, in its impact on the lives of ordinary people caught up in these events.

Contents

Part One

*is about growing up in England
and discovering the differences
between the beautiful and the ugly
between being rich and being poor.*

*It's about coming to Canada
and becoming part of the scene.*

*It's about living through the depression
and finding a small utopia
and about getting to know
the wartime generation.*

*And it's about sharing in the great expectations
of what Canada might be after the war
and about my own disaster.*

THE
FOUNTAIN
INN

THE RAILWAY
MISSION

SLATE
GAULT

STONE & BRICK
TILE

RED BR. CHS
TIMBER
BRICK

SLATE
GAULT

SHAFTESBURY

HUMPHREY CARVER
1949

1
Two Landscapes

My brothers and I used to bicycle out to the Clent Hills. From the highest point, above the little church of St Kenelm, the boy saint after whom one of my brothers is named, we could survey the whole surrounding landscape. Behind us lay the big city and on the distant western horizon the Welsh hills. But it was what we saw close below us, to the north and to the south, that demanded attention. To the south we were looking over the Forest of Arden, a green countryside of little villages with musical Shakespearean names like Bellbroughton, Hampton Lovell, Ladies Ashton, and Henley in Arden; a little further away are Flyford Flavell, Naunton Beauchamp, and so on down to Winchcombe and Stow-on-the-Wold. This was ancient pastoral England where we so often walked along the field paths and through the village streets as if it were all one big garden, with its green country-house parks and cattle nibbling under the chestnut trees. It was a kind of idealized landscape, settled and occupied by man and beast and trees and flowers in perfect ecological balance. Everyone had his place in the system: the tennis-playing families in the big houses, the vicar having tea in his study, and the respectful cottage dwellers trimming the hedges and smelling of the soil. It had been like this for centuries—gentle, static, and lyrically beautiful.

But looking north from the top of Clent, in the opposite direction, we were peering into the smoke-filled basin of the Black Country, a shadowy grey landscape under a pall of smoke, with tall chimneys, the slag-heaps of coal mines like dark pyramids, brutal rows of houses, all silhouetted against the foggy background. It was like a place in a nightmare, smelling of coal dust, horse shit, and human sweat—a city cursed like a prison you couldn't escape from. The Black Country people lived on top of the coal pits, in the shadow of the slag-heaps. The colour was indeed black. Nowadays the pollution of the air and the water is a subtle thing you can hardly see, though you are told it exists. But the pollution of the English industrial city of sixty years ago, when I was last on the top of Clent, was a very different matter. Coal was everywhere: used for cooking and heating and driving every kind of machine. Coal enveloped you–black, smutty, grimy, smoky, and stinky when it burns. It was on your hands, in your nostrils, all over every building, and you had to wear a hat to prevent it settling on your hair and going down your neck. The colour of cities was generally black. Then there was the horse shit. Every vehicle was pulled by a horse, trucks usually by two horses and buses by three. They were well fed and had good digestions; as they trotted along the streets and especially whenever they stopped at a street intersection, they added something to the mess which found its way on to your boots and your clothes and into everyone's houses. The working man, with sweat exuding into the grime upon his body and the dirt upon his clothes, suffered the humiliation of being not only poor but smelly.

What we saw from the top of Clent was unforgettable: a dream and a nightmare. Looking out over the green meadows and villages on one side and over the black smoke-pit in the other direction, one could only feel that civilization had somehow taken a wrong turning. English society was separated in two environments. At that time in my life it certainly didn't occur to me that human behaviour is essentially a paradox and that the responses to these two environments might be just the opposite to what one might at first expect. I mean that the perfect ecological stability of the green landscape to the south of Clent might contain the seeds of its own decadence and the very violence of the Black Country landscape might be the stimulus that gives vigour to the growth of a new society. The fact is, of course, that the social and economic institutions that created the English village-and-country-house landscape which I looked at sixty years ago no longer exist. And neither do the special conditions of the industrial revolution that created the nightmare of the Black Country. The environments of civilization keep on changing, sometimes for the better and sometimes for the worse.

Our family didn't live on the black side of Clent. We lived on a suburban street in a comfortable, but incredibly ugly, gabled, redbrick house built by A.E. Goodman, Builder, who lived next door in an exactly identical house except that everything was the other way round–which made one think of *Alice through the Looking Glass*. It was a house that also appears, with minor variations, in the inner suburbs of Toronto, Hamilton, and Ottawa, and in the corresponding parts of Melbourne and Sydney. Wherever it is to be seen around the world, the late-Victorian English builder's house has now become an inner-suburbs rooming house, with little prospect of surviving urban renewal.

The street we lived on was pleasantly nondescript, with an asphalt sidewalk and gas lamps every hundred yards or so. The lamplighter came along every evening at dusk with a long pole which he inserted into the lamp and it came alight with a burp; at our nursery window I was held up to wave at him, and Elizabeth, who held me and always seemed to know just when he was coming, waved prettily too and eventually married Mr Parker, one of four brothers all of them lamplighters. Apart from romantic childhood associations of this kind there was nothing very remarkable about the environment of Harborne such as to leave a lasting impact on one's life. There were, however, two very large and beautiful gardens that belonged to families more affluent than us, though when the 1921 depression hit them their riches proved to be more fragile than we had expected. Playing games between the rows of lime trees, hiding under the crabs so as to taste the bitter fruit on the ground, learning that it is more difficult and more destructive to escape through a beech hedge than a cedar hedge, and finding that there is something evil about the earth under the laurels–all this gave me a love for gardens and for what I afterwards came to know as landscape architecture, to me the most enjoyable and most civilized form of artistic expression.

In the ordinary course of events the children who lived in the green suburbs would never meet the children who lived in the black parts of the city. But some of us were not unaware of one another, as I will explain.

My father did not make a great success in business and was a man of quite modest income, yet he managed to send all four sons to the boarding school made famous by Thomas Arnold, by *Tom Brown's Schooldays,* and by the legendary hero whose memorial is on the wall of the headmaster's garden, known as 'The Doctor's Wall'; the inscription records that it was William Webb Ellis who first took the ball in his hands and ran down the field with it, 'thus originating the distinctive feature of the Rugby game'. Life at Rugby was Christian, conscientious, and austere. Each day started with a backward plunge into a round tub of ice-cold water called a 'tosh'. By 7.15, without breakfast, we were in the school chapel for a hymn, a psalm, and some prayers, followed immediately by a period in school, the chill of the classroom and the grit on the desks sometimes making it necessary to write with gloves on, to protect chilblained hands.

I went to Rugby in 1917 and many of the older boys who left school that year were dead on a French battlefield within a few months. My oldest brother Christian was just seventeen when he went into the battle and he had already spent nearly three years of his short life under fire. In February that year Christian wrote many letters to the second brother in my family who was getting ready to follow him and was 'head of the house' when I arrived at Rugby.

MY DEAR MAURICE, Many thanks for your letter. I like 'small beer chronicles', however trivial. You will be glad to hear that the grand obstacle Hun Hunt is now open. There is no charge for entry. At present we are sitting looking dubiously at the first fence. It's a devilish stiff one, old lad, devilish stiff. And lots more like it to follow. However it's all in a lifetime–and if one takes a nasty toss, there is always the satisfaction of knowing that one couldn't do it in a better cause. And if a man gives his life for a definite object, it is not natural to suppose that the object will cease to interest him, he must 'carry on' in some form or other. Otherwise death, the most natural thing in life, would be unnatural. We pass into life from the unknown, we pass out of life to the unkown, but the 'wheel swerves not a hair', there can surely be no stopping. I am reading *Europe Unbound* by L. March-Phillipps. He is very insistent that we are fighting for Liberty, though it is so natural, so fundamental in us that we cannot always realise it. And it is so, I suppose. I always feel that I am fighting for England, English fields, lanes, trees, English atmospheres, and good days in England–and all that is synonymous for Liberty. One of our battery commanders was very badly wounded to-day, reconnoitring the place we are moving into, hence these thoughts. A rotten job, for he leaves (and I fear he must) a wife and 2 kiddies. En avant!–up to the Breach, for Merrie England!   CHRISTIAN

Six months later, in the height of the summer, Christian was dead. Our housemaster at Rugby, G.F. Bradby, sent Maurice and me home with a letter to my mother knowing 'how great a comfort they will be to you and you to them'. Maurice was to come back the next Monday because 'there are things for him to do and it will be good for him to do them'. And Bradby's letter concluded:

I think Christian was one of the bravest people there ever was, because, being so introspective, he was always conscious of the danger and the shrinking of the flesh, and yet was able not to mind . . . there are times, like this, when I feel as if the burden of this war were almost too heavy to bear, as, one by one, the boys

who have meant most to me pass to the other side, and leave this side a blank.
And yet I know that my own burden is nothing compared to yours, for, though
I have loved them all, they were not my children.

Maurice was soon in France, was wounded, and survived the battle
to become an educational missionary in India; he has now lived and
worked for many years in black Africa. His successor as head of the
house at Rugby was Evelyn Montague, the oldest of a remarkable family
of long-distance runners; they were the sons of C.E. Montague, the
famous editor of the *Manchester Guardian,* who wrote the greatest of all
mountaineering stories ('Action') about man's inexplicable power to
exceed his human capacities in a moment of crisis. After Evelyn Montague was H.L. Parker, who became Lord Chief Justice of England. It
was that kind of school.

There was something about the environment of Rugby that raised
questions of social justice and impelled personal participation. I could
hardly avoid knowing about the Rugby clubs, the school missions aimed
to make life a bit more interesting for the boys in the grimy parts of
Birmingham and in the London slums of Notting Hill. The clubs also
had summer camps and, in my school holidays, I went there and got to
know and respect the boys who lived in an environment very different
from my own. The camp for Notting Hill boys was at Romney on the
south coast of England; here we slept on the beach, scooping out a hole
in the pebbles to make a kind of nest, lined with a straw mattress. We
lay awake side by side, watching the lights of ships going up and down
the English Channel. The Birmingham boy's camp was at Arley on the
grassy banks of the River Severn, into which flow all the little streams
that wind through the meadows and villages of that pastoral countryside
south of the Clent hill-top. In a big field by the river we played games
and sang songs after supper, and some of the coal dust on the boys' pale
scrawny bodies was washed down the Severn.

Because it was expected of me and because I passed the necessary
examinations to gain entry to a college, I went to Oxford, to Corpus
Christi College, where a pelican stands on the top of a high sundial in
the middle of the quadrangle. Oxford is, for me, a rather wistful and
haunting place, most beautiful at night when the spires are silhouetted
against the sky and the solemn bells echo in the narrow streets. In
academic Oxford I never connected with or discovered anything that I
was any good at or that seemed to be relevant to my particular kind of
inquisitiveness. But I did have two wonderful benefits. I threw myself

into every active sport I could find, and my overgrown 6 feet and 5 inches of body gained the exultant health of an athlete, a reserve on which I have drawn for the rest of my life. And, even more valuable, night after night, when the other college lights had been extinguished, I explored the universe with two friends, in a continuous searching dialectic. One was Nevill Willmer who as a schoolboy had been a 'bug collector' or entomologist and who became a Cambridge professor of histology and an authority on the physiology of cells. The other friend was Patrick Rolleston; he was an engineering student, though you wouldn't have known it from his room in college which had an enormous bookshelf of English literature, his most treasured possessions being the romantic poetry of James Elroy Flecker, including some first editions. Patrick was the son of a minor Irish poet, and his mother was a tall and rather distant lady of Preraphaelite quality. Patrick possessed most of the talents that a man could desire: he was intellectual, good-looking, with a talent for an exhilarating blend of talk and laughter and teasing and nonsense and romance that made a special sort of happiness around him. Women found him irresistible. Since I did not possess all these talents, Patrick helped me in many ways as our close friendship continued long after those first night-time explorations; for the next twenty-five years we travelled much the same road and knew many of the same people, and I wish he were here now to share these recollections with me.

Eventually I did discover the connection, in spite of the remoteness, wistfulness, and irrelevance of Oxford. (I remember my brother Francis telling me that, when he was at Oxford, he would often go and have a ham sandwich at the railway station instead of dining in hall, in order to restore his connection with the real world.) One afternoon I was browsing in one of Oxford's many small libraries and, in the section called Social Welfare where the boxes of pamphlets have a musty smell because they don't often see the light of day, I came across the story of Canon Barnett and his wife Dame Henrietta Barnett. They lived in Bethnal Green, a black part of London, and they had conceived the idea of taking people out of the black landscape and putting them in the green part just beyond the high point of London, Hampstead Heath. I'm afraid the people of Bethnal Green never got to Hampstead Garden Suburb because the economics of building did not make this possible. But Hampstead, together with the garden cities of Letchworth and Welwyn, set a model which changed the face of England and had an extraordinary influence upon the human environment throughout the world. Sir Raymond Unwin, the architect and planner of Hampstead Garden Suburb, together with Thomas Adams, at that time the secretary of the Garden Cities Association, are the progenitors of ideas that extended far beyond London and beyond England. Both of them left their mark upon the cities of the United States and of Canada, and both of them I came to know at a much later stage in my life.

So this was the connection. I never hoped to become an architect as a designer of building construction; I felt that I understood people and the landscape better than I could ever understand mathematics and mechanics. But this was the connection. I had to go to London. I had to find out about architecture.

The move to London took me at first to Bermondsey, not very far from Bethnal Green, because I had come to know the Oxford and Bermondsey Club, sometimes taking a boatload of small boys on the river at Oxford. (The flat-bottomed Thames punt, propelled by pushing on a pole from its stern, was designed so that two couples can stretch out comfortably on its cushions after a large picnic lunch on a lazy summer afternoon. In that situation it is the most stable craft imaginable. But fill a punt with a dozen excited London kids who have never before seen frogs, bull-rushes, or ladies and gents making love, and the instability is hair-raising.) Fortunately my older brother Maurice was just then in transition between a mission to India and a move to Africa, so we went together to live in Bermondsey, a grimy part of south London behind the docks. We had undertaken to spend our evenings working at the boys' club and so, as part-time social workers, we were allowed to live in a public housing project, on the top floor of a six-storey building called Chaucer House. There was an outside iron staircase with many cats to be tripped over late at night.

My most memorable experience of this time in Bermondsey was taking groups of boys for runs through the night-time streets of London, often in the black rain or London fog. With a little group of witty, wicked Cockney boys at my heels, we would scamper along the sidewalks, find our way through the dark narrow alleys behind the docks and, occasionally, do the whole circuit over Tower Bridge and back over London Bridge. This is a very special, cinematic way of getting to know a city; to run through the night-time streets has some of the sensations of a dream fantasy in which one floats through the air.

That was the way I came to London. I started in the black part and, for a short time, lived in the green part of Hampstead beyond the top of the hill. But as I became more deeply absorbed in architecture it was necessary to live closer to my drawing board, both figuratively and geographically, and for most of the next five years I lived near the King's Road, Chelsea.

2
Growing out of London

To be alive and well and young and living in London is wonderful. And through the latter part of the 1920s I was all of these things, and I came to think of myself as a Londoner rather than a Midlander.

The mark of a real Londoner was to get on and off a moving bus with some nonchalance and style, like the style of an Englishman with a cricket bat or an American catching a baseball. You had to judge distance and speed nicely, anticipate your footsteps, and swing around the brass pole at the back of the bus. It looked best if you were wearing a bowler hat and carried a tightly rolled brolly hooked over the left forearm. But I didn't have these things because I was a student in flannel bags and sometimes an old 'pork pie' hat. In the mornings I would get on a Number 19 bus on King's Road, Chelsea. It goes up Sloane Street, along Piccadilly, and then turns up Shaftesbury Avenue into the heartland of London's West End theatres. Up the narrow streets to the left you get a glimpse into Soho, the district of Italian restaurants, music, and entertainment. If you love the theatre this is the centre of the universe. Here was Bertie Meyer the theatre manager whose daughter Peggy is married to my brother Francis. Down there is the theatre where my childhood friend Alan Napier played his first West End role in Noel Coward's 'Bittersweet'. Here I laughed with Jack Hulbert and his funny-footed brother Claude. Up and down Shaftesbury Avenue are the theatres where I paid three bob for a seat in the pit, to see the plays of Shaw and Galsworthy, to marvel at Jessie Mathews and Sir Gerald du Maurier and, as the Number 19 bus rounds the corner into the Charing Cross Road, here is where 'No, No, Nanette' was first running in 1928. Past Foyle's bookshop, across Oxford Street, get off the bus and cross the road and you emerge into Bedford Square, the nearest corner of Bloomsbury. This is where I spent five glorious years as a student of architecture.

For hundreds of architects around the world, the AA is not Alcoholics Anonymous or the Automobile Association but the Architectural Association's School of Architecture in Bedford Square, London. It has survived for three-quarters of a century as an educational institution that is not part of a university but is run by architects and by the students themselves in a highly participatory and democratic way. It is both a school and a club, and for many who come to London from other parts of Europe, from Africa, Australia, Canada, and the United States, it is a kind of home from home, an international centre of discussion about the environmental arts in all parts of the world.

Bedford Square is a stone's throw from the British Museum and is part of Bloomsbury, the scene of so much of the intellectual life of London. Its design is simple and beautiful: the four-storey terraces of houses form a solid façade facing on to the circular garden in the middle of the square. The windows are tall, there are fanlights over the handsome doors, and inside there are Adam details in ceilings and fireplaces. The AA occupies three houses on the west side of the square with a four-storey studio block on the narrow service street behind. In the 1920s Margot Asquith lived in one of the houses on the south side, and elsewhere there were the offices of publishers, architects, and the Ecclesiastical Commissioners. Through nearly two centuries the Square has changed its uses gracefully as a model of how a city can respond to social and economic changes without suffering the destructions of urban renewal.

I first went to the AA with 'Deaf Harry', a cousin of my mother's and the only family connection who was an architect. Culturally speaking, Harry Creswell belonged to the Arts and Crafts period, a generation of architects who grew up under the influence of William Morris and Ruskin's *Seven Lamps of Architecture*. Architecture was a very personal process of designing on a drawing board and then directing a builder in putting the pieces together; if some craftsmanship in carved wood, hammered iron, or stained glass could be added to the building, so much the better. Deaf Harry designed some comfortable houses and had also bridged the gap into industrial architecture, having built a factory for an electrical firm in Rugby, where I first met him. He had been only moderately successful in his profession; but this didn't matter because he had an uproarious sense of humour as a story-teller and a writer; he looked out from behind the barrier of his deafness and found the world delightful and funny. He was a regular contributor to *Punch* and the author of

light-comedy novels written around a character named Thomas; in his
enjoyment and mockery of English life there was perhaps a bit of An-
thony Trollope and a touch of P.G. Wodehouse, mixed with Harry's
special brand of waggish fun. Perhaps his principal contribution to literature and to architecture was a book called *The Honeywood File* which
recounted the pitfalls and unexpected disasters and comedies that happen in the process of building a house.

I remember that when I first went through the front door of the AA
on Bedford Square with Deaf Harry there was a delicious aroma, a kind
of musky smell that may have been fresh paint or wax on the black and
white tiled floors. It was an enchanting and sensual little excitement that
never ceased to stir me every time I came into the building for the next
five years. I fell in love with the place. The AA was a kind of elysium.
We were a happy company of people there because we had all discovered
something in which we were supremely interested; and so, I think, we
also became immensely interested in one another. A school of architecture has one very remarkable characteristic. Each group of twenty-five
or thirty people who enter at the beginning of an academic year continue
to work side by side in a drafting room or 'studio' for several years,
revealing themselves to one another through what they create on their
drawing boards. There is no concealment possible. Everyone can walk
around and see each person's ideas and designs taking shape and, at the
conclusion of each design project, the finished work is put up on a wall
to be appraised and publicly criticized. The plagiarist is exposed; there
is no protection for anyone who labours greatly to bring forth a solemn
bathos; a person becomes known for his flashes of inspiration at the
outset and his inability to bring these early perceptions to fruition. There
is respect for those who are consistently original and tough and honest
in their understanding of design problems.

Our first two years in the school were largely devoted to the old-
fashioned practice of learning the 'classic orders' of architecture as these
had first appeared in the Greek Doric and Ionic temples upon the
Acropolis in Athens in the fifth century BC and in their later and more
vulgarized form in ancient Rome. The classic orders had been the basic
grammar of architects throughout the Renaissance in Western Europe,
in eighteenth century England, and in colonial America; and after the
heresies of the Gothic Revival, the classic orders were again the vocabulary of the 'beaux arts' tradition of architectural education. For more
than two thousand years the Doric, the Ionic, and the Corinthian orders
of architecture had been the 'lingua franca' of all educated men. So there,

in our corner of Bloomsbury, in 1925, we went to the library to borrow the plates drawn by Cockerell and the other antiquaries of Greece and Rome and on large sheets of Whatman paper we composed Piranesi-like fantasies, depicting classical temples, fragments of columns, and entablatures as if they were illuminated in the bright sunlight of Athens or Rome. We learned all the precise geometry that enabled us to draw the exact shape of a shadow cast by the sun at 45 degrees, in mid-afternoon or mid-morning–the shadow of an Ionic volute upon the curved surface of the column below, or the shadow of the Doric cornice upon the triglyphs; and we learned that the edge of a shadow is darker than its interior which holds reflected light from opposing surfaces of stone. On the Acropolis at Athens there are three different versions of the Ionic, and I could show you still the differences between the bold and simple form that appears in the Propylea entrance to the Acropolis, the pure lyric quality in the little temple of Nike Apteros, and the more florid and over decorated form of the Ionic capitals on the Erechtheum. All these are made of the white Pentelic marble, and it is the shades and shadows and highlights on the sculptured surfaces that make their shapes comprehensible in their convexity and their concavity. For more than two thousand years stone masons have reproduced these exact shapes with their tools, have felt them with their fingers, and sensed them with their eyes. If you knew this language you could look at works of architecture in Rome and in Paris, in Christopher Wren's London and in colonial America, and you could understand how the architects of each period had played upon these themes, with their own touches of innocence, of austerity, or of the baroque.

We were the last generation of architectural students to be raised on this highly disciplined knowledge of the classic orders, that great cultural heritage, and it is true that those of us who developed a wider interest in the environment of life have had little opportunity to apply this learning. Nowadays nobody expects an architect to be able to draw, from memory, the leaves and stalks of the acanthus on the Corinthian capital. The fact is, of course, that this was a rigorous training of our perceptive capacities, which enabled us to look at the whole physical world around us, with an eye for its whole form and its infinite detail. We learned to look at the shapes and shadows of everything around us and this extended into a love for the English landscape that many of us shared. Often on Friday nights, three or four of us together would take a train out into the country and we would walk for two whole days over the downs, the open grassland hills south and west of London, following the

Roman roads and climbing up to the high points where there are remains of ancient British settlements. We always took in our pockets the one-inch-to-a-mile Ordnance Survey maps, with contours drawn so that you could see the shape of the land as clearly as you could draw the shape of an Ionic volute and the shadows cast upon it. We discovered for ourselves, as if no one had ever been there before, the little village churches in the valleys, particularly those with the bold shapes and deep carvings of the early Normans.

While I was at the AA the great cultural revolution in architecture and design was beginning to take place, moving towards the forms of urban building which are now recognized all over the world as the contemporary architecture of steel and glass and concrete. Intuitively we were aware of and were part of this change, though its impact didn't become clear until the decade of the 1930s. In my second year as an architectural student, at the Easter break, I went to Paris and in a bookstore near the Madeleine discovered a paperback entitled *Vers une architecture* by le Corbusier. It had been published the year before and I had never heard the author's name. I took the book back to my hotel room and couldn't go out again until I had been right through it. It was an electrifying intellectual experience which immediately changed my whole way of looking at the world around me, at buildings old and new.

For I now saw architecture as the sculptural environment of human life, in the sunlight and in the dark of night. It was a glimpse of a world in which the social purposes of life itself would direct the shape and form of cities, moulding the materials of the earth into a new kind of environment. Like all living creatures, man seeks light and space and freedom. The sunlight on the white plastic surfaces of modern architecture and the deep shadows in the sculptured spaces could express the freedom and flexibility of a new kind of society; the whole environment of the green landscape, the sweep of the hills, and the surface of the ocean were encompassed in this vision which had the pristine impact of the Greek Doric and the great mediaeval cathedrals when their walls were still white.

But in this decade following the First World War when I was a student, all the popular and successful architects were still designing elaborate compositions in the traditional materials of brick and stone, playing eclectic variations on the classic orders and other stylistic ornaments, and being acclaimed for their brilliant displays of virtuosity. No one could do this better than Sir Edwin Lutyens who could design a bank, a country house, or the heart of imperial Delhi, festooned with fat classic forms, baroque pediments, and fruity swags of Renaissance detail. Those who could emulate him most successfully were also raised to the rank of Royal Academician. And the 'pièce de résistance' of the period was Ostberg's design for the Stockholm Town Hall which, with its romantic Byzantine touches, introduced Sweden into the big league of the arts. (This building so captivated British architects that during the next few years architectural competitions were generally won by architects who could do 'amusing' variations on its theme.) But in the decade after the Great War in which all the vanities and imperialisms of the nineteenth century had collapsed, this sort of thing began to seem very irrelevant and there was a desperate search, not only for new economic and social ideals, but for new ways of expressing the true nature of industrial society. This was what le Corbusier was able to do, and during the very years that I was a student at the AA, Walter Gropius was developing the Bauhaus at Dessau–the birthplace of the principal new tradition in architecture that eventually flowered in the work of Gropius and Mies van der Rohe in the United States and of the Parkin firm in Canada. In the annals of contemporary art and culture there is, I suppose, no event that had more historic consequences than the closing of the Bauhaus by the Nazis in 1933 and the dispersion of its brilliant company into the western world. The official architecture of Nazi Germany was in the imperial Greek and Roman style.

Though the AA of my time and the creation of the Bauhaus were exactly simultaneous, yet, as far as I am aware, no direct communication took place at that time. But the two were obviously akin in philosophy, and my generation of graduates from the AA certainly fulfilled Gropius's view that there should be a true unity of the arts. Comparatively few of my immediate friends became architects, but they include designers of furniture and textiles, teachers and writers, planners and archaeologists, and at least two distinguished art directors in the cinema. Many of them were people of great artistic talent. There was Eden Minns whose drawings seemed to have the magic of a Leonardo. He should have left his mark on history, but somehow this didn't happen. He had an ineffable charm, a languid wit, a kind of bravura in the wearing of unorthodox clothes, a liking for large handsome dogs, and a faculty for conveniently losing his way. He is also remembered because he marshalled the barrel-organs. In the first two years of our course we were given lectures on drains and plumbing and things like that by a middle-aged architect who had become tired of life and succeeded in making the subject a real bore.

Some relief was provided when, now and then, an Italian with a hurdy-gurdy would come into the narrow resonant street behind the studio block and drown out the lecturer's tedious voice. He would put his head out of the window and shout at the barrel-organist to go away. On one occasion Eden Minns combed the streets of Soho and the West End, rounding up all the barrel-organists he could find and contracting with them to move in at fifteen-minute intervals.

There was also Alexander Girard who had grown up in Florence amongst all the rich Medici colour of the Renaissance. His drawing board seemed to exude a fabulous and exotic torrent of colour, a gift that he took with him when he went to live in the United States where he added a Mexican riot of colour to his palette. As a designer and collector of beautiful things, Alexander Girard won renown.

But I think it would be fair to say that the most gifted amongst my friends found their places as educators and propagandists in developing the new renaissance of the environmental arts, rather than as architects. Three of them certainly must have a place in any cultural history of the period: Jim Richards, Edward (Bobby) Carter, and Jacqueline Tyrwhitt. As editor of that most intelligent and sophisticated magazine, the *Architectural Review*, Jim Richards became, for his generation, the principal interpreter and advocate of the new architecture and urban design. He has also been the architectural correspondent of *The Times*, Slade Professor of Fine Art at Oxford, and in much demand as a radio commentator and speaker throughout the English-speaking world. He is now 'Sir James'.

What Bobby Carter has given to the cultural evolution of his generation is less easy to define. For several years we shared 'digs' on Oakley Street, Chelsea, just round the corner from the King's Road, Chelsea. The King's Road is like a river of life, with its string of small restaurants, antique shops, and small picture galleries, its sidewalks always full of young people, the non-affluent literary people, and a quota of drop-outs. At the other end of Oakley Street is the Chelsea Embankment where one can share one's most private reflections with the dark, silent waters of the Thames. Not long after we left the AA, Bobby was appointed librarian of the Royal Institute of British Architects and editor of the Institute's journal. After the war, in 1945, he moved to Paris, to be on Julian Huxley's UNESCO staff and then, in the course of time, he was back in Bedford Square as the chief officer of the AA. Each of these posts placed him at the vortex of the flow of ideas and of people in the world of architecture and planning. As men of intellect and talent were forced out of Germany and Central Europe in the 1930s and as people moved from one continent to another in the postwar world, the Carters were a rallying point of warm affection and exuberant ideas. 'Yes, we met at the Carters.' 'Bobby Carter would tell you who to get in touch with.'

And I salute Jacky Tyrwhitt, prophetess of a new age, with her hearty laugh and restless journeying to be at the place where the action is: with le Corbusier in Paris, with Walter Gropius at Harvard University, with Doxiadis in Athens, and, in spirit at least, with Patrick Geddes in India. When the war ended she was back in Bedford Square, in a house on the north side where she lived in the attic amongst a litter of books, new ideas, and cups of tea and in the rooms below conducted the crash courses of the School of Planning and Regional Reconstruction. Here, out of Jackie's teaching, was born much of the idealism for the cities of the postwar world. In 1954, she was the first to give the graduate course in townplanning at the University of Toronto; she swept like a cyclone through the rather cautious campus of Toronto before going on to teach at Harvard. I last saw her there, in characteristic activity, picking up bundles of books in her arms and stuffing them into the refrigerator that she was going to ship to Athens–a wonderful expression of competent confusion.

I must not give the impression that all my friends at the AA followed the party line of new ideas about architecture and the urban environment. There was, for instance, Stephen Dykes Bower who supplied the principal antithesis and rebuttal for many of our arguments. He had already graduated from Oxford and was a recognized scholar in, of all things, the Victorian Gothic Revival. Dykes Bower was also an accomplished musician like his two brothers who are cathedral organists. He had an old-fashioned vicarage wit and we respected him deeply for his unwavering devotion to the gothic, which most of us felt was a dead art form. Later in life this single-minded interest led to his appointment as Surveyor of the Fabric of Westminster Abbey, with a roving commission to aid the ailing and crumbling condition of all Britain's great cathedrals. As one of the perquisites of office he has a small house in the inner inner sanctum behind the Abbey where he has entertained me at afternoon tea with cake and jam, looking out on to what is perhaps the oldest garden in England, a quiet little grassy quadrangle slap in the middle of central London that, for a thousand years, has been just the way it is today.

The time came to leave this elysium. From the AA I went to work for Felix Goldsmith, a young architect who had an office in Gray's Inn. He

gave me the job because he was designing a theatre and I was known to
have an interest in this kind of thing. A maiden lady of wealth and
culture had bought an abandoned vaudeville house in Covent Garden
and proposed to convert it into an avant-garde 'theatre in the round'. The
building hadn't been used for many years and it was a ghostly experience
to explore its dark and musty interior: there was still an aroma of the
Naughty Nineties about it and one almost expected to see Victorian
figures emerging from behind the red plush curtains, perhaps the rotund
figure of the Prince, the future Edward VII, accompanied by a Victorian
beauty with brilliant décolletage and long white gloves. The place belonged in the same period as the Paris theatres so suggestively painted
by Toulouse Lautrec. Within this improbable setting, Felix Goldsmith
had conceived a very complex spiral geometry of stairs and galleries and
stage, and I was to take his design a step further. I certainly didn't have
any technical knowledge to contribute, my theatre experience being
limited to amateur affairs in which I had admittedly taken a rather
leading part both as a performer and as a designer of a small cyclorama
stage. As a performer, I had rather fancied myself as a comic European
mayor with a tangled pronunciation and vocabulary, and the peak of my
theatrical career was a brief appearance at the Arts Theatre in the West
End, under the direction, theoretically, of Ernest Thesiger who, at about
this time, was with Dame Sybil Thorndike in 'Saint Joan'.

Felix Goldsmith had inherited the Gray's Inn office from his father
and with it an elderly lady secretary. She didn't have a great deal to do
and we seemed to spend an enormous amount of time trying to consume
the cups of tea she made. That winter, also, London was in a thick yellow
fog and the very heart of the fog seemed to be in the gloomy passages
and courtyards of Gray's Inn. So, in spite of the rather intriguing theatre
project, this was not at all like the years in elysium and I began to get
restless. I liked London and the world of the theatre. But it wasn't the
real world that I wanted to be in. As a student I had been proud of what
I did, in expressing myself, but how could I ever be proud of working
for someone else? I couldn't imagine myself pursuing a prospective rich
client. I had gone into architecture for a social purpose and now I could
see no way of breaking out of the barriers that seemed to be enclosing
me. One night I walked through the midnight streets of London with my
friend Patrick Rolleston and we discussed the idea of going to live in
another country, perhaps Canada. And while I was in this mood there
occurred one of those fortuitous glimpses through the mists and to the
horizon that can completely change the course of one's life.

In that summer of 1929, as in several previous summers, I had spent my holidays mountain-climbing in Switzerland. In October the climbing party decided to have a reunion so that we could gloat over the photographs of ourselves strung up on the rocky crests of the Sudlenspitz and Nadelhorn, as we climbed from the Saas Fee valley over into the Zermatt valley, and there were pictures of a glorious day on the Zinal Rothorn. The date of the reunion was chosen as an occasion to say goodbye to Patrick Rolleston, who had been one of the party and was to sail the next day for Canada. Our reunion took place in Ishbel MacDonald's upstairs sitting-room at 10 Downing Street, she having been one of the climbing party that summer. In the course of the evening the door opened and there came into the room a Canadian girl, a friend of the MacDonalds whom Ishbel had invited because she happened to be sailing next day on the same boat as Patrick. Mary Gordon was not remotely like anyone I had ever met before.

The following April I also got on a boat for Canada.

3

Journey into
a New Country

London had been my love. But on 3 April 1930 I flagged a taxi on the corner of Oakley Street and the King's Road, drove to Waterloo Station, and I was on the way to Canada. Rather at the last moment I had persuaded Jim Richards to come with me, just for the adventure. From Southampton we went out by tender to the Solent where we got in through a small hole in the towering flank of the *Bremen*, on its way from Hamburg to New York . We had chosen to come this way because we had thought it would be fun to travel on a brand-new ship and, rather than going up the St Lawrence of which we knew nothing, we had a romantic idea about the Statue of Liberty and New York as the gateway to the New World. We also had romantic ideas about the marvels of New York's skyscrapers. The Statue of Liberty more than fulfilled our expectations, but New York was a disappointment because we were not prepared for the triviality and tawdriness of American commerce that seemed to lay a blight on every building and pollute every effort at architectural design. Mies van der Rohe had not yet arrived, with his puritanical rejection of all that encumbers the simple structural form.

Jim Richards was a wonderful person to travel with, because not a thing missed his perceptive blue eyes. Unlike me, he had no thought of staying in Canada, but through the next year I was able to enjoy the company and the good talk of the future Slade Professor and editor of the *Architectural Review*.

On the day of our arrival in Canada we had the extraordinary good fortune to meet a person who, perhaps more than any other, could convey the quintessential flavour of the country. This was the painter, A.Y. Jackson. It was Sunday afternoon tea-time in a house on University

Street in Montreal. Jackson was just back from one of his legendary painting journeys in Quebec and 'père Raquette' had with him a satchel full of those small sketches of the deep blue shadows in the snow, the horse and sleigh in the folds of the Laurentian hills, the curved roof-shapes of early Quebec houses. From these sketches he would work up the full-scale paintings with all his bravura of rich colour and swinging brush strokes. I had never before seen landscape painting like this and, as we sat there with Alec Jackson, the sweet expression in his eyes and his cheeks ruddy from the sunlight and snowshine, I felt that I was being introduced to a rare and deep mystery as authentic as Byzantine icons or mediaeval wallpaintings.

The next day we took the train to Toronto, found a room at the Ford Hotel, and each went off to look for a job. This included searching the telephone book for the names and addresses of architectural firms and then summoning courage to make an entry to their offices. Our first impression was that Toronto architects spent a great deal of time 'out to lunch' and only gradually did we realize that many of them didn't, in fact, ever come back again. It was the beginning of the depression. However, within less than two weeks, we both had jobs. Jim was lucky to be received into the well-established firm of Sproatt and Rolph who were still finishing their work on Hart House in the University of Toronto. Unfortunately he was assigned to design some architectural details for the Canada Life building then being built on the corner of University Avenue and Queen Street, the building that now has a weather indicator on its summit. As the building rose from the ground I'm afraid it became clear that its design offended practically every criterion of good architecture that we had so recently learned. I hasten to add that all these offences had already occurred before Jim arrived, so he is blameless.

My own search for a job turned out quite differently. While walking the streets of downtown Toronto, comtemplating my situation, I came upon a brass plate at the entrance to 57 Queen Street West, just across from the old City Hall. It read: 'Wilson, Bunnell and Borgstrom, Town Planners and Landscape Architects'. I had never heard of the term 'landscape architect', but it expressed exactly what I had been looking for. To design a landscape would be far more exciting than to design a building. So, guessing correctly which of the three names would be connected with such an interesting prospect, I went up to the fourth floor and asked to see Carl Borgstrom. He was a good-looking, large, fair-haired Swede with a friendly style; he wore a green tweed jacket and a

yellow tie, and on the window-ledge behind him was a carved wooden
monkey with a quizzical expression. It was almost as if Carl Borgstrom
had expected me. I started work the next morning and was associated
with Borgstrom off and on throughout the next decade, always with a
bit of a struggle through the years of the depression, but never without
a job of some kind, however modest.

Jim and I settled down to live and work in Toronto. We stayed for
some weeks in a rooming house at 39 Wellesley Street East, our landlady
obviously suspecting that two rather untidy young Englishmen were up
to no good and complaining that we spilled ink on the sheets. To add
to her mystification we bought a china egg and a packet of poultry food
and every morning we would sprinkle a few chicken feathers on the floor
and leave another egg on the table. When the joke had run its course,
we moved to the apartment house on the corner of Church and Wellesley
where we stayed till the following summer.

Cities have their distinctive smells, to which one gets acclimatized.
Even before I went to live there, I had loved London's delicious, musky
odour that originated, I think, in the air-conditioning system in the
Underground, a smell quite different from the pervading aroma of laundry and boiled cabbage that afflicts provincial English cities. Mediterranean towns get their smell from the olive oil used in cooking. Of
Toronto in the 1930s I can only say that it had the sweet smell of sewers
and that this was strongest up and down Yonge Street. The smell was
the only way in which Toronto resembled Venice.

At 57 Queen Street West I was in a room with five draftsmen working
on plans of various kinds. My first task was to make a large plan of the
parks on the Canadian side of Niagara Falls, and I felt that my reputation in the office hinged on my success in making a realistic representation of the gigantic waterfall and gorge as seen from above. Though I
have always been regarded as a rather good draftsman, this was quite a
challenge. I was very much impressed by the drawings being done at the
other end of the office; these were maps of golfcourses being designed by
Stanley Thompson who had been a famous Canadian golfer and then
turned his hand to laying out some of the best-known golfcourses in
North America, including that photogenic course in the valley below the
Banff Springs Hotel. He had an extraordinary understanding and artistic
sense for the form of a landscape. He would walk through a dense forest
and pick out the shape and direction for each fairway to be cut through
the bush and, with the eye of an artist, visualize the site of each green,
to be cupped in the curve of the land and set off by the grouping of trees.

To create a sophisticated landscape out of the raw materials of the Canadian scene required, I thought, the same artistry with which Capability Brown had designed the great country-house parks of England in the eighteenth century and, indeed, the artistry of a Nicholas Poussin who had painted the landscapes on which those English scenes were modelled. But I'm quite sure that Stanley Thompson had never heard of either Capability Brown or Nicholas Poussin.

The firm of Wilson, Bunnell and Borgstrom had done a roaring business in the affluent 1920s, laying out subdivisions for the growing cities. The senior member of the firm, Norman Wilson, had won an international reputation for his work on urban transportation systems; he became a director of Brazilian Traction and was one of the pioneering planners of Toronto's subway system. But, in 1930, as the weeks rolled by from May to the fall, the depression deepened and a chilling and foreboding climate entered the office. The partners spent more and more time behind the glass door of Norman Wilson's office, in anxious search for some gleam of hope. After each such conference Arthur Bunnell would return to his own office that opened off the drafting room and we would hear him pouring renewed energy and even a note of desperation into an endless stream of telephone calls. He was trying to drum up support for the development of a central heating system that would serve the whole of Toronto's downtown area from a single plant. Coming from the quiet dignity of the London office in Gray's Inn, where it would have been considered unprofessional to promote anything and where the sound of the telephone ringing was an occasional surprise, I was amazed at what I overheard and at Bunnell's persistence. He was like a spider slowly and patiently weaving a web, entangling city councillors, bankers, engineers, investors, and boosters in his scheme. But as fast as someone became enmeshed, the chill wind of the depression would blow away another part of the web's structure.

Meanwhile I worked on a number of things for the partners as it became evident that I could understand planning ideas and translate them into sketches in ink and pencil and water colour. And from my corner of the office at 57 Queen Street West I began to find out about the life and growth of Toronto and about urban affairs in Canada. The current town-planning controversy in the city concerned the extension of University Avenue southwards from Queen Street to Front Street; the route was cut at an angle, so as to converge upon the York Street underpass below the railway tracks and so out to the lakefront. This was condemned by newspapers as 'the crooked lane'. The controversy arose out of a fatal error that had only recently been made when the Union Station and Royal York Hotel were built, with the railway tracks at an elevated level that effectively cut off the city from its waterfront on Lake Ontario. Chicago had handled a similar situation without making this fatal error; the tracks were put below the street level, leaving an open view of the lakeshore parks.

Before leaving England I had come across a photograph which I treasured and which raised my expectations of finding a kind of utopia in North America. It was the picture of a beach on the edge of a lake with sun-tanned citizens stretched out on the sand and, behind them the towers of a great city glistening in the sun, just as le Corbusier would have made them. I think it was a rather flattering snapshot of Chicago's lakefront. Looking forward to what I would find in Canada and noting that Toronto had the advantage of facing south towards Lake Ontario, I assumed that this façade of the city would bear some general resemblance to the charismatic photograph. However, on arriving in Toronto, I very soon discovered that this was not the kind of charisma sought by the earnest and rather humourless Toronto politicians, so many of whom seemed to be funeral directors by trade.

The fatal error on the waterfront has continued to haunt the city and, in the 1970s, has reappeared in the attempt to build a new city centre over the top of the station and the railway tracks. The controversy about University Avenue has also reappeared in the form of the battle of the Spadina Expressway; for in 1930 it was University Avenue which offered the critical route from downtown to the northwestern suburbs. At that time University Avenue, between Queen Street and the provincial Parliament Buildings, was still a splendid avenue of fine shadetrees with quite narrow roads on either side. And, for the next few years, on that grass beneath the trees sat the thousands of men who had lost their jobs and had nothing to look forward to but the next bowl of soup. It was a street of poverty, misunderstanding, and skinny charity.

While I was at 57 Queen Street West there arrived in the office the series of volumes being issued by the New York Regional Plan Association, under the direction of Thomas Adams. This was by far the most comprehensive study of an urban region that had ever been made; there were volumes on the economic base of the region, on its communication network, the recreational needs, and, most significantly, the first formulation of the 'neighbourhood unit' idea. There couldn't have been a better series of textbooks on environmental design and they gave me a perspective view of urban planning that I had not had before. This prodigious work had an added dimension of interest when I discovered that Thomas Adams had spent nearly ten years in Canada before moving to New York. What had he been doing in Canada? In May 1914, when he was president of the British Town Planning Institute and a senior government official in England (having previously been secretary of the Garden Cities Association), he had been invited to speak at a National Planning Conference in Toronto. He made such an impression that, after the conference, he was invited to stay in Canada and act as an adviser to provinces and cities on the future urban growth of this country. This invitation came from Sir Clifford Sifton who was the chairman of the Commission of Conservation, a federal body set up by Sir Wilfrid Laurier to be concerned with a wide range of environmental questions that had already begun to confront Canada: the pollution of inland waters, the settlement of people on the land, and the environmental conditions of people in big cities. (In retrospect, the creation of the Commission of Conservation appears as a brilliant flash of national insight, anticipating by more than sixty years the departments of the environment set up by federal and provincial governments in the early 1970s.) Over the protests of the British government for the loss of such a valuable public servant, Thomas Adams stayed in Canada. He left his mark here in many ways, including the first forms of provincial planning legislation, the founding of the Canadian Town Planning Institute, and the designs of two small neighbourhoods where one can still see the imprint of Thomas Adams' background in the Garden Cities movement. One of these is the Hydrastone project in Halifax which was built to replace some of the devastation of the 1917 explosion so vividly described in Hugh Maclennan's *Barometer Rising*. And the other is the charming village-like design of Linden Lea, just beside Rockcliffe Park in Ottawa.

I found encouragement in the discovery that, philosophically and geographically, I was on the same route as this remarkable man. It made me feel that there was a validity in the chain of events that had brought me to Canada. A few years later, on my first return visit to England, I called on Thomas Adams in his London office to express my gratitude for the encouragement he had unwittingly given me.

As 1930 rolled by, new aspects of Canada, new people, and new horizons began to come into view beyond the limited perspective of Yonge Street, its streetcars, and sewer smell. On Christmas Day, perhaps with some sad perversity for being away from home, Jim and I went to get a meal at Bowles Lunch on Bloor Street. At that time the 'one-armed lunch' was the poor man's place for a cup of coffee and a sandwich; it had white-tiled walls like a public lavatory and the floor was swabbed with a dirty mop by some poor wretch who usually looked like a tubercular convict. But that Christmas meal was a celebration because there we met Kenneth Mayall with his playful wit and wonderful range of knowledge. He was an English immigrant, a year earlier than I, and he had already begun his career as one of Canada's pioneer ecologists and conservationists, by living with an Indian family in northern Ontario. He was a Cambridge University graduate in modern languages and had become so captivated by the Canadian wilderness, the canoe, the axe, and the fishing line, that he had come to study forestry at the University of Toronto. It came to be Kenneth's problem in life that he knew so much about so many things, as indeed an ecologist must, that it was difficult to classify him; when he went to enlist in the army during the Second World War the personnel officers were so baffled by his range of qualifications that he was put into an 'unclassifiable' category, which meant that for a long time he cleaned the latrines and washrooms at the recruiting depot.

I also learned a lot from Brownie, an awe-inspiring Western Canadian who came to live with us in the Church Street apartment. He had a way of greeting you with a bone-smashing handshake and a frightening glare into your eyes, as if he might break your neck if you resisted. His sense of Western melodrama made even riding in an elevator with him an exciting experience because he would address total strangers in a way that was funny, threatening, and quite incomprehensible. With Brownie I had my first view of Western Canada. He had heard of someone who knew someone who had a girl friend who had left her car in Toronto when she had lost her job and returned to her home in Moose Jaw, Saskatchewan. If someone would drive it out she would pay for the gas. It looked like a good thing and we could both get a week's leave from our employers. We would drive via Chicago (at that time there wasn't any highway north of Lake Superior) and Brownie assured me that for this reason we would, of course, have to carry a gun in the back seat. When we reached Windsor we went to get a tankful of gas before crossing to Detroit and, with all the exultation of a Westerner heading home and all the dramatic style of a strong man at the wheel of a powerful car, Brownie pulled away from the gaspump and uprooted it from its base so that gasoline spewed all over the place. The car was sufficiently damaged that we had to leave it at a nearby garage while we waited in the lobby of the hotel. After a couple of hours wait two sombre figures came through the revolving doors, with the unmistakable air of plain-clothesmen, hands close to their sides. We were pointed out to them and then taken to the police station. No, the car wasn't ours and we had never met the owner. Moose Jaw did seem a rather unlikely destination. Brownie's natural instinct for dramatic obscurity didn't help much to establish the innocence of our little trip and identification required phone calls to Toronto. Only when our legitimacy was established did we discover why the garage mechanic had notified the police; the licence plates on the car had been altered, by taping over an E to make an L. On a journey with Brownie the most innocent episodes somehow had a way of taking a dramatic twist.

Jim Richards also had a brush with the police. When May came around he had fulfilled his twelve months in Canada and was ready to head home. Before doing so, however, he wanted to see the Pacific coast and we arranged to meet in British Columbia in mid-July. We said goodbye and, next time I heard from him, he was in the county gaol in San Diego, California. He had gone for a walk into the desert and when night came had simply slept under the stars. He woke to find a posse of border police discussing this unshaven vagabond, with a rucksack for a pillow and wearing a bedraggled black pullover. He spoke in the strange and unfamiliar dialect of a future Slade professor, and his pullover had a nautical air as if he had deserted from a ship. He had unfortunately left his passport with his baggage in a San Francisco hotel and he remained in the San Diego gaol for an uncomfortable week.

Meanwhile, back at 57 Queen Street West, the anxious conferences behind Norman Wilson's glass door were evidently coming to a climax. The most expendable members of the staff began to disappear. Mack, an engineer, went to keep a small grocery store in his hometown. Ted, who had learned to make the drawings of Stanley Thompson's golfcourses for affluent businessmen, had always looked undernourished because he had such a large family to support; how was he going to survive the depression? Even Arthur Bunnell's brave telephoning finally petered out and he prepared himself to return to the small-town family business. It was clear that the partners would have to split the remaining cash in the bank and each go their own way. They were good people; there wasn't a single person in the office group who hadn't shown a kindness to me. I didn't want to be present for the last farewells, so in July 1931 I left to have a summer holiday in the mountains of British Columbia.

I won't dwell on that rapturous summer. How I jumped from the train when it stopped in full view of Mount Robson; how I was received by my only relatives in Canada, the Waterfields of Nakusp, who had discovered what is surely the most beautiful mountain valley in the world; the Arrow Lakes; how I walked out of that valley a month later and, with Jim Richards, walked in valleys mysteriously darkened by the pall of forest-fire smoke and how we slept on the blackened earth and beside the lakes at the foot of great peaks. Amidst the ecstatic beauty of lakes and mountains and in the enjoyment of exhilarating health, it was difficult to be anxious for the future. But, in fact, I didn't have a clue what was going to happen next and, all too soon, there I was back in stricken Toronto. It was the end of August and I had a two-week job behind a counter at the Canadian National Exhibition. I had found a room on St Joseph Street which contained absolutely no furniture but a murphy bed that disappeared into the wall during the day, so that the resonant emptiness of the room was a kind of echo chamber in which to contemplate what was obviously going to be a momentous decision. Was I going to stay in Canada, stricken by the depression yet somehow immensely appealing?

Within a few days the answer was made unexpectedly clear. One afternoon, out of the crowd at the Exhibition, appeared the familiar optimistic face of Carl Borgstrom. Would I join him in working on the only job that had been salvaged from the collapse at 57 Queen Street West? This was the design and construction of the northwestern entrance to the city of Hamilton, a project that the firm had won in a competition a year before.

Even more decisive was the sudden re-appearance of the girl I had met at 10 Downing Street and who had, all this time, been in Winnipeg. I pulled down the murphy bed and we sat there side by side and I knew that I would stay in Canada.

4
My Chosen Land

The immigrant who moves from one culture to another doesn't just leave a job and a family and friends. He also leaves behind an environment to which he has been bound by instincts evolved over many generations and of which he may be scarcely aware. Perhaps these attachments are so much a part of one's self that they can never really disappear and are there to be enjoyed at a later stage in life. The immediate problem of the immigrant is to find new environmental relationships and compulsions to replace what has been lost in the disengagement.

England was certainly in my blood. Through the last few years I had lived there, there had been no greater enjoyment than walking over the hills and through the villages and along the footpaths and byways of the English counties. I had done this sometimes in the company of friends, all of us with haversacks on our backs, and sometimes I had walked alone in soliloquy. Warwickshire, the Cotswolds, the North and South Downs, Wiltshire, Dorset and Devon: I knew them all as my own habitat. I had slept in the village inns, examined the inscriptions and monuments in the country churches, trodden the well-worn stone floors of the great cathedrals, and looked up into their high vaulted roofs. I knew every mile along the ridge of English limestone that crosses the land from Portland Bill to the Yorkshire coast and I had often boasted that, if I were taken blindfold to any village along the way, I could tell you just where I was from the colour and the crumble and the size of the stones of which the village was built. On a number of expeditions I had been with Hope Bagenal, a great architectural scholar and already England's leading authority on architectural acoustics; we would enter one of the great empty vaulted churches and he would blow his little whistle and count the seconds of echo and resonance, as a fish in the sea might recognize the depth of a cavern under the rocks. I had always felt a special affinity with mediaeval England: the mystery of what is within the carved stone, as if it were alive and tense, a quality rediscovered by Henry Moore in the concavities of his wonderful sculptures.

Perhaps I had had a kind of love affair with England. I was part of the place, settled into a pattern of comfortable indulgence from which I somehow had to break away. There was an element of masochism in the separation. But I knew that I had to separate if I was to discover my own individuality and find ways of self-expression, however wistful the parting might be.

Migration from one environment to another starts with the period of disengagement when one really doesn't belong to either end of the axis. Then there is the act of commitment when the migration becomes irrevocable. And, finally, there is the process of adaptation as one 'plugs into' the new culture. I now entered this third phase.

Through the decade of the 1930s I worked in partnership with Carl Borgstrom, sharing what little income we could scratch from the austere years of the depression. We called ourselves Borgstrom and Carver, Landscape Architects and Town Planners; but the reference to town-planning was little more than a gesture, for it was Carl's deep understanding of the earth and the trees and the plants that kept us going. At the same time I gradually moved away from Carl Borgstrom's world as I found my way into the stream of Canada's social and political concern with housing and the problems of cities; this move I made largely through writing articles in magazines which gained me some recognition in university circles. But first let me tell about Borgstrom.

He had learned landscape architecture in the European way, working as a young man with spade and wheelbarrow in the gardens of the great country-houses. He'd planted the avenues of linden trees, looked after the roses and the fruit trees, set out the topiary hedges and all the time listened to the bubbling water in the fountains and observed the vistas and shapes of gardens in Sweden, Germany, France, and England. So he came out of the school of le Nôtre and Capability Brown and all those who had created the wonderful landscapes of England and Europe. He had the eye of an artist and had acquired an intuitive knowledge of the family affinities of trees and plants; he understood them as a psychologist understands people, perceiving the causes of their discomfortures or blooming health. As Carl Borgstrom taught me the habits and the appearance of trees and plants he would sometimes perform a kind of ballet in our office. 'What does a *gleditsia triacanthos* really look like when it's grown up?' I would ask him. 'Like this,' Carl would explain, taking the posture of a tree, with his arms and fingers expressing its thorny habit.

Anyone who practised landscape architecture in Toronto lived in the shadow of Howard Dunnington-Grubb, a witty Englishman as tall as a Lombardy poplar, with a quick teasing style and an infectious laugh. Grubb seemed altogether too good a name for anyone who designed gardens, so he had married Miss Dunnington and joined their names together. She knew as much about gardens as Howard did and had a gracious aristocratic manner. If making gardens is an essential part of a nation's culture, Canada owes a lot to the Dunnington-Grubbs, not only because they designed and built gardens but because it was from their Sheridan Nurseries that the suburban population of Toronto first learned to carry home triumphant all the blue spruces and pfitzer's junipers and chinese elms to make a garden out of the desert they had bought from the speculative builder.

I think Borgstrom was a better landscape architect than Howard Grubb because he wanted the trees and the ground to develop in their own natural way, whereas Grubb couldn't forget that he was a designer, highly trained in the 'beaux-arts' style, and he wanted to dominate the pattern and impose on the planting material his own view of how they ought to grow. It's like the difference between a permissive and an authoritarian parent. Certainly Borgstrom's sense of landscape was more in tune with our present views of environmental conservation. An example of this different approach to landscape design occurred in making the Oakes Garden Theatre at Niagara Falls.

On New Year's Day 1933 Borgstrom and I drove over to Niagara and, as we approached the Falls from Queenston, saw a column of smoke ahead of us; this came from the charred remains of the Clifton House Hotel which had burned the day before. It had been a comfortable old-fashioned wooden building with wide verandahs where the celebrities of an era had sat in deep wicker chairs to contemplate the mystery and grandeur of Niagara Falls. It was one of the most spectacular sites in the world, but in 1933 there was no investment capital for building tourist hotels. Fortunately, however, there was a local benefactor who could afford to buy the property and give it to the Niagara Parks Commission. This was Harry Oakes who in 1912 had stumbled upon the richest gold mine in Northern Ontario, the Lakeshore Mine at Kirkland Lake. With his fortune and a taste for the dramatic he had built a palatial stone mansion overlooking the Horseshoe Falls; his fortune also brought him a knighthood and a mysterious death in the Bahamas. Carl Borgstrom had come to know Harry Oakes and, not long after the Clifton House fire, we both went over to discuss with him what should be done on the site. We spent a night at Oak Hall. My principal recollection of the house is that at one end of the bedroom corridor there was a small shrine that remained dimly illumined all night; it contained a bottle of Bass's ale. When we came to the discussion of the Clifton House site, Borgstrom and I explained that the ground had a natural sloping shape, almost like a theatre auditorium looking towards the two great waterfalls. The next day I made a sketch of the idea, thinking that the enormous scale of the falls ought to be reflected in the broad and simple bowl of land and the informal planting of large trees to emphasize this configuration. About a year later the job had somehow passed into the hands of Dunnington-Grubb and he finally carried out the theatre idea with his partner Wilhelm Stensson. Instead of the bold masculine form I had visualized, it turned into a dainty and almost feminine arrangement of steps, little clipped hedges, balustrades, garden ornaments, and interlacing patterns of flowerbeds. That was Grubb's vocabulary and trademark and he had to use it, even in the most inappropriate places.

In spite of any differences of artistic opinion, I had a relationship with Howard Grubb that I can only describe as one of affection; we both enjoyed stimulating arguments about landscape design. The theme of our discussion was pursued in some articles we wrote in the *Canadian Homes and Gardens* magazine, in which I referred to Grubb as a 'leprechaun' on account of his elusive and puckish line of argument. This was thought to be such a tasty epithet that we were invited to continue the debate as a lunchtime entertainment for local architects.

In Toronto there was a small group of landscape architects who came to know one another and enjoy one another's company very much. The Grubbs were the centre of this circle, which also included Carl Borgstrom and me, Gordon Culham and Douglas MacDonald, Helen Kippax, Norman Dryden of Guelph, Frances Macleod (later, Mrs Blue), and a rather more difficult character, Edwin Kay. We used to meet in the garden of the Diet Kitchen Restaurant, on Bloor Street, and together we founded the Canadian Society of Landscape Architects of which I am proud still to be an honorary member. I was, of course, an impostor as a member of a professional society of landscape architects because I was untutored in the knowledge of plants and how they grow. However, this was not a serious deficiency as long as I worked with Carl Borgstrom, and I always felt that I had a stronger understanding of the sculptural character of landscape than some of my colleagues who were less able to see the shape of the wood because of their knowledge of the trees.

I came to know the landscape of Canada in a much more intimate way when Mary Gordon and I were married and I became, practically, a part of her large and loving family. Every summer the family congregated (and still does) on the Gordons' island in the Lake of the Woods, a half-hour's boatride from Kenora. Here I was initiated into the inner secrets of the Canadian landscape, a special revelation given to those who have moved silently in a canoe along the edge of the Precambrian rocks so infinitely detailed with their lichens and mosses, slipped close under the overhanging branches, glided quietly through the pool of water lilies and pressed a way through the long grasses in the narrow channel and so come out into the deep water beyond. Every summer the initiation was fresh and deliciously new. We gathered on the wooded island and, in a figurative sense, the family itself was like an island. Not because of its separateness, but because the family was so unified within its boundaries. I had never known a family that was so bound together. My own family in England was affectionate and proud, but my parents suffered distresses (which I will explain later) and were not able to demonstrate their love for one another. Children can have no greater gift than the manifest affection of their parents for one another and I think that the extraordinary strength of the Gordon family originated in the unceasing enjoyment that Dr Charles W. Gordon and his wife Helen King had in one another. Their love was a continuing celebration for the seven children around them and for the great number of people who were welcomed on their island.

Dr Gordon was the son of a Presbyterian minister in Glengarry County in the Ottawa valley; he attended the village school (said to be the hewn-log building now conserved for posterity in Upper Canada Village) and grew up in the decade of confederation amidst the strenuous rivalries of French and Irish and Scottish woodsmen. After theological training in Edinburgh he went into the mission field in Western Canada, where life was as adventurous and melodramatic as it had been in the Ottawa valley; his little mission church is still to be seen at Canmore in the mountain valley not far from Banff. After he and Helen King were married, they settled down in Winnipeg where he became the minister of St Stephen's. Here, as a way of attracting support for the church's missions in Western Canada, Dr Gordon started to write about his own

experiences. He had a natural gift for story-telling and for enjoying the
dramatic interplay of personalities and influences; the stories took shape
in fictional episodes of vice and virtue, love and jealousy, staged in the
vivid beauty of Canadian scenery. The stories were frankly romantic and
were written in a style intended to catch the interest of the highly moral
readers of the Presbyterian magazine. They also caught the attention of
some American publishers. *Black Rock* and *The Sky Pilot* sold a million
copies and made the author an international celebrity under his pen-
name Ralph Connor; quite inadvertently the young minister of St Stephen's had become a wealthy man and something of a national hero. For
his growing family, his son King and the six beautiful girls, Dr Gordon
built a handsome mansion at 54 Westgate, which is now the University
Women's Club. When the First World War came not long afterwards,
Dr Gordon could well afford to entrust his financial affairs to friends; so
he put on his kilt, which he wore with great style, and went overseas as
the chaplain of Winnipeg's Highland Regiment. It was an adventure that
he lived to the full, as he had in the lusty, violent mood of Western
Canada twenty years before. He returned from the war to discover that
the fortune that he had made so unexpectedly had disappeared equally
unexpectedly, and without any satisfactory explanation. He was a man
of immense magnanimity and he didn't even want to know the explanation. As far as he was concerned, it was good to be alive and surrounded
by a devoted family; there was the island in the Lake of the Woods and
he could settle down to write again. So he contracted his story-telling
skills to a publisher and what had been such a spontaneous and successful enjoyment became an obligatory task: every summer, on the island,
he was under the pressure of the calendar and the clock to finish and
deliver the next manuscript. There was a nobility in this; but the books
did not bring him another fortune. Literary tastes had changed. The
disillusionments of the Great War had set the issues of good and evil in
a new and far more complicated social context that could not be encompassed with that kind of story-telling.

Mary was the oldest of the six girls. They all adored their father, the
central figure in their lives, full of fun and an endless resource of romance
and entertainment; he sang them songs with his guitar, he teased their
mother affectionately from the other end of the dining-room table, and
he enjoyed nothing more than being scolded for his frank enjoyment of
his own public fame. Their home in Winnipeg was no longer a rich man's
place but had to be run by Helen Gordon on austere and simple lines;
but it was the social centre of a large church congregation and as

crowded as a railway station with all the friends of the seven children. They all had an immense interest in people, and the foibles and family affairs of the whole congregation were subjects of fruitful discussion, sometimes hilarious but always generous. When the family moved to the lake for the summer all this coming and going reached a special intensity as visitors were reported to be arriving in Kenora and the boat would have to go in to fetch them. My own first arrival in 1933 was undoubtedly the subject of high speculation because I was the first to appear as a bridegroom; it was a bit intimidating to sit at the big dining-table in the screened porch, aware of six pairs of penetrating eyes alert to the significance of my slightest movements. It was a family tradition that a new-comer would be judged by his reaction to a practical joke initiated by father at the end of the table. The table was covered with a waterproof oilcloth which could be conspiratorially folded into a trough below the level of the table-top and so used to convey a stream of water to be upset into the lap of the victim. Of course, Mary had warned me about this, so I was prepared to put on the right performance.

It's hard to explain the special mixture of wit, conceit, Christian dedication, romance, and generosity that made Dr Gordon such a widely and well loved person. There was the pleasure he always got from 'brinkmanship' in catching trains. When he visited us in Toronto in later years, a lean, white-haired elderly minister of the church, he always played on the anxiety and scolding he got for not being ready to go to the station to get on the CPR train for Winnipeg. He remained completely relaxed. Finally someone would telephone the CPR and say that Dr C.W. Gordon was coming; 'would they please hold the train?' This was always done and he would stroll on to the platform, receive the smiling greetings of the train crew, unhurriedly get on board, and spend the next hour or two talking to the negro porters who knew him well. He knew he was important and he made them feel they were important too.

When Mary and I were married, we went to live at Lorne Park in the country between Port Credit and Oakville, an area at that time untouched by suburban growth. And in the course of time we had a son, Peter. Our home was a small cottage built by Jim Ramage, a Scottish settler who had spent his life on the prairies and who became our guide, philosopher, and friend. He lived nearby across the field and cultivated delicious strawberries in the little valley beside the house and instructed me in planting corn and making a vegetable garden. Trillium and hepatica grew in the woods up by the Indian Road and there was a fine growth of watercress in the stream down to the lake. Across the road

were the nurseries with rows of young trees carefully tended by
Lundgren, a Swede of very few words, and there was a path through the
woods to our own beach where we planted a grove of white willows for
the shade and for shore protection. This is now called Stoney Bay Park.
It was a sweet place and many friends came on summer evenings and
weekends to lie on the beach, to swim out to the raft, and to forget about
the nagging personal problems of the depression.

The thirties was a strange, dreamlike period of suspended animation.
Because there were no opportunities and no pressures towards successful
careers, we were very intermingled and we had plenty of time to enjoy
each other's company in a relaxed and easy-going way. Artists, oddballs,
professionals, and political people–none had anything to be snobbish
about. We were all drop-outs of a kind, not by choice but by the inescapable circumstances.

We lived in an old-established Ontario landscape, the orchards of
apple and cherry trees already past their prime. Not far away in Clarkson
was the scene of Mazo de la Roche's stories of Jalna. Also just nearby
lived Mrs L.A. Hamilton and her ancient husband who had laid out the
street system of Vancouver for the CPR. 'Mrs L.A.', a tall bony woman
with smiling eyes and untidy wisps of grey hair, was an extraordinary
patroness of lame ducks. She is beautifully described in Graham McInnes's autobiography *Finding a Father*, her most notable lame duck having been Graham's father Campbell McInnes whom she had rescued
from deep trouble and set upon a new career as one of Canada's most
distinguished singers. Around her was a circle of young poets and painters and piano-players and plain quiet people beaten by the tragedies of
unemployment. There was also Ted Bedwell, a cabinet-maker, a member
of Mrs L.A.'s group of singers who made many pieces of furniture for
me, and Pietro Pezzatti who was an elevator boy until Mrs L.A. helped
him to become a portrait painter. To all of them she gave encouragement,
shelter, some rather elementary meals, and all her untidy capacity for
loving people. I think she would have liked me more if I had been more
of a lame duck. She was a great and saintly lady of the period, to whom
some kind of monument should be erected.

There were other friends nearby, particularly Helen and Morley
Lazier, Dick Blue who made us laugh and sing around the piano, and
Maggie Blue who should have lived a generous life in a big garden with
tennis courts and rhododendrons, but who died lonely and penniless.
Just the other side of Port Credit lived Tony and Augusta Adamson in
whose house we spent one winter while Tony was in Arizona, fighting

off TB; here our dear friend Pegi Nicol was married to Norman Macleod, my father-in-law Dr C.W. Gordon performing the ceremony in Tony's beautiful living room. Pegi was a delicious person and a painter of renown and spontaneity who brought into her pictures both landscape and human character. Amongst a number of her pictures that I possess, one catches the attentive attitudes of a group of children putting plants into a school garden; another simply shows two windows of a New York tenement: from the upper one a blousy woman and her little dog are looking down into the alley below, and at the lower window there is just a pot of flowers; it is a moment of wistful loneliness in the life of a big city. It's sad that Pegi died too soon to enjoy the revolt of young people in the 1960s and 70s; her natural habitat was a commune and some of her more orthodox garments were hastily stitched together from available curtains and tablecloths. She was a kind of gypsy and forever young.

My brother-in-law King Gordon was often with us, so were many of his friends who were engaged in founding the CCF (the Co-operative Commonwealth Federation) and its intellectual wing the LSR (the League for Social Reconstruction). King had been released from his position as professor of Christian Ethics at McGill because of his outspoken political views and he was travelling back and forth across the country, opening people's minds to the new kind of Christian attitude that took him at a later stage of life to the Division of Human Rights in the United Nations. Another frequent visitor was Graham Spry who had an extraordinary talent for being a publisher without any money; almost single-handed he produced a newspaper in support of the CCF and, for the price of one dollar, he bought the *Canadian Forum* magazine and made it into the principal voice of the LSR. I owe a particular debt to Graham because, after I had contributed a number of articles to the *Canadian Forum,* he invited me to join the editorial committee. The committee would meet on Sunday evenings at Frank Underhill's home; Ruth Underhill kept us going with tea and cakes and glasses of beer, while Frank's devastating and witty commentary on the current political scene would provide the background for the upcoming issues of the *Forum.* In this period of the thirties I did a lot of writing and managed to produce an article for publication about once a month, in the *Canadian Forum,* in *Saturday Night,* and in architectural and welfare journals, and in this way gained a small reputation that led me into teaching at the University of Toronto's School of Architecture and into another chapter of my involvement in Canadian affairs.

Some of the projects on which Borgstrom and I worked make an interesting reflection of the mood of the period. To begin with there was the building of the northwestern entrance to Hamilton; the shaping of the approaches to the high-level bridge and the large park areas became a work-relief program in which every able-bodied unemployed citizen of Hamilton had to earn his dole. I set out the scheme of earth-moving and planting for the work at Hamilton and I went over there on winter days to see men handling their spades like convicts, undernourished and forlorn. Though a more sophisticated age would rightly regard this kind of forced labour as an insult to men who had lost good jobs through no fault of their own, yet the system did have its merits. At least a man could tell his children afterwards; 'I helped to make that place.' But, through those sad and desperate years, it seemed incredible that the government of Canada could conceive no better way of sustaining the skills and the health of the victims of the depression; this gave to Canadians a special admiration for Roosevelt and the US Democratic party because the American 'New Deal' had a humanity to it that was not revealed by either the Liberal or Conservative leaders of Canada. With sadness in the heart I would come home in the evening to read about the greenbelt towns being started by Roosevelt or I would go to hear J.S. Woodsworth talking of the newly founded CCF.

Much of what we built at the entrance to Hamilton has been submerged under subsequent layers of highway engineering. But one thing has not disappeared and still remains a monument to Carl Borgstrom's genius: the Hamilton Rock Garden. This was originally a gravel pit, an ugly open wound on the land just beside the new northwestern entrance. Borgstrom demonstrated how such a scar on the natural environment can be made to bloom like a garden, so that it became one of the principal tourist attractions of the city and an enormous pleasure to generations of children exploring its alpine paths.

A puzzling character who emerged out of the depression was George McCullagh for whom we made a beautiful garden around the house that he built at Thornhill. McCullagh was a 'wonder-boy' with a dazzling charisma which put into his hands the great mining fortune of William H. Wright. He and Wright bought the two Toronto morning newspapers and out of them made the *Globe and Mail*. One did not quite know whether to admire him for being so rich and noble and handsome or to suspect that there must be something tricky about the miracle he had performed. It was a time when people all over the world longed for heroic figures, and George McCullagh with his horses and his tweeds and his well-polished riding-boots might have been taken from a portrait by John Singer Sargent. Then there was the morning when he went on the air to announce that he was founding the 'Leadership League'. Canadians certainly wanted some leadership, but they have generally been sceptical of charisma in politics. However, some of George McCullagh's charisma did overflow into the garden we made for him; I think it was the best work of landscape art that Borgstrom and I did together. By that time we had achieved a full artistic collaboration, with the same feeling for topography and space and the interplay of planting material. This is the kind of pleasure that musicians must experience when they have found a spontaneous unity in playing together.

There was another dimension to my partnership with Carl Borgstrom which explains the bond that held us together through the years of the depression. In spite of our very different backgrounds there was a vein of utopianism in us both. And in those troubled times people had to cling to their visions and utopias rather desperately as they kept their heads down and the gales of the economic disaster blew themselves out. Borgstrom had a special need for a vision he could cling to: shortly before we met, his wife had left him and there were three young children, the youngest about seven years old, for whom he had to be wage-earner, cook, and mother. In this predicament he had found great strength in Christian Science, but it was really the utopian aspects of our little community at Lorne Park that kept his idealism alive.

Many people with academic backgrounds and political interests sought their visions through the League for Social Reconstruction, the intellectual wing of the CCF. To some extent I was part of that fraternity. But there were other kinds of vision. There was, for instance, the group that congregated on Gerrard Street, just west of Bay Street in Toronto, and started the colony of artists and craftsmen that was known as 'the Village'; amongst these our closest friends were Rudi Renzius, another idealistic Swede who made beautiful things out of pewter, and Tom and Joan Colls who set up shop as weavers. The centre of this little community was Mary John's Coffee Shop. In other periods of history, under the impact of economic stress and disillusionment, there have been similar responses: the nineteenth-century arts-and-crafts movement associated with William Morris (which also has historical connections with the utopianism of the Garden Cities movement of which I am an heir) was a reaction to the brutalities of the first big industrial cities. And, most recently, starting in the 1960s, there has been another period of disillusionment with technological progress that has led to new experiments in working with one's hands and in living the simple life in a rural land-scape. 'The Village' in Toronto moved up to Yorkville, which became an intown handcraft place for a while, and in many parts of Canada and the United States young people in jeans and woven shawls moved out into the country.

There was some of this flavour in what happened at Lorne Park. It was a haven in the storm. Mary and I and Peter lived in Jim Ramage's little cottage by the strawberry patch and just across the road, between the highway and the Lake, were the twenty acres planted with young trees and flowering plants, tended lovingly by Lundgren and looking more like a garden than a nursery. At the edge of the woods and over-looking this garden was an old wood-frame summer residence, a charm-ing simple building, its rooms all opening off a central hall two storeys high, and with a wide verandah on three sides. In the winter months when no work could be done on the nursery itself, everyone worked on reconstituting this house, making a courtyard entrance to our office and building stone walls and steps to set it off, with a wide vista down the garden to the lake. We also acquired a large and beautifully made log-house and placed it on the garden hillside as part of the composition. We were quite carried away by the whole effect of what we had created and by the enjoyment that so many other people seemed to find in this rural utopia. So we pressed on inevitably to the next stage of putting in beds and dining tables, some handwoven materials, some wooden things made by Ted Bedwell, some country dishes from Sweden, and in the kitchen a Chinese cook. It was a lovely place, people came to share our enjoy-ment of it, and so some of our utopian yearnings were satisfied. But the whole thing got a bit beyond our amateurish capacities and required the touch of a woman and a professional. Then we found Mabel who was a dietitian and Carl Borgstrom married Mabel and they lived happily ever after. And that was the real fulfilment of his dreams.

The final event in my long association with Carl Borgstrom occurred just after the war had started in September 1939 when so many other things were coming to an end. As the news that would change all our lives came in hour by hour, I was walking along the verges of the Queen Elizabeth Way from Brown's Line to Mimico, armed with a haversack full of pegs and a long strip map. I stuck in a peg to mark the spot for each tree to be planted, and the nursery trucks came along behind me and the boys put the trees in. The route of this new freeway was through an area that had already lost its original landscape character and our planting was intended to restore the impression that here one was passing through orchard land, now through a stand of mixed woodland, and then along the route of an old concession road with hedges and tall elms on the fence-line. Our little imaginative exercise in overcoming the engineered sterility of a freeway, to restore some variety and pleasure to the scene, was made ridiculous by subsequent events. Now, thirty years later, nothing survives of this touch of beauty we hoped to give to the QE; all has been submerged by the multiplication of traffic lanes. This is the route to the airport. September 1939, when we put in the trees, was the end of an era. I often thought about those trees and, twenty years later, I had an opportunity to take up this subject again as a member of a group which made recommendations for the whole pattern of urban growth in the Toronto region and its 'transportation corridors'.

5
Self-Expression

It isn't easy to disentangle the events of one's life and set them out in an orderly sequence, because life is not a simple linear experience, a single chain of events in logical progression. There are always a number of things going on simultaneously; there are overlaps and layers and multi-dimensions to a life. This next episode has its origin long before the last one has ended. So we go back in time to pick up the thread that leads into the future.

My partnership with Carl Borgstrom was a 'modus vivendi' that supported me through the depression years while I was adapting myself to the physical and social landscape of Canada. It had been an indulgence in the pleasures of a green place, learning about the shapes of trees and enjoying the musky smells of the sun upon the earth and the leaves. But I knew that my future could not really be contained within this little utopia out at Lorne Park, which was a rather small-scale introspective affair. Nor did I need to search for some new destination in the rather theoretical political discussions of so many of my friends in the League for Social Reconstruction, though I was certainly a socialist. The fact is that I already knew the direction of my real interests which had originated in my boyhood observation of the two landscapes in which people lived, the green places and the black places, the environment of poverty and the access to freedom. I had already thought a great deal about this both in England and in Canada and knew that I wanted to be involved in both the dialectic and the political action. For this purpose I must obviously find my place within the city. I must get to know the people who shared these interests. I must find the arena of discussion and action. And I must identify myself in this context.

The events I will now describe are not, perhaps, matter of great public significance nor was my role important to anyone but myself. But this is how I first learned to express myself and set out along the path that I have followed since, in my working life.

All through the decade of the thirties, at one of the principal cross-roads in Toronto, the corner of Bloor Street and Avenue Road, there stood an unfinished and empty building that was a kind of monument to the depression and a daily reminder of the over-reaching follies of the affluent twenties. The empty tower (now the main building of the Park Plaza Hotel) haunted me, and I wrote a moody little piece about it in the April 1937 issue of the *Canadian Forum:*

Its skeleton haunted the sky . . . a truncated torso stood silhouetted against the stars, its limbs bleached in the July sun, swept by the October winds. Construction work abandoned seven years ago Tuesday. Empty floors and bare passages echoed only with banging of unhinged doors, drip-dropping from lean girders where would have been the roof. Shreds of canvas flapped and dangled against a wall like corpses. No footsteps. Visited only by broken spirits of unlucky brokers and disillusioned money-dabblers.

For seven lonely years the starveling skyscraper stuck itself up like a scarecrow in the heart of the metropolis, an awful reminder of the anti-climax to a period of reckless ambition. Pillar of bitter tragedy. Something like this happened to Lot's wife.

On upper windswept floors flotsam of the air had been taken by the eddies and deposited in corners. Fragments of newspapers. News of film stars long since forgotten, of fortunes subsequently dissipated. Pictures of grinning athletes and satisfied executives. Details of pretty ceremonies and marriages blithely undertaken seven years ago.

Among the hastily abandoned girders starlings fluttered and chattered. On the bare lattice-work of the twentieth floor a family was raised each year in the homely comfort of a cloth cap, left behind the afternoon men had been called off the job. (The owner of the cap, walking the streets to the relief depot, had often paused in his daily pilgrimage, looked up and wondered if it still lay where he had thrown it that bitter afternoon) . . .

To accompany this sentimental piece I drew an illustration that showed a family of twittering birds that had nested in the cloth cap, which was a symbol of comfortable happier days and, old and shapeless though it was, represented a man's dignity as a worker. It would have pleased the owner to know that life still went on within his personal possession. A little scrap of life.

I contributed a more serious piece to the volume entitled *Social Planning for Canada* published in 1935 by the League for Social Reconstruction and put together by a committee consisting of Eugene Forsey, King Gordon, Leonard Marsh, Joe Parkinson, Frank Scott, Graham Spry, and Frank Underhill. On re-reading the chapter called 'A Housing Programme' I am glad to find that the general principles have withstood the test of time. There is criticism of speculation in suburban land and the consequent absurd costs to the end-user and the comment that the land is subdivided to suit the convenience and profit of the speculator rather than to serve the ultimate needs of the community. And, on the internal decay of cities, there is the comment that slums are generally the property of landlords who don't bother to keep buildings in good repair because they are simply awaiting the profit to come from the expanding growth of the commercial core. 'During the last few years, the expected commercial expansion fails to materialise and the properties fall into worse and worse disrepair. The low rents attract the poorest and most destitute groups in the community: unable to meet rents elsewhere, they have to crowd into subdivided houses . . . and put up with conditions which violate all the principles of lighting, ventilation and sanitation.' The chapter in the 1935 book then outlines the general principles of town-planning and urges that there should be a federal housing authority to deal with the needs of low-income people.

The owner of the cloth cap abandoned on the roof of the unfinished tower and many others who had lost their jobs and their dignity were compelled to retreat with their families into the Moss Park or Cabbagetown area of Toronto, a place that met the specification of a slum. And just down the street from the haunted tower was the gathering place of the group of people now seriously concerned about Canada's growing housing problems; this house had been the official residence of presidents of the University of Toronto, but Canon Cody had chosen to live elsewhere and had allowed the official residence to be labelled 'The Housing Centre'. (The Canadian Institute of International Affairs was upstairs, under the direction of Escott Reid.) On the walls of the downstairs rooms I pinned up some lurid pictures of Cabbagetown and other depressed parts of Toronto and some contrasting pictures of what other countries had built for their poor people: the New Deal housing in the United States and public housing in London, Liverpool, and Vienna. I had also become a kind of squatter-tenant in the disused kitchen where I had set up a drafting table and collected books and working papers to do with Toronto's housing situation. It was a kind of 'drop-in' centre where anyone interested in the social problems of housing could meet and talk. In September 1939 the RCMP occupied the house for their own use, assuming, no doubt, that while there was a war on, there would be little time to worry about housing problems and perhaps also suspecting that this was the centre of some kind of political subversion. As, indeed, it was.

What went on at the Housing Centre had come about through the rather unlikely intervention of a very conservative gentleman, Dr Herbert A. Bruce. At the inaugural luncheon when he assumed the office of lieutenant-governor of Ontario in March 1934, he had made some impolite remarks about the negligence of the city council of Toronto in permitting such shocking housing conditions to develop in the city. The aldermen challenged the Lieutenant-Governor to substantiate the accusation and this led to the Bruce Report, a historic document in Canadian housing history.

Herbert Bruce was about as non-subversive as a man could be. He was a prim and well-brushed product of Toronto society and achieved institutional success as a central figure in the development of a hospital and an insurance company. What made him embark upon a theme of social evangelism is quite a mystery and he never seemed to be comfortable in this role. However the Bruce Report was a seminal document because it clearly demonstrated that, in the city, there were nearly three thousand housing units below reasonable standards of health and amenities, and it set out the case for public action with clarity and authority. The principal authors of the report were Dr Harry Cassidy and Professor Eric Arthur; it was an early work of two distinguished Canadians. As professor of architectural design, Eric Arthur became our most articulate spokesman for modern architecture and defender of fine old buildings; he is the author of *Toronto, No Mean City*. Harry Cassidy, as postwar head of Toronto's School of Social Work, became one of the strategists of Canada's postwar social policies and then died in the prime of life. I am proud to have known them both as close friends and to them I owe the rather unusual qualification of having been on the staff of both a school of architecture and a school of social work.

Obviously the incomes of people in the city's poorest housing would not be enough to pay for new building and a considerable public subsidy would be required. The middle-class home-owners of Toronto, always inclined to take a highly moral view of public affairs, were not pleased at the idea of contributing their tax money to build new housing for the welfare bums sitting on the doorsteps of Cabbagetown, and members of

the city council–with the exception of Mrs Adelaide Plumptre–were not
prepared to risk their political reputations in support of such a proposition. The government in Ottawa shuddered at the thought of providing
housing subsidies through a national housing act and proceeded to draft
a new 1938 act without any such offer. So, although there was some
admiration for Dr Bruce's castigation of city council, there was little
disposition to take any action. It was in this situation that the Housing
Centre was an important base for the activist group that followed up the
Bruce Report.

Mrs Plumptre was the spokesman for this group in city council. A
highly educated woman, wife of an Anglican clergyman, Adelaide
Plumptre had an impressive ability to play the part of outraged citizen;
with hat planted high on her head she would transfix an opponent
through her pince-nez and wither him with unanswerable words of truth.
In the group at the Housing Centre there were several other women of
compassion and grace, amongst whom I must particularly mention Mrs
Eisendrath, wife of the rabbi of Holy Blossom synagogue and a woman
of beauty and intelligence, and Mrs W.L. Grant, a wonderful friend of
towering strength and understanding, who had then recently moved
from the principal's house at Upper Canada College. The leading publi-
cist in the group was Claris Edwin Silcox, editor of the church magazine
called *Welfare;* she was equipped with great evangelical style in the use
of the written and the spoken work. I must also mention the group of
architects of whom Dick Fisher was the most faithful, together with Eric
Arthur and Shy Mathers, Ferdie Marani, and Bill Somerville. But the
outstanding person in the group was certainly Professor E.J. Urwick who
acted as our chairman and as leader of the delegation which occasionally
called upon Lieutenant-Governor Bruce in his palatial mansion in upper
Rosedale, where he maintained a rather lordly aloofness from this political activism.

I suppose I have an especially shining memory of E.J. Urwick just
because he was the key person in the group with whom I entered housing
affairs in Canada. But I think he has a shining image for many others
who knew him and yet, like me, knew virtually nothing about his personal history. Urwick was brought from England about 1925 to head up
the Department of Political Economy at the University of Toronto and,
from that position, he organized the School of Social Work. I see him
stepping along Bloor Street with his neatly rolled umbrella, well-pressed
grey suit, and an air of modest self-assurance–the very figure of an
aristocratic Londoner on the way to his club on St James Street. He had

a way of stroking his moustaches like a gourmet flavouring the bouquet of a wine and I can almost swear that he had a white carnation in his buttonhole. I suppose he was a Fabian socialist with a taste for an impeccably radical idea and a witty way of putting it. And I remember with particular delight his confrontations with Dr Bruce, whom he treated with punctilious respect but somehow managed to mock with the special emphasis on 'Your Honour' when the Lieutenant-Governor offered some innocuous proposal too bland for Urwick's taste.

The purpose of the Housing Centre group was, of course, to gain community interest and support for some kind of public action along the lines that had been advocated in the Bruce Report. The most practical result was the introduction of a municipal bylaw that provided a revolving loan fund from which home-owners could borrow modest sums to help them rehabilitate their properties. The operation was on a very small scale, but it was an early and imaginative adventure into private urban renewal. But it was clear that no substantial progress could be made until the federal government had provided some funds and the necessary legislation to help people of low income. The 1934 Dominion Housing Act had been entirely concerned with lending money for building middle-class homes; the act was under the jurisdiction of the Department of Finance and the declared motive was to increase employment. The legislation was an economic instrument and was not conceived as a means of dealing with the social implications of housing and the need to improve the living environment of the part of the population who suffered from the worst housing deprivations. So it was necessary to lift this whole subject out of the limited context of Toronto's Cabbagetown and to present it as a subject of national concern. Amongst the Housing Centre group it was my particular role to try to establish connections with a wider Canadian community of interest in housing affairs. This brought me into communication with George Mooney of Montreal and Horace Seymour of Ottawa, who became my close associates and friends. We worked together vigorously and by 1939 we had succeeded in staging two national conferences, one in Ottawa and the other in Toronto, and we had built the skeleton structure of what we called the National Housing Committee. Horace Seymour was, by profession, a land surveyor and his understanding of the wider fields of housing had come from his association with Thomas Adams. He was a modest, enthusiastic, and delightful person and our friendship was regrettably short because he did not live to see the results of these efforts.

On the other hand, my friendship with George Mooney extended long and firmly into our later lives. His monument is the strength of Canadian city governments in the whole political structure of the nation; for it was George Mooney who largely created that strength, during his many years as the executive director of the Canadian Federation of Mayors and Municipalities. He was their spokesman and tutor and source of morale as the power struggle developed in the fifties and sixties between the imperialistic federal and provincial governments and the representatives of the people who live in cities; he probably affected Canadian history as much as if he had been a prime minister. Unfortunately Canadian historians and political scientists have not yet taken the measure of this internal balance in our national political life. One of George Mooney's most likable characteristics was his quite unabashed enjoyment of his own skills as a 'spell-binder' in oratory. He was not afraid to feel his way into a highly emotional and sententious theme, lift his voice a bit to see how the resonance of the auditorium worked, and then take off at full pitch, shouting into the ceiling with tears in his eyes. He could put on a great act, being a far finer orator than Diefenbaker and equipped with an intelligent understanding of bilingual Canada to match that of Pierre Elliott Trudeau. Yes, he would have been a great prime minister. But perhaps he was put off federal politics at an early stage by the experience of being a rejected CCF candidate.

The Housing Conference of February 1939, which took place in the Royal York Hotel in Toronto, was the first major gathering of the forces around this subject. Amongst the two hundred who were there was a strong contingent from Nova Scotia headed by Dr S.H. Prince, who explained the pioneering experience in organizing cooperative housing for Cape Breton miners, a movement headed by Father Moses Coady of St Francis Xavier University, Antigonish. Grace MacInnis, daughter of the CCF leader, was there with a message from the Vancouver city council and with her own strong views. From Winnipeg came Ralph Ham with great ability to translate ideologies and abstractions into the practical language of construction and architecture. There was the redoubtable Norah Henderson from Hamilton, launching an attack upon the taxation system which made it impossible for city governments to fulfil their obligations to the poor people in their midst. But the dominating figure in the discussions was certainly George Mooney, always prepared to give battle in a heated discussion.

From Ottawa came two important speakers. Dr W.C. Clark, the deputy minister of finance under Mr Dunning, came to explain the terms of the new National Housing Act 1938 that contained the offer of $30 million that could be lent to limited-dividend corporations to build low-rental housing and the proposal that municipalities (but not the federal government) could contribute to 'rent reduction funds' out of which the necessary rent subsidies could be paid. The other key speaker was Arthur Purvis who had been chairman of the National Unemployment Commission appointed by the Prime Minister. His study of the causes of unemployment and his personal efforts to mount the programs that would get Canadians back to work, had given him a deep insight into the motive forces within society. His contribution to the conference was a major broadcast speech which, in effect, castigated the federal government for introducing the concept of a high-minded philanthropic limited-dividend housing corporation, without offering any kind of instrument, agency, or financial support for community organizations of this kind. It was, perhaps, too gentle a castigation; because Arthur Purvis was, in fact, exposing the Mackenzie King government's appalling failure to take any initiative or responsibility.

My personal contribution to this 1939 conference was as a kind of stage manager rather than as a participant in debate. However, I did make one intervention on a point that struck me as very important, and this episode partly explains my rather cool feelings towards Dr Herbert Bruce who was always put in the limelight and treated with adulation on these occasions. I spoke in strong objection to the theory propounded in the preamble to the new 1938 Act, that housing subsidies for low-income people ought to be provided by municipalities rather than by the federal government because this should be regarded as a matter of public health. 'I think that is not at all fair,' I said; 'the low-rental contribution is needed because of the lowness of income and this arises out of national and world-wide conditions over which no province or municipality can have any control. Of course, the Dominion government should contribute to the rent fund.' I wasn't able to speak with the fire and rhetoric of George Mooney, but it was to me a very basic position and I was successful in getting an amendment added to one of the conference resolutions, to urge the federal government to contribute a share of rent subsidy. But when the conference reached the final session, for voting on resolutions, the meeting was informed that the draft of my amendment to this first resolution had somehow got into Dr Herbert Bruce's pocket and he was nowhere to be found in the hotel. A conference delegate rose to the occasion to declare that it was always wiser to congratulate governments for what they had done rather than to complain about what they had not done. And so the conference adopted an altogether bland resolution welcoming the terms of the 1938 National Housing Act. It was a small moment in history, but perhaps a rather fateful one; for it was Dr W.C. Clark, still holding the office of deputy minister of finance, who drafted the 1944 Housing Act, and Canada entered the post-war period with no offer of federal subsidies to support programs of low-rental housing.

Looking through the verbatim report of that conference, held so many years ago, I notice that the chairman of a luncheon meeting, Mr Wilfrid Heighington, president of the Ontario Housing and Planning Association, announced: 'I want to read a telegram from the Right Honourable W.L. Mackenzie King, Prime Minister of Canada, addressed to Mr Humphrey Carver, who is so well known in this Conference and so much personally responsible for all the work that has been done.' He then read the telegram, a worthy example of such official messages sent down from the lofty towers of Parliament Hill. I don't remember being particularly impressed by this at the time; but in retrospect I appreciate the significance of such a thing happening. Only nine years before this I had been in the midst of a London fog, in the dark alleys of Gray's Inn, wondering how I could be more actively engaged in the things that interested me. And now I was the recipient of a telegram from a prime minister in almost my first experience of 'citizen participation'.

6
People
in the Long Dark Tunnel

Like many other Canadian families, we were still at the lake in the first week of September 1939, when we turned on the 10 o'clock news and heard that the *Athenia* had been sunk. We sat around the log fire and talked about the friends and relations who may have been on board, returning from their summer holidays. And as the last flames in the fireplace flickered out, we were reluctant to go to bed, knowing that more than another summer holiday was ending. I couldn't expect any longer to have the freedom to follow my interest in the environment of peacetime life. I was thirty-seven years old and I didn't seem to have any useful qualifications for wartime. As it turned out, I spent most of the war years in uniform, in a very unheroic job, but in an occupation that added enormously to my qualifications as a student of man and his environment. I had an extraordinary opportunity, such as could only occur in wartime, to talk intimately with hundreds of young Canadians, to discover what they thought about themselves and about their country.

When we got back to Toronto a few days later, I was glad that we had decided to move into the city where it would be easier to share with others some of the difficult decisions and family separations that might now occur. We had rented 44 Elgin Avenue, just a few blocks from the familiar corner of Bloor Street and Avenue Road, a pleasant three-storey attached house that belonged to Hugh and Rain Macdonell. We had felt that life in the country, at Lorne Park, had been rather lonely for three-year-old Peter and here, from behind the railing of the front porch he would be able to hail all the passers-by. He would miss his morning conversation with our kindly Scottish friend Jim Ramage, but now he would hear the high-pitched Gaelic greeting of our next-door neighbour

Dr McMillan, father of Sir Ernest, the conductor of the Toronto Symphony Orchestra.

Not being able to foresee how I might fit into this new wartime world, I took on several short-term tasks. One of these was a weekly series of radio broadcasts that I had arranged with Donald Buchanan who was at that time a program director of the CBC. These were an attempt to put the subjects of housing and city-planning into an easy and vernacular language. The words were spoken by Frank Peddy, a lawyer whose mellifluous Irish voice had opened up a second career for him; as I got the lilt of it, my writing became more rhythmic and pastoral because it was such a pleasure to hear the cadences of Frank's voice. At a few days' notice I also took on the regular course of lectures on the history of classical and mediaeval architecture at the university. The architect who had previously given this course had a military background and had eagerly departed, leaving behind a dusty cupboard stacked with old-fashioned glass slides, cracked and hopelessly incomplete. With such wretched equipment I tried to explain the elegance of the Ionic order, the majestic proportions of the great Norman cathedrals, the delicate interlacing of Exeter's rib-vaulting. To reconstruct my own memory of these beautiful places gave me a new and nostalgic understanding of their shapes and structure, and there was a poignancy in wondering how many of them would have disappeared before the war was over. I'm sure that all those cracked and faded slides and my own hastily contrived lectures couldn't possibly have conveyed my feelings.

One day there appeared at 44 Elgin Avenue a very small architect named Dr Eugenio G. Faludi. He was a refugee from anti-semitic Italy, had stayed briefly in London, and now hoped to start a new professional life in Canada. But Toronto architects took a WASPish view of his credentials and succeeded in barring him from the practice of architecture, though the reasons for this judgement seemed obscure. It was essential for Faludi to acquire some status in the Canadian community and he quite rightly conceived the idea of writing a book on housing and planning. He thought that I would be the right person to join him in this enterprise, but this turned out to be a mistake; it was a lopsided partnership in two ways. For one thing I wrote far more than Faludi ever got done. And it became quite clear that a partnership between a man who is just 5 feet high and one who is 6½ feet high is inherently laughable and absurd. I don't think it really bothered Faludi to walk down the street with me, but I always found myself walking in the gutter so that I wouldn't look like a monster. However, none of this mattered because the diminutive Gene Faludi eventually won his Canadian credentials by the stature of his brains and his persistence; in the immediate postwar years he had by far the largest town-planning practice in Canada and almost single-handedly restored a planning profession that had been wiped out by the pre-war depression and raised it to a new status. In the new élite of planners, to have worked for Faludi came to be the equivalent of wearing the right old-school tie–which rather turned the tables on the WASPish architects.

Seeking a route to a useful wartime occupation I soon found my way to the 'back campus' of the University of Toronto where a motley crowd of professors, artists, and assorted intellectuals marched up and down learning the rudiments of military routine from two high school teachers, Bert Tolton and Archie Bryce, a major and a captain in the reserve army. It was at least a declaration of one's availability and, confronted by the impenetrable future, it was a comfort to share one's innocence with such a congenial group of people. The back campus, behind Hart House, was a kind of jumping-off place from which, month by month, people started off on new lives and adventures. My immediate companions were Charles Comfort, the painter, and Felix Walter, professor of French, tall, dark, and handsome, and a fastidious left-wing intellectual. After each parade we would gather in Dorothy Walter's living-room and discuss our latest gift of knowledge from Bert Tolton. This was the point of departure for Charles' distinguished career as a War Artist. From the outset, military detail had an extraordinary fascination for him. Everything he learned was documented, indexed, and filed away in his scholarly mind. His battlefield drawings and watercolours done in Italy are, I think, the most beautiful things he ever did and his unerring eye for detail gave them a special authority. Of our company, Felix Walter was one of the first to take off into a new life, to become an intelligence officer; this was a road that led him, after the war, to faraway places, to Paris and to Beirut and to a life very different from the bourgeois comforts of the Bloor Street apartment.

In our ranks also was Earle Birney, the West Coast poet; I can still see his scrawny figure in the column marching up University Avenue as we returned from camp at Niagara, so breathless and almost strangled by the heavy pack on his back that one wondered if he would survive the next block from Queen Street to Dundas. He went off to Europe, far from strangled, and came back with his wartime novel, *Turvey*. Claude Bissell was also there on the back campus which he ruled twenty years later as president of the university. And in this motley company, too, were Wayne and Shuster, later to become great artists of the television theatre. So we all marched up and down the campus and learned to bark at one another like guardsmen and we all went to camp at Niagara and flung ourselves on the poison ivy. And, in the course of time, we all found our new wartime directions.

Waiting wasn't very pleasant and I was grateful when my turn came. I was going to do a job which appealed to me both because it contained an element of social mission and because I thought I might be quite good at it. I hoped this wasn't a selfish point of view. In fact the job itself arose out of the difficulties of raising a citizen army in a desperate hurry without suffering a critical wastage of individual talents. I know that some people would have found it a tedious and pedantic desk job. I can only say that, for me, it was a continuous revelation of the marvellous varieties of human nature, and the whole experience sustained my interest from the day I started until the day I took off my uniform in November 1945. It happened like this.

In the very first weeks of the war some members of the Canadian Psychological Association discussed how their professional skills could be put to the best use. They visited the National Research Council in Ottawa and there met General A.G.L. McNaughton who was still the president of NRC and had not yet taken his position as commander of the Canadian forces in Britain. Discussion turned to the value of psychological methods in discovering and assessing the personalities and aptitudes of those who would have to be quickly transformed from civilians to soldiers. McNaughton, quick to see the significance of this idea, thought that the system should operate within the medical framework of the army and insisted that it would have to be put through a proper scientific validation so that psychologists would genuinely be able to claim that their tests and conclusions conformed to the real-life performance of trained soldiers. The psychologists were encouraged to develop a practical scheme, and this was done largely by Professor Bott of Toronto, George Humphrey of Queen's, and W.D. Tait of McGill. 'Whit' Morton of McGill had the task of constructing the key piece in the system, which was the 'M' test. When the system went into action, every Canadian soldier, with varying emotions of apprehension, scorn, hope, or despair, turned the ten pages of the 'M' test and his profile (his score on each of the ten parts of the test) was recorded on his military documents. Everyone was measured on the same scale,whether they had been lawyers or PhDs or illiterate forest workers, maritime fishermen, or mechanics from automobile factories. After the system had been put through its validation phase, applied to the Canadian forces in Britain under the command of General McNaughton, it was introduced into the whole military system by General Brock Chisholm who was then the head of the medical wing of the army. This was the same Brock Chisholm, always a pioneer, who later won fame for his deflation of Santa Claus and for his work as director of the World Health Organization. The army's psychological staff was headed by Colonel Bill Line who had been the University of Toronto's professor of child psychology, well loved by a generation of nursery school workers. Under Brock Chisholm and Bill Line, two men of independent and humanitarian spirit, there was no risk that the system would become a cold psychometric machine for sorting out men like mice in a laboratory. The real essence of their system was the patient clinical interview to discover the 'whole man' and the environment in which he had grown and the influences to which he had responded.

I became one of Bill Line's team when the system was finally put into operation at the beginning of 1942 and for the next four years this was my whole life. I talked with thousands of young Canadians in a kind of confessional relationship that could only occur in wartime when career decisions are fateful. I discovered that there are no stereotypes: each man who told me about himself and his aspirations was a lonely individual, trying to understand himself and the world around him.

My first assignment took me to Windsor, Ontario, an industrial jungle where the motor industry has slopped over into Canada from Detroit, just across the St Clair River. The area had originally been a French settlement, but this bedrock of population had been overwhelmed by the immigrant labour employed on the assembly lines of Ford and Chrysler, an extraordinary ethnic conglomerate, a kind of microcosm of the old world with an emphasis on eastern Europe. St Luke's barracks were right beside the Ford assembly line and the pick of the incoming recruits were to be marshalled into a new light-armoured battalion. After about a month a sufficient number had been chosen and we all moved into tents in an open field near London, Ont. Here everyone had to be sorted out and fitted into the precise pattern of the regimental establishment: so many drivers and mechanics, so many motorcyclists, so many cooks, artificers, clerks, and just plain fighting men. It was quite a jigsaw puzzle and each man had his own idea of what he ought to be.

Leaving home and going to Windsor wasn't a very big geographical move, but nevertheless it was a complete break in the pattern of life and so all the events are very clearly remembered. On the way to Windsor

I couldn't get out of my mind the picture of Mary and small Peter standing side by side and hand in hand outside our front door. The two figures were etched on my mind like a primitive drawing on the wall of a cave. My own two people. And now Mary would have to shake out the furnace every winter night and shovel the coals. At that period of the war we didn't have any illusions about how long it might be before I was back for more than a hurried week-end.

An outstanding event of the few weeks in Windsor was that there I met Zack Phimister, on the same assignment as myself. There are only a handful of people in any man's life whose friendship reaches down into some subliminal infrastructure. I cannot explain why Zack appealed to me so much. He had been with a Quaker unit in the Spanish war, then he had become a school inspector in the Niagara district; later on in life, after 1945, he became the head of metropolitan Toronto's school system and, when he died a comparatively young man, he was Ontario's deputy minister of education. No psychological system could possibly delineate the magic formula that would put into one person such a superb blend of qualities: a self-effacing modesty, a quiet wit and humour, and a marvellous deep wisdom. Zack Phimister was a prince among men and it was good to meet him as I started out on my new discovery of people, with a special search for what makes the difference between the excellent and the others.

During this short stay in Windsor there occurred an incident that remains vividly in my mind. A young German Luftwaffe officer had escaped from a POW camp in Ontario and had got across the border to Detroit, where he had been recaptured; he was being held in the Windsor barracks while some investigations were in progress. One morning when the quota of recruits for the new armoured battalion had almost been filled, a visiting VIP was to inspect the men on the cinder parade-ground, just across the road from the barracks. For some reason I have forgotten, it was decided that the young Luftwaffe officer should be taken to the flat roof of the four-storey barracks where he could look down on this scene; and I was chosen to be in charge of him. He was the very picture of the proud, athletic, blue-eyed German, such as I had often seen in years before, climbing mountains in Europe and singing romantic songs in a lamplit beer-garden. In his way, he was a prince among men too, fearless and full of zest for life, a blend of superman and Peter Pan. For about an hour we were together on the roof, looking down at the raw recruits on the parade ground, an untidy rabble still without any soldier's discipline in their postures and outlook. These were the sons of Canadian immigrants and they had lived as teen-agers through the years of depression that had knocked the stuffing out of Canada. They hadn't been roused by any kind of national zest for life. Their lives had been flat and uneventful like the boring voice of W.L. Mackenzie King, their leader. They had never known anything like the young Luftwaffe officer's heroic glow of national pride; even though some of his feathers had been plucked, the cockiness was still there.

I had a few other assignments that gave me a view of the whole spectrum of army personnel, the skilled artificers and mechanics and cooks and bottle-washers; and then I moved into the work that became my specialized field, the Officer Selection and Appraisal Centre. By 1942 British forces were exhausted and Canada had undertaken to contribute a supply of young officers to be loaned to the British army. The stream of recruits being trained in Canada was combed through to find all possible candidates and, in batches of five hundred each month, these men were sent to Trois Rivières, Quebec, where the appraisal centre was, rather ironically, set up in the exhibition grounds built to glorify Premier Maurice Duplessis, not exactly an ardent supporter of the cause. I was one of about half-a-dozen examiners who had to do a dreadfully rushed job; I sometimes meet in an elevator or airport someone who remembers me from that fateful thirty-minute interview in Trois Rivières so long ago. After this emergency of 1943 the selection process moved to the Officer Training Centre at Brockville, Ontario (where the camp so familiar to hundreds of Canadians has long since been submerged by the tide of suburbia) and we settled down to perform in a more professional way.

The candidates, in batches of fifty to a hundred, would stay here for three weeks and submit to a battery of psychological, behavioural, and group leadership tests. By the time each man came for his fateful interview a great deal was already known about him. This might include a psychiatric examination if any unexplainable characteristics had turned up. Out of all this we would write a capsule biography of each man, trying in a very frank way to explain his essential strengths and weaknesses. Finally each candidate and his dossier would appear before a Board of Colonels, and a General; however hard they tried to put on a fatherly tone of voice, the experience was terrifying and calculated to put any modest man at a great disadvantage. There is something humiliating about exposing any adult to such a clinical procedure, stripping him of his secret defences and taking him apart; only the deadly seriousness of the decision could justify the process and we certainly never lost sight of the implications of a man's responsibility for other people's lives.

One series of test situations used at the appraisal centre involved groups of half-a-dozen candidates, without an identified leader, presented with a practical field problem such as the crossing of a simulated river or the raising of a high pole. Some miscellaneous material was scattered on the ground, some ropes and planks and nails and also a few odds and ends that really had nothing to do with solving the problem but introduced confusion into the group debate. The appraisal officers would sit under a tree and see what happened. Very often the first one of the group to take a lead would be a Toronto boy, a well-educated WASP, perhaps from Upper Canada College, who was compelled by 'noblesse oblige' to make the first move. But his authority would be quickly undermined when it appeared that he had no idea how to tie a knot or apply leverage. At this point a boy from the Prairies would take over to exhibit his skills with ropes and poles, so familiar to any boy on a farm. Sometimes he had been misled by the intital efforts of the young Torontonian and hadn't perceived the error; so he, in turn, would have to pass the initiative to a tall and charismatic candidate from BC who had looked like the most obvious leader from the outset. However, by this time, other members of the group had tended to attach their sympathies either to the WASP or to the farm boy and the charismatic candidate from BC would be unable to command their attention in following his proposal for a solution of the problem. Up to this point another member of the group would have remained rather detached from the huddle of eager beavers; he seemed to have a more quiet and philosophical attitude than his companions scrambling over one another to discover a solution; he was, of course, a Nova Scotian. Anxious to escape from their impasse of divided opinions, the others would finally turn to him, frankly hoping that he would make a fool of himself too. He steps into the ring, quietly disposes of the irrelevant material that has been tied into the muddle, tells each one what to do and the problem is solved. This rather characteristic episode left one with a problem of evaluating the performance of the Nova Scotian as an officer candidate: he was the first to see the solution to the situation, but what was one to make of his diffidence and natural distaste for being competitive?

The personal interviews with each man (I would prefer to call them conversations) were based on the assumption that human behaviour is generally consistent. If you know what a person's attitudes and performance have been in the past, you can predict pretty well how he is likely to react to circumstances and situations in the future. Consistency of behaviour doesn't mean that a person never changes, but that personality is continuous. Experience, suffering, and knowledge extend a person's character so that his behaviour in the future may not be the same as in the past, because of what has been added. Finding out a man's past history reveals the extent of his ability to profit from experience, to grow, and to mature. A man's history may show that he is highly adaptable, quick to learn and to make progress by applying his energies and his aspirations. Or his history may suggest just the opposite: that in an alarming situation his abilities are more likely to deteriorate than to be keyed up. Our conversations were intended to uncover these qualities, of particular importance in choosing someone to be an officer and only in a lesser degree important in the character of any soldier. In other centuries battles had been won by massed ranks of men standing shoulder to shoulder, the less resolute gaining reassurance and physical support from the stronger. In modern warfare each man had to be a fighting unit by himself and many tactical situations would depend upon one individual, alone in his slit-trench.

For about two years I spent all my working time talking to the twenty-year-old generation of young Canadians, trying to understand their innermost spirit and all that had happened to them, growing up in the Canada of that period. It was an exploration that never ceased to be exciting to me, day by day, finding out how the qualities of one generation had issued from the past generation, moulded by their social, economic, and physical environment.

Now, thirty years later, these men are the fathers of another twenty-year-old generation. The circumstances of life have changed so much that a contemporary batch drawn from the same human stock has very different views about themselves and their relationships with society. I remember that a surprising number of the wartime generation would tell me that they had played a leading role in the young people's organization of their church; this was regarded as the best evidence of their virtue and their ability to take on responsibilities; it was assumed that there could be no better assurance that, as a young officer, a man would have credibility among those he had to lead. This was the generation grown up in the depression, many of them the sons of farmers and tradesmen in small towns. There had been little money for personal possessions, such as the boats and skis and phonographs that young people have today. There wasn't any money for travelling, there were few prospects of getting a job by moving to a big city, 'opting out' was not a viable course because there was nothing to opt out of. For a great many the local church really was the only available institution where young people could gather to enjoy one another's company. And since the church was managed by a minister or priest and by the elders of the community, a due respect for institutions and authority rubbed off on them. So when that generation emerged from the depression and from the disciplines of war and entered a more free and affluent postwar period, it is understandable that they welcomed the liberties that could be enjoyed by their children–liberties they never had themselves. The present twenty-year-old generation has not been so dependent upon institutions and tends to be scornful of authority.

Looking back on this wartime search for evidences of leadership capacity and upon our judgments of character, the criteria now have an old-fashioned look, in their simplicity and directness. We had to look for people who were straightforward, firm, confident, and consistent, besides having a competent body and a mind that could score not less than a modest 160 points on the army's 'M' test. Nowadays these simple qualities are less admired by the young and perhaps we are all more attracted by people who are a bit devious and not inclined to conform to institutional behaviour, and to whom all subjects are debatable. In the luxury of peace and affluence we can afford these liberties of a democratic society. But in wartime a good deal of democratic behaviour had to be surrendered; authority had to be accepted and many subjects were not debatable–not even the orders of a junior officer no older than yourself. The wartime moratorium on democratic behaviour imposed a special obligation to be strictly fair when one had to choose the people to have authority.

One couldn't become so deeply involved with this stream of officer candidates, the preselected cream of the crop of young Canadians, without being inquisitive about the other end of the social spectrum; so I got permission to use some spare time in finding out about the men in army detention barracks. If one knew more about the human deficiencies, on the negative side, it might help to confirm the contrasting qualities on the positive side.

Soldiers are not put into detention for committing crimes that are normally dealt with by the civil courts and for which soldiers, like anyone else, may be sent to prison. The principal offence under military law is for a soldier to be absent without leave; in fact, this very often embraces a multitude of offences and minor misdemeanours. The kind of behaviour that has traditionally got soldiers into trouble is 'letting off steam': a man's masculine energies and the bravado that helps him to tolerate the dreadful stresses of war are deliberately worked up to a fine pitch so that he becomes just like a bloody bull in a china shop. If there isn't a battle to be fought as a way of releasing this resource of violence, a man has to find other outlets through 'pub-crawling', or the more athletic forms of sexual satisfaction, or by just raising hell in any available way. Though not at all endearing to civilians, this kind of behaviour has usually been accepted as demonstration of a warrior's real threat to the enemy. If it becomes too much of a nuisance the soldier has had to be put in 'the cooler' until he has quietened down and, if he's got into worse scrapes, he may be committed for some time to a military detention barracks, which is essentially a lock-up or prison though the words 'prison' and 'prisoner' are not used. This sequence of letting off steam and then cooling off was fairly familiar in the first world war which placed such great demands on patience and endurance. It also showed up in the early part of the second, when a trained Canadian army was held on the fortified island of Britain without any way of confronting the enemy—until the disaster of Dieppe.

When I talked to the men in a detention barracks in Canada in 1944, this was not at all the kind of person I found. It's one thing to lock up a rebellious and over-exuberant soldier for 28 days in the cooler, to sleep on a hard board shelf and have no one to talk to. But it's a very different thing to lock up a young recruit in a conscript army, whose personal problem is a complete inability to be exuberant about anything. To put a mild, inadequate young man in a cell and give him the treatment devised for suppressing exuberance certainly didn't help very much and only made the poor lad brood over his inadequacies and yearn for the affection of his girl or his mother, if he was lucky enough to have one or the other. Most of these unhappy boys came from broken families, victims in some way of the depression. In my notes of interviews with these dispirited wretches, I had to use a social worker's language of compassion:

Only four years education and was in Grade III when when he left school at the age of 15 . . . For two or three years had had no long-term jobs but had been an itinerant labourer, working his way west as far as Alberta. Enlisted in July 1941. Disqualified from overseas service on account of defective hearing. For more than a year employed on kitchen duties. On four occasions absent without leave for short periods and finally awarded a sentence of 94 days in detention after being absent for more than a month.

His father was a tinsmith in a small town and had eight children of whom the three first died in infancy. His father was a habitual Saturday night alcoholic and,

on these occasions, abused his wife in the presence of the children. [The boy] was
turned out of the house for attempting to interfere, in order to protect his mother
to whom he seems to have been genuinely attached. He and the two youngest
children then lived with their grandmother. His mother suffered from nervous
breakdowns and the parents finally separated in 1939. On the occasion of his last
absence without leave [the boy] says that he went to try and find his mother in
several parts of Ontario, but without success. During previous absences he had
stayed with his grandmother. [The young man's] disturbed and unhappy family
background, his limited education and the physical disability hindering him from
more active service all contributed to an attitude of hopelessness from which
there seemed to be no prospects of release and which was being accentuated by
the humiliations of a term in detention.

My notes on another man recount how

he had lived all his life in a small logging community . . . In June 1942, after
considerable hesitation, he went with his brother to enlist; his brother was
rejected on physical grounds and [the boy] found himself in the Army, alone and
friendless. He lost his courage and went home to find that his wife was very
depressed . . . his military service consisted of a series of absences alternating with
terms of detention of increasing duration. On each occasion he had been released
he had hurriedly returned to his northern home; on his last visit, prior to a term
of 9 months in detention, he had to help his wife when their second child was
born.

Another I described as

a young man of good though small physique with a sensitive and gentle manner;
evidently of emotional and introspective nature . . . For two years he had worked
as a delivery boy with a bicycle and then had been a labourer on a smelter in
Sault Ste Marie . . . After a year in the army he was absent without leave and
not found for four months. Four months before this his girl-friend had given
birth to a child, had been rejected by her parents and taken refuge with [the boy's]
parents in the suburbs of Montreal. Feeling a responsibility for the girl, [the boy]
had gone to Montreal and disappeared into the bushland near his home where
he had built himself a shanty in the woods.

Another man

small and sallow, with a long pointed chin and a timid lugubrious expression,
spoke reluctantly and mostly in monosyllables; he seemed to have only one idea
and that was to be at home with his family. (He was one of 12 children.) On one
previous occasion in detention he had swallowed three needles and during a

subsequent detention term had swallowed a safety-pin as the result of which he spent two weeks in hospital. He said that such ideas came to him suddenly and without previous consideration or plan.

So the ugliness of Hitler's war flowed into remote places far away from the heroic scenes and great events that were being enacted in Europe. The sadness and distress reached into the backwoods of Canada and hurt young people who couldn't possibly understand what the conflict was all about. For many of these innocent people Canada was certainly not comprehensible as a country that they could fight for; they had only known the world around them as an infinite wilderness where they had had to clutch for some little bit of love close to them. There were no grand ideas about Canada. There had not been the compassion of the American New Deal; neither had there been the fiery torch of a romantic dictator.

During 1944 a change came, of which most of us were hardly aware at the time. Even before D-day in Europe there was an indefinable point when, in the long black night of the war, people began to think about what would happen afterwards. At first it was only an impression that the sky was lighter on the horizon; and it was hardly decent to mention it, with so much agony yet to be faced as the awful battle of Europe was fought through Italy and through Normandy after the landings in June 1944. But as Canadians in Europe and on the Atlantic were making a new fame for their country it became imperative to think out what Canada should be like after the war. It certainly had to be a prouder and more confident place than it had been before. The word was 'reconstruction'. Prime Minister Mackenzie King appointed the Advisory Committee on Reconstruction and in 1944 its first reports began to appear. In March appeared the report of the subcommittee on Housing and Community Planning generally known as the Curtis Report from the name of its chairman, Professor Curtis, an economist at Queen's University. The report was written by Leonard Marsh, one of the editors and authors of *Social Planning for Canada*. Another member of the committee was Eric Arthur. Since I was entirely occupied in my job for the army, I was not, of course, in touch with these events. Nor did I know anything about the writing of the 1944 National Housing Act which was to be the instrument for reconstructing the housing industry when the war was over. Some of the idealism expressed in the Curtis report appeared as Part V of this act, entitled 'Housing Research and Community Planning'; this was to be the charter by which I worked, through more than twenty postwar years. In this way my own past connexions were already being linked with the future.

Towards the end of 1944 there was a reorientation in my work in the army, turning to the time when the flow of people would be reversed and Canadians would be coming back to find a new place in a new Canada, prouder and more competent than the country they had left behind. It was hoped that our whole wartime system for discovering a man's talents could be put into reverse, helping him to find a route into the peacetime world. So plans were made for staffing demobilization centres with counsellors who would have the documentary explanation of how each man had been evaluated and assigned to a military role, and how this had subsequently worked out. A counsellor with some knowledge of civilian occupations would then be able to steer him in the right direction. It was anticipated that a large proportion of the veterans would expect to go to universities and discussion of the choices involved would be enormously aided by knowledge of a man's 'M' test score and by other evidence of the kind of work in which he might be successful. The veterans returning from Europe would naturally be most respectful of counsel received from officers who had shared the same battle experiences as themselves. Consequently a new group of counsellors would have to be organized and they would need to understand the whole process of personal appraisal and psychological interpretation that had been developed by the Directorate of Personnel Selection. So, towards the end of 1944 I was asked to take up the task of writing an account of how this whole system had evolved since the initial proposals had been made to General McNaughton in 1939; to do this I moved to National Defence Headquarters in Ottawa. Because the war might be ended in a few months it clearly wasn't feasible to write all in one piece, the book-length volume which the subject deserved and have it completed when the flood of demobilization began. So I set out a writing program, with instalments to be issued every two weeks through a six-months period. I hope that the philosophy and the spirit that I tried to expound were of some help in those critical moments of decision when men left the army and had to make the choice of a career.

(In the unlikely event that anyone would want to assemble my complete literary works, he might search in the archives for what I wrote under such pressure between April and August 1945. For beside serving the immediate purpose, to help in the process of demobilization, the whole volume of about 135,000 words also served as the official military history of the Canadian army's personnel selection system in the Second World War. I expect the volume has long since been buried in some impenetrable dark corner of the army's archives–which is perhaps a pity because what Brock Chisholm and Bill Line did for Canadians was most imaginative, sophisticated, and professional and it has certainly left its mark upon Canadian personnel practices through all the subsequent years.)

Before starting on this writing task I needed to find out how the whole system had operated in the theatre of war. So in November 1944 I moved from NDHQ in Ottawa (a dreary old hotel building where the British High Commission now stands on Elgin Street) to Canadian Military Headquarters in London (in a comparatively modern office building near St James Square). I went more as a tourist than as a soldier and I felt like a ghost going to visit people and places that I had known so well only a little time ago and that were now tired, bruised, and blackened by the war.

The process of becoming a ghost began in Canada, at the military camp in Windsor, Nova Scotia, the gathering place for military personnel going overseas. It's a place that has a rather other-worldly quality, its most notable historic character being Judge Haliburton whose nineteenth-century tales about Sam Slick are now in a literary limbo. You are invited to visit his house, to see the quill pens he wrote with and to hear the tick-tock of his clock that has wooden works. Around the town are impassable red muddy channels with the Bay of Fundy tide coming in and going out again with maddeningly slow rhythm. It is a kind of purgatory where you might well expect to wait before crossing the Styx. From time to time a few faces would be missing from the ranks of the daily route march. After a couple of weeks the word came for me to pack my bag, to entrain and enter the silent passages of wartime security. There was a 24-hour train journey through hills and valleys that I couldn't identify and, arriving at a harbour in the dark of the night, an open launch ferried groups of shadowy figures across the water to the side of a large ship. A day later we woke to find ouselves on the vast surface of the grey ocean, amidst lines of ships stretching to the horizon like latitude and longitude on the curve of the earth. The extraordinary size and majestic silent movement of this armada gave me an entirely new impression of the hugeness of the war in a way that I had never comprehended within Canada, where I had been focused on the human scale of individual people. At night one tried to penetrate the darkness to see this huge company all around as the convoy ploughed on through heavy seas; and in the morning some of the older and smaller vessels were seen to have lost their positions and trailed behind. This was Armageddon. Now I understood the word, not just as a journalist's cliché. The geography of the whole thing was so immense.

I wondered where my two brothers were. I knew they were involved in some way, somwhere on the great frontier of Europe, but no information had passed between us and, in fact, I did not learn what they had been doing until after the war. My older brother Maurice, adventurous, fearless, and always determined to be an active participant in the war, was in enemy territory on the ridges of the Greek mountains near Olympus, picking his way along the goat trails and dropping down into the valley to put explosives on a railway track. He was far from his home, a Christian mission in Africa. At the very other end of the long frontier my younger brother Francis was on the windswept shore of the Shetland Islands waiting anxiously for an early morning sighting of a small boat returning from a run-in to the Norwegian fjords. I only knew that both my brothers were close to the frontier of the war. And I was just a tourist. A ghost.

It seemed to take a long time to get within sight of the Irish coast. We then lay up for a day near Holyhead, took a devious route via the Isle of Man, and finally entered the long dirty sea highway into the Mersey and tied up at the docks in Liverpool. In the days when one travelled by sea and not by air, the British dockworker had been a familiar figure in his old cloth cap and dismal overcoat–such an inefficient uniform. Here were the same colourless figures, the stoic survivors of many devastating air-raids, now even more grey, thin and dejected. And here was the very essence of industrial England, Liverpool's Lime Street Station, a black damp cavern smelling of sulphurous coal. And then, in a few hours, I emerged from Euston Station into London, that most lovable and wonderful of all cities.

I had the sensation of being a ghost in London mostly because it always seemed to be dark. Rather than living in town, near where I worked at CMHQ I thought I would learn more about wartime life in London if I went out every night to my brother Francis's home at Potten End near Berkhamsted. So every evening I would grope my way out of St James Square, through blacked-out Piccadilly and by various routes across Soho and Bloomsbury to the commuters' train at Euston. There was an overwhelming nostalgia about walking through these darkened streets, noticing the ugly shored-up gaps in the rows of buildings and the damage done to the Bloomsbury houses I had known so well. At the station, men and women hurried along the platform to get on the train as it moved away, as they had learned to do in the more anxious nights of air-raids. And the next day I was up early to walk across country in the dark and was back on the train in the halflight of morning, everyone sitting silent in the railway carriages like figures in a tomb.

There was one day that was different. It must have been a Saturday and the sun was shining. A letter had been forwarded to me at CMHQ which, for the first time, made me think about my own future when the war was over, perhaps in a few months. The letter came from Arthur Bunnell, one of the firm of planning consultants in whose office I had worked in 1930. I had overheard Arthur Bunnell on the telephone fighting to keep his head above water as the firm sank into the depression. And here he was, the first on deck again. The letter I received was to say that he had been appointed to organize the new postwar community-planning branch of the Ontario provincial government–and would I join him in this? I was very touched that Bunnell would think of me and it was reassuring to think that there might be a place for me in the new era ahead. But I had to reply that my duties in the army were still very far from being finished.

When I opened the letter I was sitting in Trafalgar Square amongst the pigeons, on a wall in front of the National Gallery: a good place to reflect upon one's place in the cosmos. I remembered that the first time I had been in this place was as a ten-year-old boy with my father on my first excursion to London and, before returning home on the train, we had had sausage-and-mashed at the Lyons tearoom on the Strand by Charing Cross. (That is why sausage-and-mashed is still one of my favourite dishes.) I also remembered one November 11th in the early twenties when the first war was not long over and Armistice Day was still a very solemn occasion: from all directions tens of thousands of Londoners walked quietly through the streets towards the cenotaph and filled the whole space of Whitehall from end to end, so that from Trafalgar Square one looked down upon the largest congregation of people that I have ever seen anywhere. And suddenly there was utter silence, there in the very middle of the city. I have never known any occasion so deeply moving. And I remembered another occasion, in 1924, when the whole of London seemed to be gathered in the Square to acclaim the results of the general election which brought in the first Labour government. The constituency results were projected on screens, with accompanying roars from the crowd and witty Cockney comments. Patrick Rolleston and I had climbed up on to a window ledge of the Admiralty Arch to get an elevated view of the scene. Come to think of it, that election which put Ramsay MacDonald into 10 Downing Street was a link in the chain of events that brought both of us to live in Canada.

Happenings like this help one to understand the meaning of life and one's place in the universe of people and their collective affairs. Even the sausage-and-mashed was, in my recollection, a kind of first communion in the big city. It made me think that the generation of young Canadians with whom I had been spending so much time had had little opportunity to feel themselves part of a great political society that responded to their own needs and expressions. Londoners knew what they were fighting for. But in the cities of Canada there was little emotional content, no central places of the heart and spirit. Just the streetcar tracks along the narrow dreary miles of Yonge Street and the bleak three-way corner of Portage and Main. London is a place full of allusions and symbols and meanings, so that you can construct some explanation of your own personal position in the context of life and feel a kind of justification for what you have done. In London you don't feel embarrassed to be sententious about this, because Londoners themselves have always had a sentimental love affair with their own city.

Trafalgar Square and Nelson's column were built in the 1830s and this has always been a big friendly place–a people-place, as we would say nowadays–with its pleasant fountain basins, its absurd lions, and the pomposity of mounting the heroic naval figure on top of a column. The symbolism of the place was even further contrived when Canada House and South Africa House were built on either side of the Square after the Great War. From Imperialism to the Commonwealth. This kind of self-conscious symbolism might be expected to appeal to a family like my own, several generations of Empire and Commonwealth builders. Of my own immediate family, after all, I went to Canada and married a Canadian girl and have a Canadian family, while my older brother Maurice went to Africa and married a South African and has a South African family. To which I might add that, on the third side of the Square, the National Gallery is the façade for London's theatre-land and my younger brother Francis married the daughter of a West End manager and his principal career has been in the art of the theatre. I might also reflect that my oldest brother Christian is remembered in the cenotaph at the foot of Whitehall, on the fourth side of the Square.

Perhaps these seem rather old-fashioned and banal sentiments, the kind of imagery beloved by Edwardian poets laureate. But how could I help receiving these ideas? I'm tuned in on London and this is the message I receive simply because the Square was deliberately contrived to convey this message to me and to people like me. The message may be banal, but I can't deny that it makes me feel that I have strong emotional ties to this place. It's a kind of territorial imperative. Anyway, I think it's important that a capital city should mean something to people who go there. Perhaps, some day, Canadians will be able to find that something important is expressed in the capital of Canada. I hope so, because I think this would make the meaning of life clearer to them.

In the months before this visit to London, I had been trying to find out, in talking to hundreds of young Canadian soldiers, what was, to them, the meaning of life and for what aims they would be prepared to give it up. (In the language of wartime psychology, this was called 'motivation', considered to be an important attribute in officer candidates.) On the whole, one would have to admit that Canada, in the decade before the war, had not given them very much to be grateful for. Now we would all very soon be back home again, and perhaps we could make it into a better place.

7
Springtime and Disaster

1 January 1946 was the beginning of a new life, in a new era, in a new kind of world full of all sorts of new expectations. I was back at the same place, near the corner of Bloor Street and Avenue Road in Toronto, but it didn't feel at all the same because I now knew exactly what I was going to do in the next stage of life. I remember walking along the street with a sense of euphoria, walking on air and talking to myself. Life was beautiful. It was the springtime of a new era.

It was beautiful to be back home again with Mary and Peter, now on Colin Avenue. To live for several wartime years, separated and yet not so very far away, had been an emotional strain perhaps more worrying than if I had been on another continent, a possible hero on a battlefield. Though I had never had any doubt that what I was doing was useful and creative, it was hard to avoid the heart-searching question: ought I to be at home? What had bothered me most was the picture of Mary, small and fragile as she seemed to me, shovelling coals into the furnace every winter night before going to bed and shaking out the ashes in the morning. In the days when all our heating was done with coal, the routine of keeping a red glow in the heart of the furnace was the expression of masculinity. The clanking sound of the furnace door being opened and slammed shut, the sulphurous smell of the coals within, and the gritty feel of the shovel in the coal bin–these were the sounds and the smells of the man at home. There's little enough a man does, God knows, to claim his position as the provider of security; and the oil companies took this away from him.

But life was beautiful too because this was a time of new beginnings, the long-awaited moment in history when great ideals could happily be brought out into the open and examined, with real prospects of public interest and realization. It was a time for the highest optimism. In Toronto, a good deal had already been going on since 1943 to set the stage for the new era and now, in January 1946, the curtain was about to go up on the performance. Certainly the subjects of housing and community-planning were going to be in the forefront of public interest. What happened in the immediate postwar period is the theme of this chapter.

My new job was to start on 1 January 1946 and, with a few weeks to spare beforehand, I joined Donald Buchanan in the first steps of setting up the National Industrial Design Council (NIDC) as a project of the National Gallery of Canada. For a few weeks Donald and I went around together, to make a collection of well-designed Canadian furniture and artifacts; we hoped to find things that had a purity and integrity of form, unsullied with ornament and artificialities of style. But because Canadian industry had been so completely absorbed into wartime production there were, naturally, very few things of Canadian design and production to be found in the stores. The most immaculate things we found were in a store that supplied hospital and surgical equipment made of glass, ceramics, or steel, and there was some astonishment when Donald and I placed an order for a most unlikely assortment of bulbous glass vessels, white pans, and various instruments of surgical torture that must have suggested a very gruesome medical treatment–and asked that they be sent to the National Gallery of Canada. Like some other people I have known of the most refined and exquisite aesthetic taste, Donald was an exceptionally untidy and unkempt person and I remember that, when he was staying with us on Colin Avenue at this time, Peter, not too good a picker-up himself, was most indignant about Donald's trail of razor blades and toothpaste in the bathroom. This small, untidy, unprepossessing man with an ineffective hearing aid was a truly great Canadian and an innovator who did more to develop the arts of this country than anyone I can think of.

Naturally, my own ideal was to pick up my interest in housing where I had left off in September of 1939. So it seemed a miracle when, during the summer of 1945, while I was still in the army, I received an invitation from Dr Harry Cassidy to join him at the University of Toronto's School of Social Work, of which he had just become the director. He wanted to make the school into a place which not only trained professional social workers but was also a focus of community research and initiative. At his suggestion I outlined my idea for a centre of study and teaching in housing, a place where all the literature on housing would be found, where researchers could gather, and where educational courses could be developed for those working in the housing field. In explaining this idea I recalled what a stimulating influence Catherine Bauer and her book *Modern Housing* had been in the evolution of housing affairs in the United States; in Canada there was no literature on housing, and no base from which to work, to stimulate public interest and to expound social policies for housing. I suggested that the best way to begin would be to do some quick and practical studies of the immediate housing needs in the Toronto area; out of this could grow the long-range programs of a permanent study centre.

Cassidy's fund-raising for this project was, in itself, a test of the idealism of three levels of government in jointly supporting this kind of community study, at that time an entirely unprecedented kind of collaboration. The main contribution was to come from the new federal housing agency, to be called Central Mortgage and Housing Corporation when it came into existence on 1 January 1946. I was the recipient of the first research grant made by CMHC. (The second grant was made to Leonard Marsh to support his pioneering study *Rebuilding a Neighbourhood* which dealt with the Strathcona area of Vancouver and was published in 1950.) The Province of Ontario contributed a third of the funds and the City of Toronto's share was arranged through the Toronto Reconstruction Council, a citizen body to which the city had assigned the task of thinking out the problems of transition into the postwar era. Out of these rather modest funds I was to be paid a monthly salary of $400, a princely sum as it seemed to me then. The funds were deposited with the bursar of the university, Mr Higginbotham, and perhaps he displayed the least idealistic attitude of all towards the project, with the suggestion that, before publication, all my research reports would have to be read and authorized by the university's Board of Governors. Presumably this reflected the austere moral code of the president, Canon Cody.

So at the beginning of January 1946 I walked up the steps and into the dingy gothic halls of the Ruskinian sandstone monster on Bloor Street, the old McMaster Building, greeted Harry Cassidy, and my career in the postwar era began.

I was accommodated in a narrow slit in the gothic stonework near the southwest corner of the building and nearby was another slit that could be used by a graduate assistant. For a few months this slit contained the uproarious humour and brimming intelligence of a young economist from Winnipeg, Bob Adamson, who came to my rescue. The slit was too small for him and, after he and Rigmore Christopherson were married in the church across the street, he took her off to Ottawa where he has worked ever since, as principal economist and policy adviser to Central Mortgage and Housing Corporation.

To keep me on the right track, Cassidy had provided me with a small advisory committee with whom I could confer. One of these was a charming and friendly gentleman, Mr L.A. de L. Meredith of the real estate firm of Chambers and Meredith, and the other was Bill Anderson, president of North American Life Assurance Company. They were a rather ill-assorted pair. Mr Meredith, the practical no-nonsense Toronto businessman, was presumably there to be a steadying down-to-earth influence on me and I welcomed his warm-hearted friendship. His principal contribution to our discussions was: 'I say, don't let's go off half-cock, eh?'–a comment that always convulsed Bob Adamson. On the other hand Bill Anderson shattered my morale every time we met because I simply couldn't follow his convolutions of thought and the technical language that flowed so rapidly from his actuarial mind.

I had first met Bill Anderson the previous summer in a big sunny room in the East Block on Parliament Hill where he had been installed to think up some idealisms for postwar housing; out of his brainstorming, Housing Enterprises of Canada Limited was born. This was to be a collaboration of the insurance companies, a kind of national public utility, to provide rental housing for the middle class in all parts of Canada. At that time there did not exist, of course, any of the big apartment developers who appeared in the 1960s; there were no firms financially and technically competent to produce massive quantities of community housing and it seemed an excellent idea to develop such a system out of the great financial strength and stability of Canada's insurance companies. The head office of HECL was set up in an old industrial building on Front Street in Toronto under the command of Brigadier 'Granny' Storms and was largely staffed by engineers demobilized from the armed services. Some small apartment projects were built, the best of which are still to be seen on Fourth Avenue in Vancouver; but it was a difficult time for building and the program foundered for lack of patience and persistence in dealing with the adjustments to postwar conditions. This was, I think, a tragedy: Canada's housing history might have been very different if there had been a strong input to fill the gap between public housing and the middle-class home-owner suburbs. Housing Enterprises folded up and, a few years later, its property was absorbed by CMHC. It was one of the heroic postwar ideas that didn't come off.

In the expectant mood of January 1946 I was very aware that I had
to deliver something quickly. This was no time for long-drawn-out scholarly investigations or for reports studded with perceptive footnotes, even
if I had been capable of producing such a thing. By June I had single-
handedly produced a nicely printed booklet with the rather ham-fisted
title *How Much Housing Does Greater Toronto Need?* and, only a few
months later, another called *Who Can Pay for Housing?*, both of which
were published immediately by the Toronto Reconstruction Council. I
have always thought that this was an accomplishment that gave credibility to the project however unsophisticated the matter. It showed that the
research process works: you put in a penny and something comes out
quickly. Too many subsequent housing researchers have set themselves
ambitious targets, gone underground for two or three years and, by the
time they reappeared, their credibility has gone. The formal product of
my two-and-a-half years work at the School of Social Work took the
form of a book entitled *Houses for Canadians* published by the University
of Toronto Press in 1948. Perhaps it was a rather dull book, but it was
the first Canadian attempt to set out in an orderly fashion the whole
fundamental problem of housing, to show that, in the nature of things,
the economic market would never fulfil all housing needs and this could
only be done through adding a substantial public program. In the two
concluding paragraphs I tried to summarize the two great challenges–of
design and of social equity:

The economic market for housing is likely to lag from sheer inertia and boredom
unless the programme is generally regarded as a great creative national enterprise, exciting all the imaginative, aesthetic, and emotional faculties of the people. There must be a dramatic satisfaction in the building of new communities
rather than a sense of futility in the scattering of bungalows upon the reluctant
suburbs.

It has been argued here that the amount of obsolete housing which has been
allowed to accumulate within our cities and the mounting numbers of families
housed in emergency accomodation [by the end of 1947 there were in Toronto
alone nearly 5000 families in emergency shelter provided by the city] together
represent a backlog which cannot now be cleared by the supply which will come
in from the private housing market . . . ultimately the solution to this central
problem of housing involves the forming of a philosophy concerning the rights
and equities within our society.

While my formal commitment was to produce this substantial piece
of writing, there were a number of by-products that arose out of local

events in which I became involved; and I'm sure that these by-products were, in the end, more useful than writing a book. From my little slit in the stonework of the old McMaster Building I was able to go out and take part in the stirring life of this postwar period. The principal tide of events that carried me along was the launching of Canada's first public housing project, as the consequence of the citizens' movement led by Harold Clark.

Regent Park North is a quite modest low-rental housing project on the east side of downtown Toronto. The original project of three-storey walk-ups and row-housing was built on 44 acres and housed 1289 families or about 5000 people. Architecturally it is of no significance at all: just three city blocks with utilitarian brick buildings on the street frontages surrounding three open spaces. But it is of great historical interest because it was created out of the idealism of the postwar years, through the sustained evangelistic effort of a remarkable group of people, endorsed by a public vote of the community's electorate. There was, at the time, no provision in the National Housing Act for subsidies to low-rental housing and no framework of government organization for such an undertaking. It was in all respects a precedent-setting accomplishment that came, not out of the political strategy of senior governments, but out of a citizen movement. This whole experience influenced me very much to believe that history is not all made by the prominent people whose names appear in the history books and the political biographies. It gave me confidence in the belief that, in our kind of society, small beginnings of a seminal kind can indeed grow and blossom into great achievements. (Little streams flow into great rivers, acorns grow into venerable oak trees, and planting the small seed of a really good idea may be as important as the grand oratory of a statesman.) The pioneering history of the Regent Park project was also important for me, because it confirmed my belief that it is right for communities to be directly involved in the housing affairs of their own people; it is for this, above all else, that communities are incorporated as municipalities: to express their compassions and manage their own environment and habitat. Since the experiences of 1946 and 1947 I have always been an advocate of local responsibility for housing affairs, with the necessary back-up from higher levels of government.

The Citizen's Housing and Planning Association led by Harold Clark had been formed in 1944, at the time when Canadians began to turn their minds to postwar aims. In that year the Curtis Report on Housing and

Community Planning was published, the new Housing Act was introduced and, on the first day of that year, Toronto's new City Planning Board issued its first master plan, which incidentally designated where the slum-clearance process should begin: in the area chosen by the Bruce Committee before the war and now to be known as Regent Park. Harold Clark's group was highly activist. They summoned conferences, sent telegrams and briefs to the federal government, organized delegations to hammer on the doors of the City Hall, aroused the public, and generally treated their theme as one of immediate urgency, not as a matter to be left until the halcyon days of peace. Their manifesto of July 1945 was entitled 'A Proposal by the Citizens' Housing and Planning Association for Action Needed NOW'. They wanted 2000 houses built for poor people immediately and kept up a patient and relentless pressure.

The decisive moment in this affair was the municipal election of 1 January 1947. A few weeks after being urged by the Citizens' Housing and Planning Association to allow the people of Toronto to express their views on Regent Park, Mayor Robert M. Saunders issued an explanation of the proposal, prefaced with his comment that 'the true greatness of a city is measured not by its artistic and commercial attainments alone but also by the homes of its citizens and the conditions under which the least affluent of them live'. At the polling booths the electors were asked to vote on this question:

Are you in favour of the City undertaking as a low cost or moderate cost rental housing project, with possible government assistance, the clearance, replanning, rehabilitation and modernisation of the area bounded by Parliament, River, Gerrard and Dundas Streets known as the Regent Park (north) Plan at an estimated cost of $5,900,000?

From the mayor's explanation it was understood that rents would be set so that anyone then living in the area would be able to move into the new housing and that this would require an annual subsidy of about $150,000 which would have to be met by the city's taxpayers because there were no provisions for rental subsidies in the National Housing Act 1944. In answer to the referendum question 29,677 Torontonians voted 'Yes' and 18,028 voted 'No'. An active participant in these affairs was Dr Albert Rose (now director of Toronto's School of Social Work) who has written the definitive history of the Regent Park project (published by the University of Toronto Press in 1958) in which he describes the ceremony of laying the cornerstone in September 1948. Dr Rose quotes a report in the *Globe and Mail:*

The back premises of the surrounding block presented a motley array of dilapidated sheds, flat roofs and clotheslines hung over the top of them. But every back window was lined with eager faces–mostly mothers and children, the people who stand to gain most by the Regent Park Housing Project.

And then Dr Rose goes on to say that, as he stood beside the ancient funeral parlour on Gerrard Street, which was to become the first office of the housing authority, he felt less enthusiastic about the way the ceremony was conducted:

Members of the Housing Authority and members of the Toronto City Council took most of the bows at the dedication ceremony, while the audience, for the most part composed of volunteer lay and professional members of a host of organisations which had worked for from five to fifteen years for the launching of a redevelopment programme in the City of Toronto, was almost entirely ignored in the ceremonies. The residents of the area, future tenants of the project, also received scant attention.

In October 1947, just a year before this cornerstone ceremony took place, Mr Louis St Laurent, then Minister for External Affairs, had declared in a luncheon address in Montreal: 'No government of which I am a part will ever pass legislation for subsidized housing.' A few months after the cornerstone ceremony Mr St Laurent, as Prime Minister, visited Regent Park and, in a Toronto luncheon address, lauded the project as a milestone in slum clearance in Canada. And later that same year the National Housing Act was amended to provide a system of subsidies for low-rental housing. So is history made.

As well as being in the ranks of Harold Clark's enthusiastic little company as he led them into the political battle and as well as being in the cheering squad for Mayor Robert Saunders, the first Canadian mayor to stake his political career on a housing issue, I had another part in these affairs. From my base in the School of Social Work and through my sponsors, the Toronto Reconstruction Council, I was able to inject ideas into the public discussions. Soon after the public vote of January 1947 I wrote a pamphlet on the nature of a local housing authority as a new feature in public administration; the authority was set up along these lines in April 1947. At about the same time Bob Adamson moved out of the little slit beside me in the McMaster Building and his place was taken by Alison Hopwood who joined with me in making a study of rental systems used in Britain, Australia, and the United States; from this we devised a rent scale that incorporated these features:

1 Adjustment to family size and income, in conformity with the aims of English and Australian rent rebates and American proportional rents.

2 The recognition of a minimum standard of living, comparable with the 'subsistence Minimum' used by English Authorities and the 'basic wage' in Australia.

3 The progressive application of subsidies so that a greater degree of rent relief may be granted in the lower ranges of income, in accordance with a system used by the National Capital Housing Authority (Washington, DC).

The rent scale we proposed for the Regent Park project and the explanation of its rationale were published by the Toronto Reconstruction Council in a fifty-page booklet entitled *Rents for Regent Park*; of all the things I did during that period this proved to have the most lasting value, for the so-called Carver-Hopwood scale was used for all public housing in Canada through the next two decades.

I have always been interested in how things get started, and I have been much involved in the seminal process in housing and urban affairs. In fact, I can probably claim to have been at the greatest number of meetings with the smallest number of people in them. There is a certain excitement about waiting in an empty room, wondering whether three or six or sixteen or sixty people are going to turn up. This has been my life, rather than attending the rotarian kind of gathering where the same people arrive each week to take their lapel badges off the pegboard and the same things happen, according to comfortable expectations. Of course, the seed-sowing process brings its share of disappointments, of which I have had many. The seed may fall on sparse or stony ground, or it's snowing horribly the day of the meeting, or the seed is a dud. Because the Regent Park affair was, I think, a classic example of the seminal process, a great tree with many splendid branches grew from the small seed, I have often wondered about its real origin. And I have asked Harold Clark about this. Harold has told me about the occasion when he recognized with fresh clarity the social purposes that so captured his imagination and led him into a long sequence of events in the course of which he performed such great services to the Toronto community. It was an evening lecture on the campus of the University of Toronto, early in 1944, one of a series on town-planning arranged by Tony Adamson of the School of Architecture. The speaker that night was Elizabeth Wood, the executive director of the Chicago Housing Authority and one of the great leaders of the housing movement in the United States in the Roosevelt period. Her subject was 'Public Housing Estate Management' and she spoke about the human qualities of tenants and of managers. She said there were plenty of statistics about the people moved from Chicago slums into public housing–data about illegitimacy, venereal disease, juvenile delinquency, adult crime, tuberculosis. 'But it isn't easy to understand what the slum-dweller is really like,' she said, 'because he isn't one kind of person. [There is] the good housekeeper and the bad housekeeper; the bitter and the hopeful; the defeated and the undefeated; the moral, the immoral; the god-fearing and the godless. But we have no data on these characteristics.' Elizabeth Wood wanted her project managers to be people of imagination who would 'set at work the wishes, desires, and culture of their tenants to make the buildings and their grounds into their personal home and neighborhood.' 'I have often thought,' she said, 'how a home changes in appearance and character as the content of family living changes, as the children grow older and new interests and tastes develop. A piano, flowers, new dishes, books, playthings are added as they grow and their life expands. The same thing should be true of a housing project. When this process takes place, you will know that the buildings have truly achieved their purpose. They have become homes and the slum-dwellers will truly have come into their own as creative citizens of the day.'

Harold Clark has also told me that his grandfather in England was a friend of the Cadburys who built Bournville Garden Village for the workers in their chocolate factory which was within a half-hour's bicycle-ride of my own childhood home in Birmingham. I like to think that Elizabeth Wood's words stirred an echo in Harold's genes; the same feeling for the environment and for the ecology of human life is passed down from one generation to another, with different words, but the meaning is the same.

Looking in my archives I am interested to note who, in addition to Elizabeth Wood, were the speakers in this series of lectures; for they were, in a sense, the transmitters of a culture that had to go underground in 1939 and could not reappear in action until 1946. It was a truly remarkable line-up and since the names read like a roster of my close friends and professional colleagues, I will list the twenty-two names in full:

Eric Arthur, that most distinguished professor of architectural design, was the general chairman. The series was led off by George Mooney whose oratory would never fail to touch your pride and your emotions,

and by Tony Adamson with his extraordinary talent for mixing laughter
with scholarship. There was Leonard Marsh who was, at that very time,
working on the Curtis Report and who is one of the Canada's most
eminent formulators of social policy. He was followed by Eugenio
Faludi, that very small architect who was yet to become that very big
planner. There was Lawrence Orton, the New York City commissioner
whose kindly friendship I enjoyed in a later decade; there was Griffith
Taylor, the great geographer; and there was Robert Legget, later to be
the custodian of Canada's building standards. Dr A.E. Berry and J.F.
McLaren shared the platform one night to talk about sewers and utilities
and were followed by my first two Canadian employers, Arthur Bunnell
to explain street systems, and Norman D. Wilson, the planner of Toronto's subway system yet to be built. Professor Curtis of Queen's spoke
about municipal finances, and Ben Higgins of McGill lectured on housing finance. Three Americans spoke about planning needs and systems:
Walter Blucher, the executive director of the American Society of Planning Officials and a long-time friend of Canadian planners, as well as
Ralph Walker and Carol Aronovici, New York planning consultants.
Then came Elizabeth Wood of Chicago who was followed by Shy Mathers, Toronto's leading architect of the prewar period and a lovable man,
and Howard Dunnington-Grubb, the father-figure of landscape architects in Canada. Towards the end of the series came Donald Fleming,
then an alderman and later an embattled member of the Diefenbaker
government, followed by Henry Churchill, a New York architect who
was at that time the best known propagandist for the humane design of
cities. The final lecture was given by Tracy LeMay who goes down in
history as the first incumbent of what is surely the most difficult position
in the world, planning commissioner of the city of Toronto, caught
between the devil and the deep blue sea; there is no community in which
politicians fight more pugnaciously for local democratic interests and
there is no community that more piously pursues the blue horizon of
great ideals. The chief planner is caught in the middle. Harold Clark
came to know a lot about this because in the 1960s he was chairman of
the Planning Board and had to defend Tracy LeMay's successor, Matt
Lawson, through many a struggle to reconcile local self-interests with the
high ideals of planning.

There was a further stage in the sequence of events I have been
describing, when the seed of an idea had the opportunity to take root.
This occurred in June 1944, at a meeting of the Toronto Citizens' Forum
in the Carlton Street United Church. The Citizens' Forum meetings were

a joint effort of the CBC and the CAAE (the Canadian Broadcasting Corporation and the Canadian Association for Adult Education) which had been initiated during the war when we clung to our radio sets to catch some glimmer of optimism in a tragic world. On this occasion the subject of discussion was housing, and there was a resolution to form a new citizens' group. In the audience was Harold Clark. He was elected chairman of a provisional committee and the forces gathered around him. Amongst those who joined in this campaign for social housing were George Grant, later to become an eminent philosopher, Stuart Jaffary of the School of Social Work, a most gentle, wise, and compassionate person (whose son Karl played a prominent part in Toronto's reform movement of the seventies), and that magnificent lady, Mrs Bessie Luffman who had a great big heart and a queenly presence; she was a church organist and she became one of the founding members of the Toronto Housing Authority.

Another event which involved a good many of the same people and greatly influenced the transmittal of ideas about housing and about Canadian communities was the founding of the Community Planning Association of Canada. This arose from discussions in Ottawa about implementing some of the ideas that had first appeared in the Curtis Report in 1944 and had been embodied in part V of the 1944 National Housing Act. The words of this part of the Act placed upon Central Mortgage and Housing Corporation a responsibility to encourage public interest in community planning. But it was felt that, constitutionally, it was awkward for a federal agency to mount such a campaign in a field that clearly belongs to provinces and cities. So it was suggested that federal funds (and provincial money, too) might be used to sponsor a citizens' association to educate the public and stimulate planning across the country. (At that time Toronto was the only city that had any planning staff at all; in fact there were virtually no professional planners in Canada and no means of training them.) So, in the fall of 1946, a meeting of about fifty people was convened in the Chateau Laurier in Ottawa to discuss this proposition; there were representatives of the architectural and engineering professions and some provincial administrators. The vice president of CMHC, General Hugh A. Young, was chairman, and his Minister, C.D. Howe, appeared briefly to bestow his blessing on the proceedings. I was there as the representative of the Canadian Welfare Council and sat next to Stanley Lewis, the perennial mayor of Ottawa. The staff person who made all the arrangements for the meeting and who dedicated the next ten years of his life to its consequences was Alan Armstrong whom I had known as a student in the Toronto School of Architecture.

There were some serious doubts about the CPAC. Would those who were deeply concerned about the social issues of housing find in the Community Planning Association a reliable support for transmitting ideas on this sensitive subject? Would the federal government money be embarrassing? This very much concerned George Mooney and myself because we were the surviving heirs of the prewar housing association (which had staged the 1938 national housing conference) and so we had a right and an obligation to protect the freedom of discussion of housing subjects. And this question concerned Harold Clark as the leader of the very vital Toronto group. Rather than try to develop both a national planning association and also a national housing association, should we combine forces and go along with this new proposal that had the promise of public funds and the blessing of the powers in Ottawa? I urged that we should concentrate our forces and, as an assurance of this alliance, the provisional committee of the CPAC agreed to name George Mooney as the first president and me as the vice-president. If the CPAC didn't come through as an advocate of social housing we reserved the right to initiate other steps (in fact, this didn't happen until 1968). The first constitutional meeting of the CPAC was held in Montreal and when General Hugh Young learned that Mooney was to be nominated as president he was alarmed because he knew that Mooney had been a CCF candidate in a Montreal constituency and had the qualities of a strong political figure. At that point we were being entertained at the Montreal City Hall, which has a cloak-and-dagger atmosphere anyhow, and I found myself drawn into a conspiratorial whispering behind a white marble column in the reception hall, with Hugh Young urging Dick Davis of the Canadian Welfare Council (and chairman of the provisional committee) to get himself nominated instead of Mooney. And this is what happened. I have often wondered whether this was a fateful moment for George Mooney; in 1947 he was at the height of his very considerable powers and if he had had a national platform from which to speak about urban affairs he might have had an even greater influence on political events.

Looking back on this period immediately after the war, I like to think that I had a part in three important initiatives which grew in strength and significance as the years went by. Undoubtedly the Regent Park project was important to Canada because it showed the strength of a compassionate democratic community in looking after its own housing affairs, and our rental system acknowledged the basic concept of human rights to decent shelter, even for people who do not have enough money to pay for it. Secondly, in launching the CPAC we created a framework of discussion in which laymen and professionals and politicians could meet on equal terms to talk about their aspirations for Canadian cities and how to direct and control their growth. The CPAC did not evolve into an instrument of local activism, but it did enable the concerned people in Edmonton, Halifax, Vancouver, Hamilton, and so on to get to know one another and to exchange ideas–and this transmittal of experience could not have happened without the federal funds that supported the CPAC.

The third important initiative that occurred in this period was the first process of discussion that led to the metropolitan forms of government in which Canada has been a pioneer. I was only involved in this initiative in a peripheral way: the necessity for metropolitan forms of government appeared in much that I wrote about housing and planning in this period. It was my sponsor, the Toronto Reconstruction Council, that started the studies of this subject which were carried out by Dr Albert Rose and by P.A. Deacon, both of whom were close colleagues both in housing interests and in the CPAC.

For all these reasons, this was a happy time of growing confidence and the sense of an expanding future full of interesting opportunities. Much of what I had done before the war now seemed to have had a place in the pattern. I felt secure, and with the help of my friend Jim Murray I started to build a house within the co-operative project in Moore Park where Jim Murray and Harry Cassidy and other friends also lived.

But there were shadows on the path.

In September 1947 Patrick Rolleston died, my companion over many years, my link with the past. We had first met in the summer of 1921, the year we both left school. We had first stretched our minds together in Oxford, exploring the universe of thought, far into the night. We knew one another's family and friends, we had lived together in London, climbed mountains together in Switzerland, and together we had conceived the idea of coming to Canada. And it was through Patrick that I had met and married into the Gordon family. After coming to Canada he had risen rapidly into the upper echelons of the Aluminum Company, as head of a research subsidiary and, at the time of his death, was head of the Aluminum Company's plant near Oxford in England. In the summer of 1947 he had returned to the scene of our last mountaineering expeditions of the 1920s and, with his wife Alma, had climbed perhaps too hastily up the mountain paths out of the deep valley of Saas Fee. And a few weeks later he was dead.

I thought of the day Patrick and Alma Howard were married in the springtime, just before the war. They both had a great sense of occasion and had worked out an original scenario for the event. After all, Patrick was the son of an Irish poet and he had a theatrical imagination. The wedding was to take place in a flowery meadow, at a high point overlooking Lake Magog. The bride, accompanied by her family and friends was to walk along a fieldpath from the Howards' summer home nearby while the bridegroom made his way from a smaller cottage near the road where he had been lodged with his best man and other men friends, including me. The two processions were to converge on the hill-top where they would be received by the black-coated minister who was none other than my brother-in-law, King Gordon. He would perform the ceremony, with all of us standing in a big circle around them in the splendour of the long view up and down the lake. It was to be like something in a French mediaeval tapestry. As the moment approached, Patrick, waiting nervously in the bridegroom's cottage, suddenly realized that he had omitted an important part of the script that required him to send a spring bouquet for his bride to carry on her walk to the hill-top. He leaped the railing of the cottage verandah and hastily plucked some lilac blooms from their stalks and handed them to me with the explanation that I was to take them to the big house for Alma. I had never met the Howards and felt rather silly walking up to the house with a bunch of flowers. I knocked on the door and it was opened by a lady who said quickly: 'Oh, I'm awfully sorry. My daughter's being married today!'

Since that day I had not seen much of Patrick because the war set our paths in different directions. But he was always a kind of subliminal presence and I had looked forward to many future opportunities to re-explore our mutual past. Patrick had always occupied a very large place in my mind because we had done so many things together. It was as if some of this past had been blotted out.

At Eastertime in 1947, Mary and Peter and I drove down south to Virginia to find warmth in the spring sunshine and see the first buds and flowers that had not yet arrived in Canada. When the time came, all too soon, to start the long drive back to Toronto, we were sitting in an old garden on the James River, with the sun drawing the sweet musky perfume out of the clipped yews and junipers. Mary had not been well through a cold grey winter and this little foretaste of colour and warm days meant a lot to her. There was something about that moment of return that suddenly had a sadness–life was too short. It was a kind of foreboding. Through that summer and into the fall Mary didn't seem to recover her health and good spirits, for reasons that were not at first clear to the doctors, though both of us had unspoken premonitions. It was not until Christmas Day 1947, however, that I learned the truth: she could not last very long. And during the night of 18 January the warmth of life and love was drained from her cold hands and she left me, without knowing that we were saying goodbye.

As if to add a last lick of hurt to this shattering event, the house that I was building for Mary was burned a few weeks later. The salamander heater on the unfinished floor of the house was carelessly knocked over, the oil spewed all over the sub-flooring from wall to wall and went up in a flash of flame that left the building a dead, charred, black carcase.

Part Two

*is about how it feels
to be inside a government bureaucracy
and how a person in this position
    can strive
    for the things he believes in.*

*It's about the people I was with
    and how we tried to make Canada
    a better place to live in
        with better houses and finer cities.*

*And it's about our many frustrations
    and some of our successes.*

*It's about the turbulence and the strength
    of the democratic idea.*

p. 94   Anne and I were married in November 1951. We drove down into Virginia where we shared Thomas Jefferson's infectious delight in Monticello, the house he built for himself, with its brick-walled garden and his ingenious contriving of rooms and furniture. The house, as all houses should be, is an extension of his own personality, full of beautiful and interesting things.

95   We extended our own house in Ottawa to contain the new dimensions of life that came to us. This is Anne's mother who lived with us for a time; her family has lived on the Atlantic shore since the seventeenth century. With her is Debby and, behind, one of the many pictures (a Cosgrove) on the walls of our living room.

96   The three pictures show: the rural landscape of the edge of Toronto; the way this was subdivided into rigid characterless streets by the postwar NHA housebuilders; and, at the bottom, the layout of Don Mills, the first major demonstration of suburban community planning. Under the guidance of Macklin Hancock, trained as a landscape architect, this organic design provided a setting for the individuality of houses and families.

97   When Newfoundland came into confederation there was some very poor housing in St John's. I took this photo in 1949 when CMHC had the first discussions there about public housing.

98   Public housing helped to move Newfoundland into the present era. This federal-provincial project is on the steep hillside above St John's harbour, designed to give views of the boats on the waterfront. (CMHC photo)

99   Many Canadian architects have devised new forms of family housing, less wasteful of city-space than single houses and more livable than high-rise buildings. This movement has been led by the Canadian Housing Design Council of which James Murray and Jack Klein have been successive presidents. This is Yorkwoods Village designed by architects Klein and Sears. (CHDC photo)

100   Moshe Safdie's design of Habitat in Expo 67 was a spectacular feature of Canada's centennial celebration, our coming-of-age as a nation skilled in the arts of urban design. Habitat expressed Safdie's aspiration that, within a great city there could be 'for everyone a garden'. (CMHC photo)

101   Another kind of celebration was Peter and Penny's wedding in August 1964. Our daughters Debby and Jenny, then 12 and 10 years old, were bridesmaids.

8
Inside the Bureaucracy

Shattered by the disaster of Mary's death, distracted by confusing emotions and the perplexities of loneliness, I found it very difficult to press
on with my mission at the School of Social Work. I thought that I might
gain some new orientation by taking Peter to England for the summer,
as a way of discovering a new starting point in life. Before doing this I
decided to visit Ottawa, to report to the officials in the federal government who had provided a one-third share of the funds that had supported
me for the last two years. I visited David Mansur, the president of
Central Mortgage and Housing Corporation which was then housed in
the old No 4 Temporary Building, a stone's throw from the Supreme
Court. There I sat down with Mansur and Eric Gold, the chief administrative officer of the corporation, and explained that I was well on my
way to completing the principal report on my work (*Houses for Canadians*).

This meeting proved to be a momentous event for me. When I left
Ottawa that night and drove back in the dark along the lonely road to
Toronto, I felt greatly encouraged by the proposition Mansur had made,
offering me an opportunity for change and action, the only kind of escape
from the condition I was in. Mansur had suggested that I move to
Ottawa and take charge of the research and educational funds provided
through Part V of the National Housing Act; I would reverse my role
and become the dispenser instead of the receiver of funds. It was a
completely new and unexpected idea and, in my desperate need for some
new adventure, I accepted the invitation on the spot. I am eternally
grateful to David Mansur for thus rescuing me from the depths of my
personal disaster and giving me the opportunity to enjoy the next twenty

happy and fruitful years within CMHC. I have never known whether Mansur's offer was influenced by any knowledge of what had happened to me, though I do know of his kind acts in helping other people he knew to be in trouble; so nothing I may say below about Mansur's housing policies reflects upon my deep respect for his human qualities.

So in July 1948, I moved all my belongings into a weirdly ugly house in Ottawa, took my bereaved twelve-year-old son to England for the summer and, in September, reported at No 4 Temporary Building. There I found that I had a secretary and, in the room beyond, was the shining morning face of Peter Oberlander who, quite unknown to me, had been hired as my aid and support. He was an architectural graduate of McGill, then fresh from the city-planning course at Harvard, bursting with ideas and full of a lust for life. We hit it off immediately and for the next two years were practically inseparable, the tall and distracted widower and the small effervescent Peter. I was told that Peter had arrived at CMHC with a large Air Force moustache, no doubt to give a facade of solemnity to his boyish appearance–solemnity not being one of Peter's strong characteristics. But when he appeared before Major-General Hugh A. Young, vice president, it was suggested that he should remove this thing. Another winning characteristic of Peter was that, in the middle of crossing a street, he would often leap into the air and clap his heels together for sheer joie-de-vivre; I'm sorry that I never saw him do this while wearing the moustache, because the effect must have been even more striking.

We did not receive any directives on what we should do, and at first we had no staff other than our shared secretary. I was to be called Chairman of the Research Committee and Peter was to be the secretary of the committee, the members of which had already been selected for us. We were to take as our text, Part V of the National Housing Act, which was entitled Community Planning and Research.

The story is told that, when the 1944 Act was being drafted at the turning point of the war, it was suggested to its principal author, Dr W.C. Clark, deputy minister of finance, that it was a pretty unromantic document with which to greet the returning warrior heroes expecting to make their homes in a new kind of world. So Dr Clark said he would touch it up a little over the weekend while he was at his cottage up the Gatineau. On the Monday he returned with Part V, just two short pages to challenge the imagination. It simply suggests a variety of directions in which research and education might go, in market economics, or in industrial technology, or in housing design, or in professional training

or in the education of the public to understand the problems of housing
and the planning of communities. To give a sense of proportion, the sum
of five million dollars was specified as the authorization of Parliament
to support these investigations and the search for new horizons. And,
perhaps because this all sounded a bit too bland, Dr Clark divided his
list of researchable subjects into two categories, half of the subjects of
inquiry requiring an approval of the Privy Council for the expenditure
of funds ('an order in council') and half being in a category of expenditure that could be approved by CMHC itself. Through the two decades
in which I looked after these grant funds no one ever discovered the
rationale for this distinction and it remained one of those subtleties in
which bureaucrats delight, providing opportunities for delay and confusion. But what Dr Clark wrote, over that weekend, must have had the
imprint of genius upon it because, nearly thirty years later, this is the
only piece of the Housing Act that has never been amended, except for
a couple of minor administrative references. The words have an impeccable vagueness.

The Research Committee was not a success. It consisted of the recognized technical experts in several aspects of housing and it was assumed
that an interprofessional group of this kind would be able to 'brainstorm'
in a creative way and produce a well-rounded research program. But
through a long succession of meetings the rather ill-assorted collection
of diverse interests failed to strike any intellectual fire. As chairman, I
worked hard over several months to get a combustible response out of
the group sitting around the table, but the little flame fizzled out.

One member of the group, Robert Legget, was at an early stage of his
distinguished career as director of the Division of Building Research, in
the National Research Council, and he was understandably preoccupied.
Ira Ashfield, CMHC's own expert on building components, was not well
equipped for abstract discussion. Then there was Dr O.J. Firestone, the
economist who had risen rapidly to be a kind of 'eminence grise' at the
shoulder of C.D. Howe, the cabinet minister under whom CMHC was
established; he sat at our committee table with an oracular smile and
always gave me the impression that he was 'slumming' and must hurry
away to higher things. The most effective member of the group was Tom
Pickersgill who brought the Pickersgill wit to bear upon any subject
under discussion; within CMHC he had been assigned the subject of rural
housing and he had already been successful in setting up a collaborative
research program in the three prairie provinces.

Perhaps one could attribute the failure of the committee to something lacking in the personal chemistry of the mix. There was certainly a missing element, with no social scientist in the group, to put subjects in a social context; it took a long time for the Ottawa establishment to comprehend that housing is a human and social subject and not just a matter of money and physical materials. But I think the real difficulty was that the members of this group were unable to locate themselves in the three dimensions of geography, social philosophy, and history. They didn't know Canada well enough to have a perspective view of the whole scene; in the next few years we all got to know our own country much better through the speed and convenience of air travel. Nor did the group share any kind of over-all philosophy or point of view about how an urban society constructs an environment of living. And, perhaps the greatest difficulty, it was then too early in the postwar period to have any sense of history as events unfolded in the evolution of postwar urbanization. At a later stage in my career within CMHC, as I will explain further on, I worked with another interprofessional group of people very happily and creatively because we all knew Canada well, we shared some common knowledge of the whole subject, and the evolutionary history was much more understandable. (This was the Advisory Group of which I became the chairman in 1955.)

Without any directives from above and without a research committee to guide me, I was left very much on my own, to discover how best to use the position I had been given and how best to apply the funds available for research and education. My response to this situation can best be explained after I have described the general climate within CMHC and what was going on there during this period before David Mansur resigned from the presidency in 1954.

Every six months or so, the senior officials and branch managers of CMHC were summoned to Ottawa, to meet the top brass of the head office. I was invited to these privileged gatherings and this was certainly the best way to learn about the attitudes and interests of CMHC. On these occasions the principal event was always Mansur's opening address on the state of the nation. He had the unmistakable air of the paramount government official who had direct access to the Delphic oracle. It was a period when the concept of the gross national product had just come into fashion and we all sat and listened in awe to Mansur's beautifully constructed paragraphs, his precise vocabulary, and his esoteric references to this new thing, the GNP. It was made even more unlikely that anyone would challenge Mansur's interpretation of the world around us,

because beside him sat Dr O.J. Firestone, nodding his bald head sagely
and smiling gently in approval, as if to indicate that he also had private
access to the oracle. The only other person in the room who seemed to
be privy to Mansur's sources of knowledge was Bert Woodard who had
also learned his mortgage financing with the Sun Life and had been with
CMHC from the outset (and ten years later was the author of the definitive
work on residential mortgages). Woodard would reveal his membership
in the inner circle of cognoscenti by protesting some quite minor and
devious point in Mansur's dissertation; but since Bert never removed his
pipe from his mouth and spoke in a rapid staccato Yorkshire accent, his
interventions were obscure and Mansur remained master of the field.

By the time I arrived at CMHC in 1948, the immediate postwar emer-
gencies had already been dealt with. Under the 'emergency shelter'
scheme, great numbers of returning veterans had started their married
lives in army huts that had been moved on to university campuses. Other
temporary wartime buildings had become the rather pitiful refuges for
families on welfare who had nowhere else to go in the dislocations of the
time; with screens made of blankets, the interiors of warehouses and
drill-halls were divided into family spaces. CMHC had also inherited the
operations of Wartime Housing Limited which had built 20,000 houses
for munitions workers; these became the nucleus for the Veterans' Rental
Housing program that produced another 25,000 houses in the next three
years, so that by 1949 CMHC was the landlord of more than 40,000
families in fifty communities across Canada. All of these projects had
been carried out under the management of CMHC branch offices, in
collaboration with municipal governments. It had been done with the
kind of vigour and momentum that had made the wartime fame of C.D.
Howe, the greatly admired czar of so many Crown corporations. So
CMHC had quickly won a reputation and a credibility in Canadian communities, as a peacetime Crown corporation that got things done with
authority and worked harmoniously with local governments. It was, in
fact, an enviable reputation but one that in the course of time brought
its own backlash from the provincial governments.

When the emergency phase was over, the focus of attention shifted to
the central postwar aim: to create a mass-production housing industry
out of the comparatively few hammer-and-nails housebuilding firms that
had survived the war. There were plenty of carpenters with boxes of
tools, but there weren't many firms with annual budgets for assembling
and servicing land and with the managerial competence to produce and
market housing projects of any size. It was the task of CMHC, directed

by David Mansur, to develop the Canadian housing industry, practically from scratch, to sow the seed and cultivate the crop. This was done through Mansur's ingenious pragmatism: there were all sorts of ways in which small firms without the security of capital or experience could be induced to build another dozen or fifty houses, each complete with a front-door bell and a street address. The principal method of doing this was to eliminate the element of risk for most of the parties involved. There was the 'pool guarantee fund' to protect the money-lending institutions; there was the 'integrated plan' by which CMHC undertook to buy back from the builders any unsold houses if they had been built within certain prescribed standards. And, for investors, these was the 'rental insurance' system to encourage private enterprise to build apartments, protecting them against an inadequate rental revenue. There was even the practical possibility of what is called 'mortgaging out', that is to obtain an NHA housing loan with practically no equity investment and so gain a real-estate asset under the protection of government. The president of CMHC invented and prescribed the rules of these games and it was up to the branch managers to lure the players on to the field and keep the ball in play.

The only interested party in the housing scene which didn't seem to get much attention at the staff meetings of CMHC was the Canadian family which couldn't afford home-ownership. Since I had originally come into housing affairs because I was interested in the circumstances of people who needed low-rental housing, and since I had played a part in mounting the Regent Park project, a pioneering community action, I might have had something to say on that subject. But I had no knowledge of mortgage techniques so I remained silent in the background, awed by Mansur's mastery of the subject and by the obvious competence of the whole CMHC staff. The criterion of success was the number of new housing units provided under the National Housing Act, which increased from 11,827 in 1946 to 65,438 in 1955. To give some humanity to these statistics the expression used was 'the number of new front doors', suggesting the grateful smiling faces of the families who would respond to the postman's knock. A subject that did not appear on the agenda was the question of what was behind the front door and what it looked out upon. The environmental quality of the product was not considered important and, looking around me at these meetings, I could not feel that anyone present was very qualified to judge such matters. It clearly wasn't a subject that interested David Mansur. (There was attributed to Mansur, however, the introduction of the 'squeal factor' in community planning; streets should be curved, he would tell us, so that hot-rods driving too fast for safety would be immediately identified by their squealing tires. A planner named Wregglesworth worked on the staff of CMHC at that time and his street layouts came to be known as Wreggles' Wriggles. Their serpentine shape can still be seen from the air in some postwar suburbs.) The architectural staff of CMHC were generally regarded as mere technicians unlikely to be able to comprehend higher policy matters. Jim Dudley, an architect, was the only senior person on the staff who was qualified in matters of environmental design; he became the regional supervisor in the maritime provinces, but he suffered from his differences of orientation and resigned from CMHC to manage the building of Kitimat, the Aluminum Company's new town in British Columbia. In this exciting task he sought the advice of the American Clarence Stein, the most significant urban designer of this period, of whom I will have more to say later.

It would not be quite correct to say that aesthetic matters did not come on the agenda of these discussions. There is an aesthetic quality in the mortgage 'instrument', as it was called, a certain elegance in contriving a lender's security so that it is infallible. Around the table of CMHC there have been many who would speak of the mortgage instrument as if it were the Holy Grail.

During Mansur's régime there was one important political event that came within my field of interest: this was the 1949 amendment to the Housing Act which belatedly, and rather deviously, made public housing legitimate, together with rental subsidies for low-income families. Section 35, added to the Act in 1949, was less than a page in length and looked so innocent that it didn't arouse a great debate in Parliament or receive much public attention. The words of the amendment simply declared that the federal government, in partnership with any one of the provincial governments, might buy or build or sell or rent housing or could assemble land, sharing the cost on a 75:25 percentage basis, and stated that the federal government was also prepared to share any deficits in the same proportion. The use of the word 'deficit' rather than 'subsidy' seemed to imply that there was no positive intention to help low-income families and a deficit would only occur as the consequence of some unfortunate administrative error. The motive for introducing the amendment was rather back-handed and certainly didn't arise out of any enthusiasm for public housing in the mind of Robert Winters, the member of Mr St Laurent's cabinet who had to introduce the legislation in Parliament. The fact was that the Veterans' Rental Housing program had proved all too successful and the prospect of the federal government becoming landlord to even more than 40,000 families horrified a Liberal government that was dedicated to private enterprise and would do almost anything to avoid getting into a policy of public housing.

The Parliamentary debate on the 1949 amendment took place on 29 November (my birthday). Donald Fleming, the Conservative party's spokesman, was in great form, knew his subject well, and taunted Prime Minister St Laurent unmercifully for his famous protestation of 27 October 1947: 'No government of which I am a part will ever pass legislation for subsidized housing.' Apart from Donald Fleming it was clear that hardly any members of Parliament had knowledge or insights about housing and about the processes of urbanization in their constituencies. This had not seemed to them to be a political subject. It was only David Croll, that fine old radical from Windsor, Ontario, who had the assurance to speak passionately on the subject. 'So at long last,' he said, 'the government to its everlasting credit has taken a direct stand in the field of subsidized housing, something that will be hailed from one end of this country to the other, as one of the most progressive and far-reaching measures ever introduced in this house, in my opinion comparable to the family allowance legislation.'

From a constitutional point of view it was, no doubt, strictly correct to unload upon the provinces some of the responsibilities for public action in housing. But for those of us who were more concerned about human needs than about the niceties of the constitution, it seemed like a shabby trick. Surely everyone must know that the provinces had not shown the slightest interest in social responsibilities for housing; provincial legislatures were still dominated by rural voters and were most unlikely to show any leadership in solving the very difficult problems of low-income people in the centres of the big cities, the problems of slum clearance, of rent scales, and the need for local authority management. It seemed that federal authorities had been very ingenious in taking the risk out of private enterprise, but the president of CMHC didn't seem to be equally ingenious in finding methods of helping public enterprise serve the needs of low-income people.

It was also very disappointing that the whole momentum and experience that had been gained in the Veterans' Rental Housing program was to be abandoned and the houses sold to their occupants. These were single-family houses in quite small projects on suburban sites. They had been excellently designed under the direction of Sam Gitterman, the chief architect of CMHC, and represented the accumulated know-how of several years in site-planning and house-grouping. Many of us felt that this program should not have been interrupted but should have been redirected to the needs of low-income families. But the continuity was unfortunately broken. In its environmental design this housing was vastly superior to what was currently being produced through the private enterprise system, forced into production by the incentives of the integrated plan and by rental insurance. And because of this high standard of design, the veterans' housing had been welcomed by people living in suburban areas; this was an important acceptance of public action in housing. I recall that soon after Peter Oberlander and I had joined forces in Ottawa, he went with his camera on a country-wide tour to record the most interesting veterans' projects. To him, fresh from the sophisticated judgments of the Harvard school of planning, these Canadian projects were a remarkable achievement and he wanted people to appreciate what had been done. We had the impression that the management of CMHC did not understand the significance of the achievement.

I longed to talk with Mansur about these questions, but it was not possible because our basic assumptions and intuitions were far apart and we talked a different language. He had brought me into CMHC to look after affairs that were outside his central purpose, which was to build up a productive housing industry in Canada, a task that he carried out with extraordinary competence. He was, to me, an aloof, distant, but always kindly character; he never asked my opinion about anything and there was only one occasion when he took me along with him on an important business mission: that was when Newfoundland had just come into confederation and when the 1949 amendment to the Housing Act first offered opportunities to build public housing, an opportunity that Newfoundland was the first province to use. I went with Mansur to St John's, took part in the discussions, and walked up and down all those steep harbour-side streets where women then drew their household water from stand-pipes in the streets. Apart from this visit, Mansur left me to my own devices, feeling, I think, that I was a trustworthy solemn fellow devoted to things like community-planning and the arts of housing that he didn't care much about.

The culmination of Dave Mansur's term as president of CMHC was the introduction of the 1954 Housing Act. This removed from the NHA mortgage-lending system the direct contribution of federal money which, up to that time, had been 25 per cent of each loan. The 1954 Act introduced the CMHC 'loan insurance' system which for the first time made it possible for Canadian banks to invest their funds in housing, they being protected by the insurance security and enabled to liquidate these investments through the buying and selling of NHA mortgages. This was Mansur's 'nunc dimittis' and, having thus placed the imprint of his philosophy upon the system, he resigned from government service on 1 November 1954 and, a month later, was succeeded by Stewart Bates.

An appropriate monument to this period is the head office building of Central Mortgage and Housing Corporation on the Montreal Road in Ottawa. When the time came to move out of No 4 Temporary Building on Parliament Hill, Mansur chose a building site two miles away from Parliament Hill; it was a deliberate move to express the independence of CMHC as a corporate institution that could perform its role best if it was beyond the reach of cabinet ministers and political influences. Even the architectural style of the new head office was a departure from the conventions of Canada's federal government buildings. It was designed in red-brick American Colonial style, looking not unlike a glorified Howard Johnson's highway restaurant. The effect was rather humiliating to those of us who thought that, as a patron of domestic architecture, CMHC should have known better. But it was understood that Mansur wanted the building to look like the head office of an insurance company; and I suppose it did. Having worked in this building for so many years, I can say that it had one outstanding merit and one very serious defect. It's a low, spread-out, three-storey building and the long internal corridors are like pedestrian malls; if you are restless or in search of a new idea, you can take a walk from one end of the building to the other, the length of a city block, and you'd be sure to meet someone in the corridors with whom you could have a friendly chat. That is a social amenity much to be preferred over a high-rise tower in which the occupants of one floor may never set eyes on the occupants of another floor. On the other hand, the great defect of the building was the isolation of the management group on a small upstairs floor, with the president and vice-president at either end of the board room. It's a stereotype that may fit the image of a private corporation, but it's a form quite alien to the true political nature of a federal government agency in urban affairs. The real executive authority is not in the board of directors of CMHC, but in the minister and the cabinet. To be stuck with the model of an insurance company has, in a later period of history, made it very difficult to put CMHC into the context of a Ministry of Urban Affairs.

The creation of a mass-production housing industy was, in this period, the remarkable achievement of David Mansur, CMHC, and the National Housing Act. It was a performance of great authority. What still remained to be done was the creation of a policy and action system which could respond directly to the social evolution of communities and be more sensitive to the diversity of human life. This further process of creation is still going on.

9
Visions and Designs

When I arrived in Ottawa in September 1948, I expected that there would soon be some people knocking at my door, seeking funds for research and educational projects, to pursue their favourite ideas about housing and the forms of cities. But, strange as it may seem, this practically never happened. The surge of interest in housing and urban affairs had not yet come to the surface. It was like a quiet time in an empty house before the guests have arrived for a party. The rebellious young people of the sixties and seventies were still infants. There were no liberated urban protesters and there were no planners for them to protest against. Old people and young people still lived together in extended family groups. There were no high-rises and no freeways. The evident frontier of activity was on the outskirts of cities where the postwar suburbs were begining to grow at an alarming rate, in an unplanned stereotyped way. As the National Housing Act incentives gave confidence to the new and inexperienced generation of housebuilders, new subdivisions and streets and small houses were beginning to cover up the landscape, mile by mile.

Since there was no one knocking at my door and the research committee that had been set up for me didn't prove to be very helpful, the direction of my work had to come out of my own intuitions and perceptions. What I thought about and what I worked at were naturally a response to the attitudes I found in the bureaucracy around me and to what I saw happening in the growth of the new suburbs. I was an environmentalist lost in a crowd of mortgage-lenders. Looking back now from a period in the 1970s when it is fashionable to produce research studies of block-busting dimensions and task-force reports pregnant with dark accusations to be surreptitiously leaked to the media, my product

of the years from 1948 to 1955 was of child-like simplicity. With my own
small staff, which was never more than three or four people, I produced
quite a number of publications. And with the use of grant funds I worked
with many people outside CMHC, in many different ways. There was no
grand strategy about all this, but it did, as a matter of fact, all fit into
a pattern even though this was not evident to the management of CMHC.
What I tried to do can best be described as three counterpoint themes,
each dependent on the others for the total effect.

The first theme could be called 'design for living'. As I looked around
at the acreages of new housing, the stereotyped forms were clearly being
determined by the mortgaging system and by the packaging of the National Housing Act incentives. There must be, I felt, some principles of
organic design that might help to make places more hospitable to a good
life. How could house-space be arranged around the privacies of individuals and around the structures of families? How could family
houses be grouped together so that social relationships in the suburbs
would evolve spontaneously? And how could these housing groups and
neighbourhoods be assembled into the forms of communities? How
could the new suburban landscape be made more compassionate towards
human life?

The second theme had to do with the disciplines for applying the
general principles of social design, supposing that some such principles
could be discovered. After nearly twenty years of depression and war,
Canada entered the postwar era with practically no plans for the growth
of cities and practically no constituted authorities for making plans.
There were plenty of surveyors who could measure out rectangular
acreages of streets and lots, and there were the traditional systems for
recording the ownership of property. But community-planning, as a
process of design within a framework of legislation, and bylaw controls
virtually didn't exist.

The third theme had to do with education, with the lack of people who
had thought about these subjects at all. There were practically no
Canadians who had had any professional training in community design
and, at the beginning of this period, not a single university offered a
course in community-planning. So even if some principles and doctrines
of good design could be brought to light, and even if there were constituted authorities for working out the designs of cities, not much could
happen if there was no staff available and if the general public didn't
understand the subject of discussion.

I worked on all three of these themes simultaneously. I worked with the Community Planning Association in staging discussions and conferences in every major city across Canada, helping people to become familiar with the language, the methods, and the aims of planning, and urging cities to install planning staffs. I worked with the universities, encouraging them to develop graduate courses so as to produce a stream of qualified people to fill the new positions as they were developed. And I worked, mostly with my own small staff, trying to puzzle out some basic principles for the arrangement of living space within houses and within neighbourhoods. (If all these objectives seem very elementary and self-evident today, I can assure the reader that they were virgin territory at that time.)

Because I had a rather isolated position within CMHC, the Community Planning Association was particularly important to me at this stage; it provided me with a circle of friends who shared a common interest, many of them people I had known before I moved to Ottawa. Besides Alan Armstrong, the talented first director of the CPAC, there was the first president of the association, Dick Davis of the Canadian Welfare Council. There was Harold Clark, the staunch leader of the Toronto group which had initiated the Regent Park project. There were P.A. Deacon, that literate architect and radical; Eric Thrift, then Winnipeg's planning commissioner; Jacques Simard, musician, patron of the arts, and creator of Préville; Sir Brian Dunfield of Newfoundland, the last Canadian knight. As one of the founders of the CPAC I enjoyed still being part of a group outside the bureaucracy of Ottawa, though my role had changed and I was now the person who had to make the annual advocacy for an increased grant to the CPAC. In the course of our mission we all got to know Canada together and, over a period of ten years, the CPAC was substantially successful in its first objective: to get community-planning launched in Canadian cities.

In the other two themes of my activities I was also fortunate in the people who now came into my life. It will be clear from what follows that I owe a special debt to Harold Spence-Sales who, of all my friends, shared most fully in understanding what I was trying to do, whether it had to do with cities or landscape or the aesthetics of housing design. Harold has a capacity to transfigure a subject with his lyrical imagination, a faculty that has bothered people who do not quite understand the mind and the eye of an artist. But Harold never failed to stretch my mind and our discussions would often go late into the night as I lay stretched out on the sofa or on the floor of my living-room and Harold's poetic ideas became less and less distinguishable from my own intermittent dreams.

Like me, Harold had studied at the Architectural Association in London and, after the war, he had come to McGill University to start the first graduate course in planning. I was also very lucky that through this whole period Jean Strange worked for me, with her meticulous sweet patience for the small-scale problems of housing design and the page-by-page layout of the publications that issued from our office. I had first known Jean as an English school-girl and wartime-evacuee who came to the Toronto School of Architecture in 1939. Later, she joined the navy, married Captain William Strange, historian and broadcaster, and now they live in Mexico.

Here I must also acknowledge the presence of another person who was with me through this period, not in the flesh but in the spirit. That was Clarence Stein, the American architect-planner and author of *Towards New Towns for America.* He stands in the direct line of succession from that great English architect of garden cities, Sir Raymond Unwin; and those who know the literature and history of town-planning may trace that same succession back through Frederick Law Olmsted, the great American landscape architect who designed Central Park, New York, to John Nash, designer of streets, architecture, and parks in Regency London, and so back to John Wood who set out the beautiful squares and terraces of eighteenth-century Bath. Stein and Olmsted and Unwin and Nash and Wood all had a comprehensive perception of town design, the total composition of streets and open spaces and buildings. I had known Clarence Stein's pioneering work of the 1920s in the design of Radburn, New Jersey, and his poetic design of the little town of Greenbelt near Washington, done in the Roosevelt period, and I had followed the further evolution of his ideas. It was not so much the special feature of the Radburn plan that was so important to me. (This is the system of grouping houses around an interior landscape space, with their service-sides backing on a street – an arrangement that was first used in Canada in Wildwood, Winnipeg, in 1946 and reappeared in Stein's own plans for the new town of Kitimat, BC.) For me, the important thing about Clarence Stein's work was the whole interplay of landscape and townscape, the sculpturing of three-dimensional spaces with simple building forms, with trees and hedges and lawns – so as to make a place that would be a pleasure to live in and to walk around within. Perhaps I was influenced in this direction by my early love affair with the English Cotswold village, also an inspiration for Unwin and the first garden-city designers. This, it seemed to me, was the clue to solving the problems of our new suburbs. If we could come to accept the vernacular of the Canadian housebuilders in simple straightforward small-house designs, to suit our climate and our way of life, then it should be possible to create places of great beauty by grouping and clustering and arranging landscape spaces and living spaces. The art of the suburbs, I felt, is nearer to landscape design than to architecture. So I used to chide Canadian architects who thought that their great gift to Canada would be some unique and original house design, remarkable in being different from everything around it.

As I worked along on the three themes, some of the small and detailed tasks might have seemed very trivial and boring if I had not had some ultimate vision in mind. That is why I am grateful to Clarence Stein because he was the bearer of a testament that had been handed down through the centuries. So I was glad when I finally came to know him; a small, grey, cultured man, with an elusive smile and wearing a loose tweed coat. I have beside me a copy of his book *Towards New Towns for America* which he sent me with my own name written on the flyleaf; it is rather as if I possessed a copy of St Mark's gospel with the author's message to me in it.

There is no learning without language. The first publication to come from the small group in my office was a manual called *Urban Mapping,* a project started by Peter Oberlander and largely carried out by Blanche Lemco (later Mrs Sandy vanGinkel). The aim was to codify the language of maps, assuming that in the on-coming growth of cities an enormous amount of mapping and planning would have to be done and that there would be a bedlam of misunderstanding and wasted time if the people who drew maps and the people who read maps did not use the same graphic language. The manual took the form of an atlas, using Brantford, Ont., as an example, showing how every aspect of an urban community with its services, land uses, and densities, can be described in black-and-white maps suitable for reproduction. *Urban Mapping* was published with the endorsement of the Ontario Department of Planning and Development (of which Arthur Bunnell was then a key figure) and was distributed through the CPAC. It remained the definitive codification of urban mapping for many years.

Another codification problem was that every Canadian province had acquired a different regulatory system for conducting community-planning. Since planning is constitutionally a provincial responsibility, each province had gone its own way and we discovered that many of the officials responsible for administering planning in each province had never even met one another. It was the Council of the CPAC which first brought them all together to a meeting in the Chateau Laurier in Ottawa in 1950; and thereafter this became an annual event. It was hard to imagine the development of a planning profession in Canada if there was not some common knowledge of these provincial planning systems and, in 1948, Harold Spence-Sales obtained a CMHC grant to travel across the country and gather this information together. He was in the midst of this inquiry when I first encountered Harold's genius for making a work of art out of the most unlikely subjects. In his room at the Royal York Hotel in Toronto he unrolled several yards of drafting paper on which he had plotted what he had found, from Newfoundland to British Columbia; the length of paper stretched from the bathroom at one end, right across his bed and then fluttered out of the window. It was a nice demonstration of the endless trail of inconsistencies within a federal country emerging from a rural background and having to learn the ways of building cities. Since Spence-Sales and his colleague John Bland, head of the school of architecture at McGill, had both worked in the British ministry which introduced the postwar Town and Country Planning Act, they were well qualified to advise the provinces on how to modernize their systems. Consultations were arranged through George Mooney of the Federation of Mayors and Municipalities; their advice had particular effect on the subsequent development of Edmonton and Vancouver.

Harold Spence-Sales also applied his imagination to the rudimentary business of residential land subdivision which had been the traditional occupation of land surveyors, measuring out the raw land into standard-sized rectangles just as the original concessions of farm land had been measured out long ago for the first settlers in the empty spaces of Canada. This was a geometrical exercise that had never seemed to call for much imagination until Harold demonstrated that to design this basic unit of a community is a social art and a landscape art. For a seminar course given at MacDonald College, Montreal, for subdivision planners and administrators he used a sand table (well known in wartime for teaching military tactics) to show how the special character of each landscape could be modelled to make a setting for groups of houses. His further explanation of this art appeared in a splendid little book called *How to Subdivide*, published by the CPAC under Alan Armstrong's management; the book acquired an international reputation both for the originality of the ideas and for the design of the publication by Allan Harrison.

To Spence-Sales also goes the honour for having established the first graduate course in community planning. There was no fixed curriculum, but rather a personal entrée into the fascinating mind of Harold Spence-Sales; this was teaching more in the manner of an atelier than a university. The McGill students followed the master as his interests shifted from year to year; I particularly remember the year of their great excitement in examining the traditional settlement patterns of rural Quebec, with its elongated communities stretched out along the 'chemin' and the river routes. Though I used to argue with Harold fiercely about the lack of a core curriculum, his course was a continual voyage of discovery and its alumni moved quickly into key positions and are now among the élite in the planning profession. There was Murray Jones who became the director of planning for Metropolitan Toronto, when metropolitan government was first set up under 'Big Daddy' Gardiner. There was Len Gertler who has left the imprint of his fine analytical mind on many parts of Canada, upon the shape of the Toronto region, on the conservation of the Niagara escarpment, and at the University of Waterloo where he founded the first undergraduate course in urban planning. There was Harry Lash, now planning director for Greater Vancouver, Brahm Wiesman, Nigel Richardson, and Tom Shoyama who is now a deputy minister in Ottawa, to name but a few.

In the next few years other universities followed suit, setting up graduate courses partly sustained by the grants that I was able to arrange, to pay the basic salary of the principal teacher and to provide fellowships for students. Peter Oberlander left CMHC to set up the planning course at the University of British Columbia, and Joe Kostka started a course at the University of Manitoba school of architecture under John Russell. The president of the University of Toronto, Dr Sydney Smith, was hard to budge, but eventually an arrangement was made to bring in Jacqueline Tyrwhitt, a fellow-student of mine at the Architectural Association in London. Jacqueline's tempestuous energy swept across the campus, but it was too placid for her. Matt Lawson filled in for a spell before becoming planner for the City of Toronto and he was followed by Gordon Stephenson of Liverpool University, a great scholar and a man of international reputation. The University of Montreal followed in the sixties, and other universities are now in the field.

Many of the graduates of these university courses have helped to shape the destinies of Canadian cities in the last twenty years. So the evangelism of the early members of the CPAC and the patience of the pioneering teachers in the universities gradually built up Canada's capacity to confront the surging tide of urban growth. Though our early efforts were exposed to a good deal of scepticism from people in authority, in just a few years we had laid the foundations for a new profession and for the public acceptance of community-planning.

Meanwhile the little group in my office were producing a number of publications to stimulate a wider interest in the design of housing and the urban environment. The most long-lived of these publications has been a fifty-page paperback still obtainable from CMHC, entitled simply *Choosing a House Design*. As I write now, it is being reprinted after being in circulation for nearly twenty years and having had a distribution of nearly three-quarters of a million copies. It was largely the work of Edwin Raines, now a practising architect in Alberta. Our most comprehensive publication appeared in 1952 and 1953 as supplements to the CPAC's *Review* and to the *Journal of the Royal Architectural Institute of Canada*. It started with an analysis of existing dwelling plans; as a botanist classifies the various arrangements of leaves and petals and the seeds of plants, so we classified the known varieties of household space arrangements, the relationships between day-time space (living and dining and kitchen space) and night-time space (bedrooms and bathroom). We looked at these varieties in single and two-storey houses and in the composite forms of rows and terraces and apartment buildings, and we set out all the known varieties of grouping and street pattern–including, of course, Clarence Stein's variations. It seemed to me that this should be the vocabulary of the housing designer, like the keyboard of a piano or the letters of the alphabet. Out of these elements it would be possible to evolve wonderfully diverse and imaginative compositions. It is an art like the music of Bach.

We worked a good deal further on the idea of clustering houses in the landscape, in compositions of groups and vistas and street scenes; 'eye-fulls' we called them. And we tried to discover the connection between the aesthetics of groupings and the social patterns of people's lives. I have always felt that when one says 'This is the place where I live' there is usually an emotional attachment to a territory which one shares with the immediate neighbours. It is true that home can be a very private retreat; but perhaps there are social benefits in a somewhat wider territorial imperative.

While we were building these rudimentary foundations for the growth of cities in Canada, the United States had already entered a much more advanced stage in the evolution of city affairs. Of course, American cities were larger and had already experienced more of the problems of middle-aged deterioration; but I think the greater maturity was also the consequence of what had happened during the depression when Roosevelt's New Deal programs had focused so much on the problems of the slums and on an appreciation of environmental quality. That had been an important part of Roosevelt's own philosophy and was in the tradition of American presidents who had a patrician interest in fine houses and landscape: Washington at Mount Vernon, Jefferson who was the architect of his own lovely house, Monticello, and the Roosevelts at Hyde Park on the Hudson. No Canadian political leader had had this kind of personal interest, unless one could count Mackenzie King's strange love affair with the Gothic ruins he collected on his Kingsmere estate.

Naturally I was very inquisitive about what was going on in the United States and took all the opportunities to attend the annual conferences of the two principal American organizations concerned with urban affairs; these were the American Society of Planning Officials (ASPO) and the National Association of Housing Officials. These connections led to my appointment as the Canadian director on the board of ASPO through the years 1952 to 1955, which took me to many cities for conferences and board meetings, particularly to Chicago and to Philadelphia. So my view of North American cities was greatly extended and I gained an understanding of how urban policies originate in the minds of innovative people, are projected into public discussion, and are finally brought into the mainstream of political policy and action. In this period American cities were moving away from the first bulldozer methods of slum clearance and redevelopment, through the first exercises in rehabilitation, and then on to the much more ambitious concept of total city design which was the original intent of the expression 'urban renewal'. I was present at the meeting at the headquarters of ASPO at 1313 East 60th Street, Chicago, when the idea of urban renewal was born. This meant the rediscovery of the good things already built within the older areas of cities and the effort to revitalize them rather than to erase them with the bulldozer. In Canada, the term 'urban renewal' came to have a pejorative meaning because of the failure of our legislation to provide sufficient funds for the conservation part of the action.

The first phase of this transition, the massive clearance and rebuilding, was most dramatically seen at the south end of Chicago's central area. It was an ugly, violent, overcrowded tenement district and block by block, acre after acre, it was simply obliterated and in the place of that industrial jungle, high-rise apartments rose on the artificial hills that covered the ruins. The wind blew in off Lake Michigan and there was much talk about the safety of the high balconies where little black faces

peered through the bars like caged young animals now forbidden to roam
the streets as they had been accustomed to do. The second phase,
rehabilitation, started in Baltimore, a city largely built of long strips of
row-housing made of a brick that looks very handsome in old age and
combines well with white paint and new colours. The city officials who
developed the 'Baltimore Plan' of rehabilitation told us that they had
based their scheme on an earlier rehabilitation bylaw of another brick-
built city, Toronto (Ottawa also made some claim upon the copyright).
But I think it is really Baltimore that can rightly claim to be the origina-
tor of a great wave of popularity for the repainted townhouse that swept
the continent, and eventually found its way into some of the old streets
of Canadian cities, into Toronto's Yorkville and into Vancouver's Gas-
town. That is, as art dealers would say, the 'provenance' of the style that
has done so much to brighten our cities.

But certainly, in this period, the stage on which the art of city design
had its most theatrical and exciting revival was Philadelphia, in the
brilliant performances conducted by that distinguished impresario, Ed
Bacon. The motive was to bring back an age of elegance to the heart of
a historic centre of American culture. Between Independence Hall and
the Delaware River the old colonial town had descended to the level of
a grubby slum, its narrow streets packed with trucks serving the food
market on the river front. Most Philadelphians, on their way to and from
the suburbs in the wooded hills in the other direction, had never seen the
relics of the old colonial city of William Penn until a group of intelligent
business men formed the Philadelphia Movement and city-planner Edmund Bacon gave them a new pride in their heritage and showed them
that there was gold down there in the narrow colonial streets of Society
Hill. Bacon was a great student of European cities and a keen photographer; he perfected a brilliant style of illustrated lecture (a bit like Lord
Clark's famous series on civilization) with which he made Philadelphians
feel that they were the true heirs to the Medicis, the princes of a new
Renaissance. So they cleared away the mess around old Independence
Hall and worked their way down towards the river front, cleaning up the
streets, scrubbing up the old colonial brickwork, painting the doors and
windows. But on the banks of the Delaware River the fish and vegetables
in the food market had a pervading odour and somehow this had to be
removed. At this point the strategy was to convene a princely banquet
to which would be invited all the barons, the presidents of all the national
corporations in the food-processing and food-marketing business. They
would be told about the newly awakened glory of historic Philadelphia

and they would be invited to finance a new food market far away from Society Hill, the birthplace of America. Philadelphians have a way of doing these things in a noble style, to the manner born. Having visualized all the food presidents at the feast, banked in a series of head-tables each a little more elevated than the one in front, they then had to find a speaker who would give just the right touch of vision and good taste to the affair.

I don't know how the leaders of the Philadelphia Movement came to hit upon me as a suitable candidate for this role. The secretary was sent up to Ottawa to look at my credentials and I was offered $1000 as a fee for making the principal address. My family persuaded me that this would be a good opportunity for me to buy a new dinner jacket. So I composed a piece called 'Vision of a Great City' and, on 27 October 1954, spent the day practising it in a hotel bedroom and then found myself standing up in front of the largest banquet I've ever seen. I got through my speech all right and the food barons did build the new food market. But I had discovered that food barons don't dress for dinner and that even the élite of Philadelphia can be forgetful. I had bought the dinner jacket–but they forgot to send me the $1000.

In the following year my connections with American planners came to a kind of culmination in the staging of the first joint conference of the two national organizations ASPO and CPAC; it took place in Montreal, on 24-25 September 1955. With an attendance of 1400 people, of whom 400 were Canadians, it was said to be the largest gathering of people interested in planning cities that had yet taken place. Philadelphians are not alone in having a sense of occasion and I remember that the American visitors were greatly impressed by the panache they found in Montreal. The Canadian chairman was Sir Brian Dunfield of Newfoundland who could always give an air of judicial dignity to the proceedings, with an added spice of his tart wit. Mayor Jean Drapeau had already acquired his princely style and, to the amazement of planners who like to see how a city works, had all the traffic stopped to make way for a cavalcade of buses going to the belvedere on the mountain. I was also amazed to note that in the province of Quebec a cardinal could not come to lunch at the hotel without having a length of red carpet rolled out for him by a posse of black-coated acolytes, all the way from his car door to the elevators.

Such pomposities are, I suppose, sometimes useful if they make an occasion memorable. But what I had chiefly enjoyed at American conferences was their informality and the extraordinary pleasure that Americans have in prolonged and intense discussion. They would fill a meeting-room at eight o'clock in the morning to talk about zoning bylaws, not ordinarily considered a very exciting subject. Perhaps this was partly due to the personal style of Hugh Pomeroy who always conducted these sessions: a big cheerful man, with a clear mellow voice who seemed to know everyone in the room by first name and who had, I believe, been a minister of the church. He had a genius for bringing to light the human issue behind the bloody-minded bylaw and everyone who had been at the session went back home with some fresh view of his mundane problems. Then there was small pugnacious Charlie Abrams with his New York vocabulary and impassioned intellect, always picking a fight on behalf of the poor and the destitute, not only in New York but in all the depressed places of the world. These and other great Americans I got to know, and I often wished that Canadians had more of a gift for passionate discussion and more opportunities to communicate with one another.

In those postwar years Canadians, though well led by men of authority and rectitude, had been tucked away tidily in their neat rows of NHA -mortgaged homes–with only an occasional wriggle in the rectilinear street system. Canadians had been too tame. Now they needed to break loose, to argue and protest a bit. I hoped that I could help to foment the discussion.

10
A House Is a Place for Flying Apart

The way I have lived with my own family, in our own house, has helped me to understand the subject of housing which is, after all, just a generalization of how people live in their own houses. So my appreciation of this whole theme changed and deepened after Anne Sedgewick and I were married in 1951.

To be a widower and in the middle of life I can only describe as a ghastly experience, and all the emotional confusions and personal perplexities of that time have no place in this book. Then, to find someone with whom to start life afresh was like being born again. On 26 November 1951, Anne and I were married by our friend Dr Ian Burnett, and out of snowbound Ottawa we headed down the Blue Ridge into Virginia and a whole new life of unthinkable joys and adventures opened up before us. As we have done on many occasions since, we turned off the Ridge down into Charlottesville to share some of Thomas Jefferson's enjoyment in his wonderful house, Monticello; and then we wandered in the warm sunshine along the streets of Athens, Georgia, with its delicious Greek Revival houses. Then we returned to Ottawa and life began again, with new dimensions and unexpected events. To our great delight, two children soon arrived and our small house in Ottawa was enlarged to contain their active and explosive lives. By this time my son Peter had left home to explore the world; and when he returned and married Penny Woolgar, two grandchildren added a further dimension to our lives.

Anne's parents were both Nova Scotians. Her father, George Sedgewick, was born and brought up on a farm in Middle Musquedoboit. He had died in 1939 a greatly loved and respected man, a Justice of the Supreme Court of Ontario, a great student of politics, and the first chairman of the Canadian Tariff Board. Anne's mother was a Robertson of Halifax; her ancestors are buried in the old churchyards along the South Shore of Nova Scotia all the way from Lunenburg to Barrington Passage and Tusket. She lived with us, off and on, until she died in our house one early morning in April 1959, an intellectual, proud, affectionate, but very demanding person. In her later years she was immobilized by arthritis and had become dependent upon Anne not only to keep house but also to satisfy her appetite for lively conversation. When she died, our two daughters were seven and five years old.

Since I was then in my fifties I was able to view the childhood of the two girls with a greater detachment and perhaps a greater enjoyment than younger fathers can; we saw them move joyously through Betty Hyde's co-operative nursery school and on into the eager expanding years of public school and Lisgar High School. By merging with a Nova Scotian family I got to know that part of Canada where we went every summer, away from the affluent competitiveness of Ontario, and close to the seashore which had always been the scene of my own English childhood summers. So I relived with the two girls all the glories of childhood adventure and our house was always full of children; their parents were our friends, much younger than I and mostly a good deal younger than Anne.

As my own life in my own house changed very much in the 1955-65 decade, so, I think, did the experience of many other people too, because this was an important phase in the evolution of postwar society: the new families and the reconstituted families that started life together in 1946 had moved through the first cosy baby-feeding stage and, by the sixties, the parents had begun to find out about the new generation of teen-agers. The grandparent generation, too, had by this time begun to get the sense of a new kind of world in which they wanted some independence. Consequently housing became an altogether more dynamic subject, with far more subtleties and social dimensions than had been thought of when Central Mortgage & Housing Corporation was established in 1946.

This was the background of my life when, in 1963, I was asked to be the representative of CMHC on the council which was to stage the Canadian Conference on the Family, a celebratory event initiated by Governor General Georges P. Vanier and Madame Vanier. General Vanier's predecessor in the office of governor general, Vincent Massey, had won a place in history as a great patron of the arts; he had been chairman of the commission which resulted in the establishment of the Canada Council, and there was no doubt that his monument was the consequent advance of painting and music in Canada. Georges Vanier wanted to be remembered in a quite different way and, since the Vaniers were indeed a remarkable family, this was an appropriate theme that reflected the deep spirituality and the strong bonds of love within their own family. The theme was a noble one, though it was a bit difficult to see how it could be translated into some tangible monument. But there was a great desire to do what the Vaniers wanted because Georges Vanier had something sublime and saintly about him. Perhaps there could never be another governor general whose personal qualities were greater than his office; under the hard lights of public exposure all others who have been elevated to this high position have somehow revealed their human frailties and pomposities. But Georges Vanier was an angel.

To carry out the idea of a National Conference on the Family, the Canadian Welfare Council was enlisted to look after the housekeeping arrangements and a National Council was set up, with Arnold Heeney as chairman, our most impeccable public servant and former ambassador to the United States. (I should also mention that Arnold had been a great friend of the Gordons in Winnipeg and, because of his great devotion to my first mother-in-law Helen Gordon, I know she would have been one of his candidates as the model mother of a loving family.) I was appointed to this Council of about fifty people because the concept of the family home could hardly be discussed without reference to housing. When we first met in the very formal gilded salon at Rideau Hall, I found that I was the only person who had this kind of background; almost a quarter of all the council members were clergy. The chair next to me was empty and the meeting had already started when an impressive black-garbed figure, with a high black hat, entered and took the chair beside me. In order to be friendly and democratic I leaned over and whispered in his ear 'Carver', to which he replied curtly 'Athanagoras'. He didn't speak to me again. When we came to the hot June day in 1964, for the opening ceremonies of the conference on the lawns of Government House, the massed bands of the Salvation Army played the vice-regal salute and, in the words of the official conference report, 'representatives of 19 religious communions bore witness to the ecumenical spirit of the occasion'. A brilliant solution had been found to the protocol problem of which religious voice would be heard first and which should have the last place. They all gave tongue simultaneously. In their sacerdotal gowns and ecclesiastical splendour the host of clergy was like something to be seen in a mediaeval cathedral window, the crimsons and blues and magentas so rich and irridescent in the June sunshine.

As one who had been thinking for a long time about the environment of family life, and as a father living in the vortex of my own family's noisy lust for life, I found all this institutional sanctity a bit hard to take. Somehow my own family, and all the families I knew, bore little resemblance to the Holy Family, which seemed to be the image we were being invited to contemplate. So one evening shortly before the conference, sitting in a plane on my way back from a meeting in Winnipeg, I wrote the following essay in which I tried to express my perception of a vigorous, healthy and 'flying apart' family. The essay was published before the conference in the magazine of the Canadian Welfare Council and has subsequently appeared in a booklet issued by the Canadian Housing Design Council. It was also the spoken script of a film made by the National Film Board, with a charming pictorial accompaniment devised by Lawrence Hyde, artist husband of Betty Hyde in whose nursery school our two girls first discovered their individualities.

A HOUSE IS A PLACE FOR FLYING APART

Each generation has to re-invent the family house.
What goes on inside it changes so much.
In fact a house is used in a different way
    at each stage of a family's evolution.
It has to shelter the complicated process by which
    the unity of a family
    gradually flowers into separate individuals
    each to fly apart and regenerate.

Scene One

A house is for living together
and for drawing apart,
for love
and for loneliness.
The first stage is a 'cabin in the sky' affair.
It doesn't much matter where it is or what it is:
    a few symbolic marriage possessions in a room,
    a place to eat, a place to sleep,
    and a night-time window looking out on the rest of the world.

The place is empty all day.
Detachment and mobility and opportunity are the criteria:
uptown, downtown,
Calgary next week or back to the Maritimes in the New Year.

Scene Two

Then the cabin comes down to earth
and there is a daytime at home.
'7 lbs. 6 ozs, on June 12th
sincere thanks to Dr G. Mitchell
and wonderful staff at Grace Hospital.'
In the Winnipeg papers the other participants in the event
are always gracefully acknowledged.
The particular piece of ground on which the family lands
now comes to be of great importance:
a sheltered porch, some grass, some earth to scrabble in the fingers.
The corners of the bedroom floor,
the height of the window sill and the angle of the sun
now all come into microscopic focus.

Scene Three

Then comes the main period of family life
spanning through about thirty years.
In looking for a house to fit their needs
the customers are pretty innocent.
The salesman shows them the imitation fireplace,
the simulated stone around the front door,
the stunted shrubs around the foundations,
and other symbols of domestic sentiment.
It's difficult to visualize the structure of family disciplines
and the struggles for individuality
that will strain this little empty shell.
In the bare cubes of standardized bedrooms
it's hard to see where the furniture will go.
At a loss to make a judgment
father fingers the basement walls
as if they would render some clue;
mother turns on the kitchen taps

as if blood might issue from them.
Each year a million Canadian families thus embark upon the unknown.

Scene Four

The children grow up
and the strength that sharpens their individualities
is the irresistable force
of life itself.
At first, two children in a room together
share their surprise in life
with some mutual content.
But each soon comes to recognize
    the struggle for individuality
    and a separate place:
A place for possessions
a place to bring friends
and, at night, something different about the relationship
    with each parent.
'Stop throwing things at your sister!'
'Let her come in!'
This conflict within the family explains
    some of the difficulty about planning houses.
It isn't easy to reconcile
    the drawing together and the flying apart
    all within the little perimeter of a house
    that must be tight and compact in the Canadian winter,
    stuck half in the ground against the frost
    and with much of the money used up in the mechanical equipment
      to keep the house warm and the food cold.
However improbable the place may be
    as something to cherish and remember
This first phase is the sweetest time of all.
The first layer of memory is about the shape of the rooms,
    the sound of the front door closing,
    the voices in the hall,
    the security of the inward-looking family
      preoccupied with its own little world.
Life has indeed been wasted if the house in this recollection
    is not a thing of beauty.

But it is not long before this sweet span of family unity
suffers a change.
The inner conflicts take on a new dimension
    as the children's individualities become confirmed
    and the teenager begins to discover the world beyond his own house.
He gets that separate feeling,
a bit glum around the mouth,
and a funny haircut.
The backyard and the whole neighbourhood become too small
    and stale a territory.
The rooms that were able to contain the inward-looking family
    are now struck by the flying apart.
Along the streets of the city
the inscrutable facades of houses conceal the stresses,
    the banging and bouncing and straining of social evolution
        that is going on inside.
There is a sound of hammering by night
    as fathers desperately
    try to fix up something in the basement
    that might capture the migratory teenagers
    for a time
    if a bit of their alien outside world can be brought inside.
Some affluent fathers buy boats and cars in a speculative bid
    to attach the violent interest of the young.
But many families sell their houses and start again.
The very act of moving into another house
    that doesn't have the overtones of childhood discipline
    is in itself a defence against the flying apart.

Scene Six

Finally the children leave
and there are only two for dinner,
Empty bedrooms are still and silent
    with the photos and trophies of school triumphs
    fading on the walls.
A juvenile family moves in next door.
Feeling a bit strange
    they look for a new kind of place to live.

It should be compact, so they can lock up and go away,
    yet the door should open on a garden and a tree
    not on the dark anonymous corridor of an apartment house.
It should be relaxed and isolated
    but near the shops, the church, the doctor's office.
And for each one there is that private, haunting, lingering question:
    how to be left alone
    when there is no longer a family, a house
    and a neighbour?

Scene Seven

The mythology of the family home dies hard–
The place that is the permanent establishment of a family
    from its inception to the old age of the parents,
    a place encrusted and enshrined
    with the emotions and traditions of a family group.
But the picture has gone with all its sentimental aroma.
The truth is
that a family is a group of individuals
    in a highly active evolutionary process
    requiring to change their physical environment
    as the pattern of life changes.
The city must be hospitable to these changes
    and respond to the forces of growth and separation.
A house is a machine for living in
    with its pipes for bringing in fresh water
    and for removing waste
    its climate controls and mechanical equipment
      for making meals and entertainment.
It is also a more subtle kind of instrument
containing the forces and moods,
the straining activities and the private tranquillities within a family
    to grow together
    and to grow apart.

11
The Creative Spirit

In December 1954, after the resignation of David Mansur, Stewart Bates was appointed president of CMHC. He had a poetic imagination, he suffered dreadful frustations, and he died unhappy and disappointed nearly ten years later. Mansur had been a mover of money and power. Bates was a mover of ideas. He saw the extraordinary opportunity for CMHC to be an influence upon the evolution of Canadian society through the shaping of the urban environment.

Stewart Bates had grown up in Glasgow so he knew all about the ugliness and the seamy side of cities. He was a good scholar and he won a Commonwealth fellowship to Harvard; then he had taught economics at Dalhousie and from there he entered the bureaucracy of economic controls in wartime Ottawa. At the time of his appointment to CMHC he was deputy minister of fisheries under Hon. James Sinclair, to whom he was greatly devoted. He had loved going out on the trawlers, exchanging yarns in his broad Glasgow accent, with a nip of scotch in his hand. He understood the roughness and beauty of the ocean and his eyes would glitter as he told us about the marvels of the salmon run in the headwaters of the rivers. Perhaps it seemed a strange transition, from fish to housing. And yet I think there was a kind of connection in Bates's intellectual capacity to see the wholeness of a subject. He had been fascinated by the whole universe of life in the oceans and rivers; and I think he intuitively had a view of the whole universe of people in the habitat of cities. Having marvelled at the strange divine forces that impel the fish to move and migrate within their environment, perhaps Bates even saw himself as a kind of God-like mover of the social order. One of his favourite expressions that turned up in many of his speeches was 'the Vatican of Science'; perhaps Bates did have some symptoms of paranoia. But, like many others who have had such illusions, Stewart Bates was strangely shy in his private relationships with people, anxiously seeking courage and self-confidence in friendships which eluded him.

Bates took for granted all that Mansur had done to develop the mechanics of mortgage financing. His mission was to set CMHC upon the search for a social philosophy in its objectives.

Not many days after his appointment, Bates came into my office, looked over the shelves of books that covered one wall of my room and said: 'You'll help me, won't you?' It was the beginning of an awkward relationship such as one can only have with a brilliant, emotional, and erratic man: half respect and affection, and half maddening fury. I know that I was able to give to Bates ideas that he made his own and, in turn, I owe to him the opportunities that made my whole career with CMHC worthwhile. But there were some dreadful times.

Things moved fast. At the beginning of February, just a month after his arrival, I gave Bates some suggestions on how I would like to work and I also gave him some proposals that I had made to Mansur the year before, for widening the functions of the architectural and planning division of CMHC.. These suggestions were the origin of the new Development Division and of the Advisory Group which were both established in April 1955. The effect of the reorganization was to put the whole headquarters staff of CMHC into two packages, one part to do the business management of loan insurance and mortgage-lending, while the Development Division was to contain all the elements of the corporation that might be regarded as 'creative', a combined research and educational and developmental organization, to improve construction techniques and materials, to advance the qualities of housing design and community-planning, and to undertake social and economic research. The Advisory Group was to be a constituent part of the Development Division, to act as a kind of internal task force for evolving and advising on housing policy, and to look after the grant-making functions of CMHC. The director of this new Development Division was Jack Hodgson, later to become Prime Minister Pearson's principal private secretary, and later on a deputy minister.

I became chairman of the Advisory Group, and the five advisers were Alan Armstrong (community planning), Andrew Hazeland (house design), Sam Gitterman (building technology), Fred Coll (public housing), and Bob Adamson (economic research).

The reorganization was an oversimplification of a dynamic idea. The main elements in the Development Division did not, in fact, remain together very long as a single entity; in the course of time they drew apart into the two main strongholds of the Architectural Division and the Public Housing Division because of the inescapable dichotomy of physical planning and social planning and the rivalry of these two professional groups. On the other hand the Advisory Group remained intact throughout the next twelve years of my career in Central Mortgage and Housing Corporation. It was based on the idea that the subject of housing really involves five disciplines. We coined the expression 'The Five Fingers'.

The reorientation of CMHC shifted the emphasis from suburban mortgage-lending to a concern for the whole city, its interior change as well as its external growth. To deal with the interiors of cities it was clearly necessary to acquire a more sophisticated piece of legislation than the existing section of the National Housing Act which provided funds for redevelopment: this simply offered a 50 per cent federal contribution to the costs of acquiring and clearing slum areas with the proviso that this land had to be used exclusively as a site for low-rental housing. This offered no choice but to bulldoze the old housing and build new public housing in its place. Anyone who had followed the evolution of the urban renewal process in American cities, particularly in Philadelphia, knew that there had to be a wider range of treatments for the older areas of cities: the good things ought to be carefully conserved, what was obsolete beyond recall should be removed, new playgrounds and other social amenities ought to be added in districts with high concentrations of poor people, and some land ought to be turned to quite different purposes. At that time the term 'urban renewal' was fresh and untarnished and we used it as a synonym for 'renaissance', 'regeneration', or 'resurgence'. It's unfortunate that the words 'urban revewal' have lost their charisma because of their association with bulldozing projects that were the very opposite of what we had in mind.

Urban renewal has now been part of our national history, an experience in which many people in many cities have had some personal experience, affecting their political attitudes or their professional careers or in some way touching their private lives. So it may be of some interest to record how it all started in Canada. For there was an identifiable moment of birth. Perhaps the occasion did not seem very prestigious at the time and may even have been forgotten by some who were present. But this is how it happened.

The birth took place on 7 and 8 of July 1955 (the long labour account-

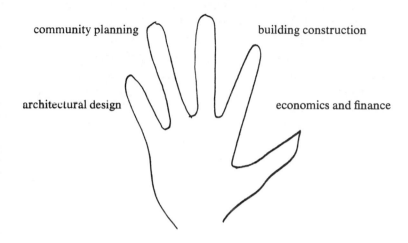

community planning

building construction

architectural design

economics and finance

ing for the double date) in the presence of twelve people and the secretary of the meeting whose name was Hicks. We met in the small conference room on the third floor of the CMHC headoffice in Ottawa. I still have a note of the way we sat around the table.

There were six CMHC people present and we had invited six others to help us understand the whole concept. I was moderator of the discussion.

Mr Carver   Mr Bates

Mr Coll

Dr Rose

Mr Sutton-Brown

Mr Beecroft

Mrs Gillbride

Mr Armstrong

Mr Lawson

Mr Adamson

Mr Hodgson   Mr Feiss

A key person at the meeting was Carl Feiss who had been in the urban renewal administration of the United States but, in the turnover from a Democratic to a Republican government, had moved into a consulting practice. I had got to know Carl as a person who, like me, had had a lifelong interest in housing and in city-planning, as an educator and a practitioner; while he was at MIT in the 1930s he had been responsible for bringing Sir Raymond Unwin to the United States, a move that had led to the Roosevelt program for the Greenbelt Towns and so to the emergence of Clarence Stein. The other visitors were: Mrs R.K. Gillbride, the leading activist for low-rental housing in Montreal; Dr Albert Rose of the University of Toronto School of Social Work who had already established his reputation as the leading Canadian scholar of housing problems; Gerald Sutton-Brown, the director of planning in Vancouver; Eric Beecroft, at that time executive director of the Community Planning Association; and Matthew Lawson, city planning commissioner of Toronto.

Apart from Carl Feiss, the most knowledgeable person present was Matt Lawson who was already, in the summer of 1955, studying the central areas of Toronto to see how the older neighbourhoods could best be revived, rehabilitated, and renewed. A year earlier Matt and I had discussed this idea as we were returning from a conference in Philadelphia, sitting in a taxi on our way across New York. I had been able to arrange a grant to support this study and, at our urban renewal meeting, Matt was able to tell us something of what he had already discovered.

It was an uplifting and visionary discussion as we talked about all the beautiful and creative things to be done and the great adventure on which we hoped to embark. But urban revewal is a subject that also has its tedious aspects. At one point in our discussion Sutton-Brown was explaining the need for 'code enforcement' and was telling us that other cities should follow the example of Vancouver in establishing a 'centralized inspectorate' to deal with both building standards and with code enforcement. Sutton-Brown has some of the attributes of the strong, silent police inspector with the inscrutable eyes, and I could see Stewart Bates getting restless before he burst out: 'This is an antiseptic, namby-pamby attitude. It's colourless and dead. Urban renewal isn't something to be discussed so politely. Life cannot be understood by staying home and drinking tea. We're concerned with rogues, vagabonds, sorcerers, the pimps, the bawds, and the perverts. It's a human problem . . . What we need is a good fight with the reactionaries!'

Out of this discussion a number of actions followed. Certainly the most important was the amendment to the National Housing Act that was presented to Parliament by Robert Winters the following March 1956. I can admit to a small thrill in seeing the words I had written for him on the pages of Hansard. Winters, a graduate of MIT in electrical engineering, had an oddly inexpressive electronic voice and one had to write very plain housekeeping prose for him. It was a housekeeping speech, pointing out that in spite of all the new suburbs that had been built, two-thirds of all Canadian families still lived in houses that pre-dated the war and the depression, more than half-a-million families lived in houses more than fifty years old and one-tenth of the existing houses were more than seventy-five years old. All of this housing was in a state of decline. It was a vital part of our national wealth and must be carefully conserved; the most obsolete would have to be replaced but a great deal of this stock could be rehabilitated and adapted to new uses.

The amendments to the Act therefore provided federal funds for dealing with declining areas in many different ways and removed the previous restriction in the use of cleared land. Also the amendments extended the funds available under the 'home improvement loans' section of the Act which we thought would be a workable method for dealing with rehabilitation; in this, I'm afraid, we proved to be wrong and the error was not repaired until the 1964 amendments provided for financing the improvement of houses in urban renewal areas. However, the 1956 amendments started a new flow of events in cities all across Canada. Action soon started in the blighted areas near to the hearts of Halifax, Saint John, Hamilton, and other cities.

To improve the legislation was one thing, but to make it actually work was another matter. With this aim, the second action that followed from our 1955 meeting was a campaign to stimulate public interest in renewal and to encourage city governments to examine their problem areas and help them work out plans of action. In this effort the leading evangelist was Stanley Pickett, an English town-planner who had been brought to Newfoundland to give a professional expertise to the haphazard problems of that province's scattered communities. We succeeded in disengaging Stanley from this assignment (but I'm happy to say that he never really abandoned Newfoundland as his first love) and for two years he was on the staff of the Community Planning Association with a roving mission to tell the people of Canada about urban renewal–what to do and how to do it.

Another kind of activism was to extend the process of 'urban renewal studies' to every city in Canada, based on the prototype model of Matt Lawson's Toronto study published in 1956. The next studies to be carried out were Professor Gordon Stephenson's study of Halifax and Gerald Sutton-Brown's comprehensive renewal study of Vancouver. In Halifax there was a strong CPAC group to support the renewal strategy worked out by Gordon Stephenson, and Halifax has been blessed with a succession of very able mayors to maintain the momentum of action. In the course of time other cities followed and the completion of an urban renewal study became a kind of municipal status symbol. The real value of such a study was not only that it could suggest a variety of renewal treatments and a sequence of action programs, but that it was a way of becoming involved in a small and understandable task, without too deep a commitment of funds. Like many operations that begin with imagination and vision and then become absorbed into a bureaucratic system, I'm afraid the long series of urban renewal studies eventually deteriorated into a routine exercise, going through the prescribed motions of what Harold Spence-Sales called a 'vermin count'. But this decline happened some time later.

In order to prepare the staff of CMHC to respond to the growing demands for urban renewal which we hoped to stimulate, the corporation embarked upon a comprehensive program of staff-training and reorientation. The senior and middle ranks of all the regional and local branches were brought to Ottawa in weekly shifts and given an entirely new view of their organization, which was no longer to be dedicated primarily to the mortgage business but was now to become involved in the creation of better cities, through growth and change. It was expected that every branch manager would be able to talk about these things within his own community, not just as a person who knew the financing regulations, but with the new enthusiasm inspired by Stewart Bates's panegyrics.

In entering this new era in which CMHC was to have a new role and a new image, the Architectural and Planning staff were obviously going to be an important factor. Sam Gitterman withdrew from the position of chief architect, a post he had filled with distinction since CMHC had been established. It was not that Bates considered him unworthy of the new age (he has remained the acknowledged master of small-house design) but that the new impresario needed to find a new star, a Nureyev for his 'corps de ballet'. Because Sam was a popular figure, everyone felt embarrassed about this and the star role was not immediately filled.

Finally I offered to go to Toronto with the rash promise of finding the right person. When I got there I went into a phone booth on Yonge Street and called Professor Eric Arthur and explained the situation. Eric had a wonderful gift for keeping up his relationships with the most talented graduates of the architectural school. Could he think of any suitable candidate? He certainly could. It was Ian Maclennan who had just come back from Venezuela the day before. Ian had been born in Gull Lake, Saskatchewan, won distinction as a flying ace in the Mediterranean, returned from the war to become an architect and had then quickly gained professional experience in New York and in Caracas–and here he was, ready and willing. When Ian appeared in Bates's office a few days later I remember raising some doubts about his knowledge of housing, hoping that, if I said these things first, Bates would be bound to make reassuring comments. So, in a flash, Ian Maclennan became chief architect and he rapidly gained for CMHC the reputation for having one of the best design staffs in North America. It was an important point of prestige for impresario Stewart Bates, who thereupon won the acclaim of the architectural profession and an honorary fellowship in their royal institute.

Opportunities to display the talents of the new 'corps de ballet' were soon at hand. The first major work was the large Regent Park South project in Toronto, just across the street from the first Regent Park project started in 1948; in Toronto there was already a momentum of public support for public housing. Then followed the extremely difficult task of building the Jeanne Mance project in Montreal, the first redevelopment and public housing project in Quebec. This could not have been accomplished without the persistence of a citizens' group first set up in 1952, with Mrs R.K. Gillbride as its activist leader. This committee, representing fifty-five civic associations, patiently kept up the pressure through five long years while the Duplessis government in Quebec, Mayor Drapeau in Montreal, and the joint forces of CMHC and Montreal's city planners struggled through plots and counterplots. (The Duplessis government refused to be a partner of the federal government, as prescribed in the 1949 legislation for public housing, and of course Mayor Drapeau wanted to impose his own authority on the plans. The hero of the battle was Paul Dozois, a Montreal city councillor who succeeded in becoming provincial Minister of Municipal Affairs and then stripped Mayor Drapeau of his powers to obstruct the project. Drapeau was defeated in the 1957 civic elections.)

Then there was the Mulgrave Park project in Halifax which was the first strategic step that made it possible to clear the ground for transforming the old Jacob Street slum area into the new heart of the city, Scotia Square. These three projects (in Toronto, in Montreal, and in Halifax) are of historic significance because they were Canada's first large-scale essays in urban design, embodying mixed compositions of high-rise apartments and townhouses with spaces around them for children's play and for carparks. They pioneered in what has subsequently become a familiar field of urban architecture, and it was done with great skill and authority. I have always thought that Mulgrave Park in Halifax, which I have visited many times, is a masterpiece in its handling of a very difficult hillside site; the place has a vigorous harbourside character and its walls and steps and colour are full of sculptural surprises. These and many other substantial projects that came from the drawing-boards of CMHC's architectural and planning staff in this period are the physical monuments to Stewart Bates because it was he who put the team together and demanded that their standard of performance was to be excellence, and nothing less.

Of course, these large projects of redevelopment and public housing for which CMHC was responsible have subsequently been at the centre of an awkward controversy about the segregation of low-income people in so called 'ghettos' of public housing. It is ironical that the very excellence of their design came to be regarded as a dreadful mistake because it was this difference in quality that made them stand out from the general dullness of the surrounding city; it was said that low-income tenants don't like thus being in the limelight–it only exposes their humiliation. I have always been rather doubtful about the sincerity of this argument. I think most parents are willing to swallow their pride if their children obviously benefit from a better environment. However, the difficulty really occurred because these first large projects were indeed left as rather isolated monuments when the whole expected tide of urban renewal and rehousing failed to gather strength. The dedication of Stewart Bates and those around him simply didn't bring results on a large enough scale. This was largely because the Diefenbaker government, which came into office in 1957, was more interested in housing Conservative middle-class voters than in tackling more fundamental social issues; it was certainly true that we were not in rhythm with the political tide. And yet, I think, perhaps we were closer to the mood of the people than the politicians were. Within CMHC we had a strong impression that our interests and missionary efforts to bring about major changes in the cities were relevant and timely, and people in the cities were responsive. There

was a surge of intellectual interest in the subject; the popular paperback
literature of that decade included William H. Whyte's *The Organization Man,* David Riesman's *The Lonely Crowd,* Paul Goodman's *Communitas,* and the subject had really come to the boil when Harvey Cox's *The Secular City* was published in 1965. By that time the catchword was 'The city is the people' (the title of Henry Churchill's book published in 1945). And to the extent that this tide of interest had flowed through Canada, it was the thrust of CMHC people around Stewart Bates that had helped to bring this about. But none of this appeared to touch the political establishment in Ottawa; and the minister within the Diefenbaker government to whom CMHC had to report, Howard Green, seemed to be living in an altogether different world.

Having previously worked for a liberal government and having inherited such an experienced minister as Robert Winters, Bates had felt pretty sure that he could win support for the new directions on which he had set CMHC's course. He certainly felt that his predecessor, David Mansur, had solved the basic problem of investment funds for NHA financing, now that there was access to the supposedly infinite resources of the big banks. So it seemed appropriate to turn towards other and deeper social issues. Unfortunately neither of these comfortable assumptions proved to be correct. In 1957 the Liberal government stumbled into the disaster of the pipe-line debate and Mr Diefenbaker took over. And also in 1957 the economic climate changed, the country was slipping into a business recession and the banks failed to come through with the expected funds for private housing. The house-building industry that had largely been created by CMHC had acquired great lobbying strength and did not have much difficulty in persuading Howard Green, that it had to be kept afloat. To him this looked like a most opportune political bonus, for a party that had no housing philosophy. What could be better than supporting the house-builders who provide shelter for that home-owning lower-middle class–the very core of the Conservative vote? So began an era in which the federal government became committed to placing enormous public funds in suburban homes, instead of shifting course towards the larger cross-sectional problems of the cities, towards a policy in which all of us in CMHC so fervently believed and for which the reorganized CMHC now had a capability. So in the decade following 1957, the federal government used its own funds, through CMHC, to finance 223,000 home-owner units while the banks and private lenders found money for less than 200,000 home-owners. This was a complete reversal of the theory that had been generally followed within CMHC.

The 1957 Annual Report of CMHC expressed the feeling of consternation. It contained a full-page photograph of an extremely handsome fourteen-storey Regent Park public housing project rising above the wreckage of Toronto's Cabbagetown and these comments: 'Parliament, in passing the National Housing Act 1954, had never intended that the Corporation should become a major supplier of mortgage money. Although Parliament in framing the Act allowed for such an eventuality, the purpose of the mortgage insurance arrangement was to reduce the house-building industry's dependence on public money by mobilizing private funds more effectively.'

Within CMHC the situation had an air of comedy. Howard Green seemed to be a delightfully old-fashioned American gothic character, tall, lean, and ascetic, with a sepulchral voice. He spoke about the 'Small Homes Loans Programme' as if it had some Old Testament authenticity, and he invented a mythical Canadian called 'the little man,' whom we couldn't recognize but who must have been Green's idealization of the Conversative voter. But the worst part of the joke was that this highly moral man believed that a 'little man' must have a 'little house.' And this was interpreted, literally, to mean that the publicly financed home-owners must not occupy more than the magic figure of 1050 square feet of floor-space. Within the CMHC architectural staff there was a rush to design the smallest possible dwelling unit. Someone worked out an acceptable plan at 900 square feet (we called it the 'mouse house'). And then, one morning, word went around the corridors of CMHC that Ian Maclennan had done one at, I think, 850 square feet, (the 'louse house').

Having committed the federal government to using public money in support of suburban home-ownership, Howard Green moved, two years later, to be the Minister of External Affairs where his fine old-fashioned patriotism enabled him to defend Canada's adherence to the British Empire. Then, for three years, David Walker as Minister of Public Works, was the person to whom the president of CMHC had to report, and he did not appear to have any great interest in housing and urban affairs; what had brought him to Ottawa in the landslide 1957 election was his close personal and political friendship with Mr. Diefenbaker whom he had nominated for the party leadership back in 1942. Both these men were political tacticians and hardly likely to appreciate the philosophy and long-term urban strategies to which CMHC was dedicated. So, isolated in our headquarters out on the Montreal Road, remote from the heart of politics on Parliament Hill, we had no choice but to pursue our own relationships with people in the cities of Canada. Throughout this period it was CMHC which sustained and cultivated community interest in social housing and the renewal of the older parts of cities.

Throughout this period the views of the Advisory Group were continually sought by the board and management of CMHC and we expressed our views in a number of papers which were pretty frank. 'There is no national policy for public housing,' we wrote in a March 1962 report. 'The previous Liberal Government did not enunciate a policy and quite deliberately avoided doing so. The Conservative Government has not materially changed the terms of the Act concerning public housing and has not declared any point of view.' In fact, without any official policy guidelines laid down by the government it had become very difficult for CMHC, in its partnerships with provincial and local governments, to conduct public housing business with reasonable efficiency. Our 1962 report commented:

The Corporation has been left to deal with applicants, to negotiate with them, to try to understand their requirements, to try to fit these requirements into something which the Minister will accept, when the limits of ministerial acquiescence are not really known, and are subject in any case to change. It is impossible in this situation to have a set of criteria which, taken together, could be regarded as a coherent and responsible policy. If the criteria are too accommodating, projects are in risk of being vetoed by the Minister; if they are narrow, the Corporation is subject to charges of bureaucratic and irresponsible control, and justly so. The Corporation is in the position of having to negotiate issues over which it has no ultimate authority. It is therefore not surprising that decision within the Corporation has been fragmented, uncertain, and contentious.

At this time each public housing project had to be a joint undertaking in a partnership of the federal government with a province. The city concerned had to ask for a project but was essentially a bystander; this was the consequence of a view traditionally held by federal officials, that local governments, like women before 'women's lib', were by nature inferior and incompetent. Since I had myself lived through an experience of being on the other side of the fence, having taken part in Toronto's early efforts to get action from an indifferent federal government and a completely uninterested provincial government, I had always disliked the partnership arrangement that was introduced in 1949, in the Mansur régime. So, as soon as the Advisory Group came on to the scene, I had started to advocate a change. And this became a recurring theme in the Group's policy advice. If local governments had greater direct responsibility, we argued, they would have a 'more spirited interest in public housing, urban renewal and suburban development'. The senior governments 'had never encouraged communities to generate their own agencies to give life and vigour to public housing and renewal'. Perhaps the difficulty in getting these programs off the ground, we suggested, was this lack of 'an evolution of local leadership 'and the time had come for a new deal'. Finally, the Advisory Group's persistence was rewarded and in 1964 an important amendment was made to the Act, offering direct 90 per cent loans to the cities so that they could carry out their own programs without being mothered and smothered by the federal and provincial bureaucracies who seemed to have the greatest difficulty in expediting their partnership projects. Out of respect for provincial authority over the rights of municipalities, the amendment was worded so as to permit the provinces also to work under a loan system.

Unfortunately our hope of passing the initiative and the responsibility to the cities was not fulfilled, for reasons not entirely to do with housing. The year 1964 also ushered in a new era of constitutional controversy and provincial power thrusts, following the Liberal government's return to power under Lester Pearson; it was a process that started with the social revolution in Quebec and was echoed in the new economic power of Ontario. In this political climate the provinces grasped the initiative in housing and the leading role, instead of passing to the cities as we had hoped, was taken by the new provincial housing agencies, of which the Ontario Housing Corporation (OHC) was the prototype. It was certainly ironical that, since the provinces lacked experience and personnel for this role, CMHC had to provide from its own resources all the key people for this new hierarchy of public housing management. A decade later, these difficulties have still not been resolved; in the course of time, no doubt, the responsibility for these programs will be passed down to communities, so that local citizens will be able to take a more active part in looking after their own housing requirements.

Stewart Bates died one Sunday evening in April 1964, two days before the parliamentary debate on the amendments to the National Housing Act. He had wanted to do something great for Canada, but the political indifference had a crushing effect upon his creative spirit; and it was partly these stresses, I think, that killed him.

I believe that Bates was essentially a religious person. In fact the first time I saw him, he was dressed in a black morning-coat, taking the collection at St Andrew's Presbyterian church in Ottawa, the very model of an orthodox Presbyterian; he was a friend of the minister, Dr Ian

Burnet, another talented and imaginative Scot who, like Stewart Bates,
suffered great trials in his life. When Bates came to CMHC, a stranger and
lonely, he conceived the idea of installing in his office a hi-fi sound system
so that in periods of depression and introspection he could be uplifted
by great music of compassion and inspiration. I think he hoped to be able
to share this inspirational experience with the friends whom he might
discover and he may have known that some of 'the intellectuals', as he
called the Advisory Group, were lovers of music. So on several occasions
when one of us was in his office, Bates would consider that this might
be the time to try out the treatment. Bob Adamson, Alan Armstrong,
Stanley Pickett, and I would find ourselves torn away reluctantly from
some serious task and seated in the president's office with a glass of
scotch, to await the music. At this point Bates' dedication to the great
masters would begin to fade, or perhaps he began to feel a bit silly in the
reality of this locker-room situation and out would come, not the heav-
enly choirs, but the voices of Flanders and Swann and particularly the
song called 'I'm a Gnu', which very much tickled Bates's fancy. An hour
or two later we would seize on some excuse to escape from an embarrassing situation and we hoped that Bates would be be able to find his way
home.

But the most distressing of all my associations with Bates occurred in
a quite different way. Early on in the whole process of reorienting CMHC
to an activist role, a searching discussion took place about 'the publics'
to which CMHC should address itself, as an interpreter of urban growth
and change. Jack Hodgson, then director of the Development Division,
drafted a scholarly paper setting out the whole array of technical, professional, political, institutional, and lay 'publics' and the variety of media
that could be used to carry the message. It was decided that CMHC's
information functions should go far beyond factual reporting on the
numbers of houses built and the blessings bestowed on Canadians by the
decisions of the government. The output of an Information Division
should be far more educational and evangelistic. I can't say that my heart
was entirely in this idea because I really believed in a rather different
theory of 'outreach' as I shall explain below, but when Bates asked me
to take on the new Information Division, I said I would. At the same
time, and unknown to me, Bates had approached Fred Wooding who
had been his information officer and a close friend at the Department of
Fisheries; Fred was highly experienced in the production of information
about fish and was the author of a well-received book on that subject.
I can only say that Bates' well-meant scheme to join together Fred's

production expertise and my knowledge of the subject of housing was a disaster for both of us. Our differences at first seemed to be about trivial matters, but these gradually accumulated into an insuperable barrier that brought us in anguish to a standstill. I think the difficulties all had to do with style, which is an inescapable aspect of every information product; not *what* to say but *how* to say it. This came down to details about choosing type-faces, photographs, mood and emphasis, language and colour. I recall that our differences of judgment in these things came to a head in producing the first issue of a new house organ to be called *Habitat.* On the cover there was to be a picture of the new Regent Park project in Toronto which was the pride and joy of the CMHC architectural staff and I felt that a rendering of this subject by an artist skilled in depicting the underwater life of fish would not be well received. Our partnership became untenable, and the only practical solution was that we both withdraw to lick our wounds after some tense weeks. I think the person who was most embarrassed and stricken by this episode was Stewart Bates; he felt that his error had lost him two good friends, and I have always suspected that this made a serious crack in his morale. In order to restore my own morale I went into retreat to write a book which emerged as *Cities in the Suburbs,* published by the University of Toronto Press. I then returned to the chairmanship of the Advisory Group and remained in that position until I retired from CMHC.

One sometimes remembers the most trivial things about a person, a little snapshot which captures the actuality of a man more vividly than a formal portrait. This snapshot was taken one day outside the CMHC head office where, after lunch, we would often stroll up and down the broadwalk in front of the building, for conversation and a sniff of fresh air. In one direction we would walk towards the Montreal Road where a chain hung across the path to separate us from the heavy traffic on the highway. One day, as we came to this point, two or three of us in conversation with Stewart Bates, an old man shuffled along the edge of the highway, pitifully dirty and desolate and almost under the thundering wheels of the big trucks that overshadowed him. Bates stopped, suddenly quiet, as if hurt by what he had seen. 'Poor devil,' he said. I think Bates had an extraordinary sense of companionship with the sinful and the distressed; he understood the grace of God.

12
Reaching Out

If my account of Stewart Bates' frustrations has given the impression that this was not a fruitful period for me and for my fellow-members of the Advisory Group, then I have erred. There were certainly disappointments, and we could well understand that Bates might have a sense of failure because, with all his imagination and his high aspirations, it was extraordinarily difficult to translate his ideas into political action. I think perhaps he felt that he had let us down because we depended upon him to advance the causes in which we shared. As president, he alone had the responsibility of explaining these new ideas to his minister and of advocating shifts of housing policy. He was not very successful in this simply because the political circumstances were not favourable. But nevertheless Bates' effect upon the decade was pervasive.

It was a period of ferment in the evolution of Canada as an urban nation and we were in the midst of things, with new faces and new ideas coming to the surface. Certainly CMHC was an initiator of much that happened at the time and it was a unique and lively institution. I was in the company of people I liked and admired. So I look back with gratitude to the twelve years between 1955 and 1967, when I was chairman of CMHC's Advisory Group, as the most constructive part of my working life.

The composition of the five-man group has been explained by the analogy of the five fingers representing the five subjects of housing design, community planning, social purpose, building technology, and economics–the specializations of the five advisers. It could also be said that the fingers and the hand were in the gesture of reaching out. It was understood that each of us in our own individual way would go about the country, getting to know situations in the cities, finding people with ideas, and stimulating a process of discussion. We were to be activators, not bureaucrats sitting at our desks. This would not always be considered a proper thing for public servants to do; but during those twelve years when I was chairman of the Advisory Group this was an important part of our role. The great debate about city growth and renewal, and about citizen participation, had hardly yet begun; I think we helped to cultivate the ground and sow the seeds for that debate. The previous decade had been largely devoted to re-establishing family life after the deep disturbances of the war and the depression; great attention had been given to building the dormitory suburbs and providing schools for the surging generation of postwar children. But now there was a feeling in the air that, out of the enormous growth of metropolitan cities a new kind of civilization was going to appear. The surge of the postwar 'baby bulge' was going to move through the university age and become the youth of the seventies. The big immigration of urban Europeans was beginning to change the style of city life. The problems of poverty and old age began to look different from the conventional stereotypes. We were engaged in a process of social expansion and diversification.

In my files I have come across some notes for a talk I gave to a CMHC staff course in February 1958 which will serve as a recollection of how I was thinking about this process of social change. I was speaking to the managers of branch offices in the principal cities of Canada, suggesting how the social dynamics of an urban community can work effectively in the process of urban renewal; it was part of our plan to encourage the field staff of CMHC to talk about such things within their home communities, and to give aid and support to the process. Bureaucrats tend to be scared of citizen activists and I was trying to explain that CMHC must welcome the initiatives of citizens and help them to organize and to express themselves and to sustain the processes of growth and renewal. These were my notes for a 'chalk-talk' in a basement room of the Butler Motel in Ottawa:

I for INCIDENT, IMPACT, and INITIATIVE. Some event acting upon some latent force within a community usually supplies the original motive power to get something started. This may occur within an elected body, but is more likely to start outside. May be only a few individuals or may be in strength of some organization. Motives likely to be emotional (pious) rather than economic.

A for ACCEPTANCE of responsibility by local government and for the ACTION it

will take. Usually requires the staking of a personal and political reputation.
The 'father person' in the mayor, e.g. Mayor Saunders (Toronto), succession
of mayors in Halifax.

E for EDUCATION, EXPLANATION, and EVALUATION. Raising an understanding
in the public mind, explaining the intentions, and giving an opportunity to
evaluate the consequences. Choice between social benefits and improvements
to utilities and services. Interpretation of economic effects.

V for the VOTERS and their VOICE. Winning electoral support for the spending
and action proposals. Newspapers and ward campaigners.

T for the TEAM. Marshalling the staff and the administrative arrangements to
carry out projects. Intergovernmental rapport and mutual understanding
through discussion, conference, and staff-course methods.

PR is for PR, which is interpretation to those who are going to be affected by
actions: those who will be expropriated, relocated, and rehoused. Negotiations
with private builders working in the area and with agencies and institutions
who have contact with population in area.

O is the WHEEL, the presence of continuing forces within the community to
sustain the momentum once the original action has been taken. To keep
rolling.

Each member of the Advisory Group reached out in his own way and
into his own special field of interest, to find the people and the ideas that
were fermenting in that period. We each took our own initiatives but,
collectively, we knew what each was doing because our offices adjoined
one another and because about once a month we gathered round a table
to report to the group and to discuss the funding of research and educational projects that largely evolved out of our own outreaching. From
time to time, the president would refer policy questions to us and these
would be debated furiously and a paper written; on many occasions we
tried to redefine the social philosophy of public housing and the rationale
of public land-assembly. And, during this period, most of the proposals
for new legislation originated in the suggestions made by the Advisory
Group. The five advisors had an unusual combination of talents and,
collectively, a great deal of experience in housing affairs. We were a
congenial group, not afraid to tear strips off one another when opinions
differed, and all had a great capacity for laughter. We were tenacious in
argument and equal in status. Though I think that the organizational
concept of the Advisory Group might be applied in other situations, yet
it might be difficult to find the people to fit the pattern so well.

All my recollections of that period are inseparable from recollections of my close associates who are also my friends. We got to know one another rather better than most office colleagues do because, in argument and in search for the ultimate social justifications of housing policy, we had to dig deep into our own beliefs. It is a delight to get to know some of the infinite details of a person's mind, to come upon unsuspected corners and configurations; it is like looking into an extensive view of the sea or the hills and loving it the more you get to know it in different moods and lights.

But to offer a description of one's friends is both impertinent and difficult–particularly if they are alive and well and living in Ottawa and able to protest. If, at a public meeting, one has to introduce a friend about whom one knows a great deal, it is possible to take refuge in selections from his 'curriculum vitae', a respectful but usually boring procedure. On this occasion I will take refuge in another device, which is to show you around my private portrait gallery.

This is a picture of Andrew Hazeland who was adviser on housing design and who succeeded me as chairman of the group when I retired in 1967. He is seen inside his own house which is light and sunny, and there is a glimpse through the living-room into a small garden with clipped hedges and there are some birds pecking at berries scattered on a paved walk. That small figure in the deep chair in the living-room is Andrew's wife, Mary: she is drawing in a small sketch book and on the wall of the room is one of her own paintings of a meadow with flowers and there is a rather wistful figure of a girl, perhaps herself as a child. Andrew is in the doorway to the hall, evidently coming in to greet a guest who has just arrived. He looks well brushed; he is wearing a well-cut tweed jacket that has that well-used look, like the clothes of an Englishman–though I know that he was brought up in Hong Kong and went to a well-known China missionary school. The interior of the house, though it seems luminous, is really quite small and has a comfortable quality. It's the kind of house in which it would be a pleasure to do a simple thing like boiling an egg and putting it on the table because everything is in the right place and has a shine to it. Obviously Andrew and Mary take pleasure in the place they have made around themselves and they enjoy sharing it with other people.

The second portrait in the gallery is of Bob Adamson, economist and greatly valued adviser to three successive presidents of CMHC. He is sitting with his feet up on his desk with one elbow raised as he ruffles the hair on his head. Unlike the clear light surface of the Hazeland portrait, the brushwork here is rough, active, and loose, and the colours are rather wild and clashing. It is like an Augustus John portrait. The room in which we see Adamson is active, too, with papers and reports and files strewn at random on chairs and tables. And in his loose jacket pocket I see a paperback Western. The view outside the window is western, too: a big sky, a stormy evening, a swampy growth of bushes and bullrushes. Being a Winnipegger, being red-headed, and being an economist is an unbeatable combination for having a detached point of view and being able to laugh at the rest of the world. Bob's teasing wit and deadly aim in deflating my romantic illusions always gave me laughter and immense enjoyment of our many long and involved discussions. And successive presidents and ministers have enjoyed receiving his advice which was never given in the dreary and colourless language of so many economists, but in vivid literary language, with the vigorous brushstrokes of this portrait.

To have his portrait painted I asked the subject of this next picture to wear a white coat, as if he were a surgeon or some kind of scientist in his laboratory. The man in the white coat wears glasses, he is looking straight at you and he is surrounded with a network of pipes and tubes and the torsos of building structures. The painting has a surrealist clarity and is equipped with a sound system that emits bubbling and gurgling and other subdued laboratory noises. The person in the white coat is Sam Gitterman, adviser on building technology. He is the son of an immigrant family, he worked his way through the McGill school of architecture, and he became chief architect of CMHC under David Mansur. He is an inquisitive person and what he knows he found out for himself. When he joined the Advisory Group he wanted to discover two things. One: a multifunctional material for housebuilding, to combine the properties of structural strength, insulation, and surface quality, and so avoid the extraordinarily costly combinations of wood-framing with layers of interior and exterior cladding. Two: he hoped to develop a recycling system which would eliminate the whole costly network of sewers and sewage disposal plants and make it possible for us all to drink our own bathwater. The significance of Sam's scientific search has become even clearer as urban societies have become more aware of the frightening consequences of waste disposal in damaging the environment of life on earth.

The next portrait in my gallery is painted in the style of Velasquez. It shows the finely drawn figure of a tall, good-looking man in black doublet and hose. The pose is graceful, the left hand on the hilt of a slender rapier and the right hand lifted as if in a gesture of greeting and explanation, the head a little on one side as if expecting an answer. It is the figure of a man entirely at ease in a public situation; an actor perhaps, or a lawyer. I think of Fred Coll in this way because of his great talents in speech and exposition. People are his medium, the interchange of mind and language. He was one of the original members of our group, as adviser on the social programs of public housing and urban renewal, but at a quite early stage he left to seek his fortune elsewhere within CMHC, where he could use all his talents in negotiation, in meeting politicians, mayors, and decision-makers. The Spanish style of the portrait, the debonair pose, and the cosmopolitan 'savoir-faire', seem to fit one who was brought up by the Mediterranean. By an odd coincidence in our lives, Fred Coll grew up in the very same house in Gibraltar where my grandfather and great-grandfather had also lived.

The fifth portrait in my gallery is of Alan Armstrong who has appeared earlier in these recollections and who continues to be a companion in many of the later affairs of my life. In this portrait, which might have been painted by Lemieux, Alan's head and shoulders appear in the bottom left-hand corner of the picture and most of the canvas depicts shelves and more shelves of books. Alan is a scholar, but if you could read the titles of the books you would still have difficulty in knowing what was the subject of his scholarship which seemed to be encyclopaedic. As if to tease you, in refusing to be pinned down in answering this question, Alan will not speak because he is playing a clarinet, neatly held in his mouth and with his fingers. In fact the specialization of Alan's scholarship has been its non-specialization and an extraordinary faculty for piecing the specialized parts together. I think that has been Alan's great strength as the first director of the Community Planning Association, as an adviser to CMHC on planning, and as the director of the Urban Research Council set up in 1962. He has understood the relative positions of the arts, the sciences, the politics, and the economics of community planning to an extent unmatched by any other Canadian.

Those are the portraits of the five original members of the Advisory Group. There were changes and some others joined the group for short periods; but Stanley Pickett was a member of the fraternity for such a long period that I must include him in my portrait gallery.

This is a closely detailed picture of a landscape, looking across a cultivated green valley to a wooded hillside; in the valley there are farm houses, and a stream flows towards the sea where there is a harbour with boats. Here and there are groups of people talking or working together and there are animals in the fields. It is the kind of folk-picture first perfected by the seventeenth-century painter Pieter Breughel and recently revived in the delightful Canadian pictures by William Kurelek, illustrating scenes of life on the prairies and in the Maritimes. Stanley Pickett appears as a small figure down there in the valley, listening to some children playing their band instruments in the yard of the village school. Stanley's portrait takes this form because, as an adviser on urban renewal, he always appreciated the indigenous character of a place and its people and didn't carry around with him the stereotypes and administrative formulas that have been so destructive in the transformation from old to new. There is music in each place, which some people can hear. My last correspondence with Stanley, who now lives and works in the highlands of Scotland, was about Brigus, a little harbour village on the Avalon peninsula about fifty miles from St John's, Newfoundland, beyond Topsail and Kelligrews and on the way to Spaniard's Bay, not far from Cupids. It is a hauntingly beautiful place, the village tucked away behind the bare rocks, at the head of the deep-water retreat from the ocean. I hope its innocent architecture will be saved from the hands of those who cannot see and do not hear the music.

Amongst those who joined the Advisory Group for shorter spells was Roger Marier who came from the McGill school of social work to seek a wider career; he became CMHC's senior official in the province of Quebec and, later, was deputy minister of social welfare in the Quebec government. Alain Nantel also started in the group and then became a vice-president of the corporation. And there was Rex Opie who filled in for Sam Gitterman for a time. Rex was a great big Tarzan of a man who had had a legendary career as a bush pilot, mountaineer, and explorer of equatorial jungles; his wife could play the piano with such vigorous rhythm that the instrument would jump from the floor. Rex always seemed an unlikely person to be found in the captivity of a government office and we appreciated his shrewd open-air judgments.

Perhaps these portraits of my colleagues in the Advisory Group may dispel the popular notion that people who work for governments are colourless, toe-the-line conformists. We had, in fact, a pretty robust mixture of personal qualities and professional expertise. And I don't think these qualities are at all unusual among those who live and work in Ottawa and who have found that there is as much room for originality in the public service as there is in the ranks of private enterprise.

At the outset in 1955, it was agreed that each adviser would reach out on his own to people across the country who could join him in his endeavour. Perhaps the outreaching that fulfilled this pattern most clearly was Andrew Hazeland's establishment of the Canadian Housing Design Council. It had been part of my original proposal to Stewart Bates that we should organize a council somewhat along the lines of the National Industrial Design Council (NIDC) on which I had worked with Donald Buchanan some years before. The reasoning was that the pursuit of excellence in domestic architecture is a cultural objective and that CMHC, as a government agency, could not easily express cultural preferences without being discriminatory in making housing loans. So this kind of thing would be better done by the three parties involved: namely the builders, the architects, and the consumers themselves. So in April 1956 we brought together a small nucleus group to discuss the concept, in the same manner in which we initiated the process of urban renewal, as I have described earlier. In this case we invited Fritz Gutheim, an American with wide experience in such matters, to give a detached point of view, and amongst the founding group were R.C. Berkinshaw, a prominent businessman who became the first chairman of the CHDC; Alan Jarvis, then director of the National Gallery; John Bland, head of the McGill school of architecture; and Mark Napier, Canadian head of the J. Walter Thompson Company (whose childhood memories go back to the same place as mine; for it was in his family's beautiful garden in Harborne that I first hid behind the beech hedges and tasted the bitter fruit of the crab-apple). The Housing Design Council consists of twenty-four people who each serve a three-year term and in the seventeen years since its establishment, forty builders, thirty-eight architects, twenty-one businessmen, and thirty people in the general category of consumers, have served on the Council. By focusing public attention on well-designed housing, through its annual awards, exhibits, and publications, the CHDC has been a major influence in advancing the quality of Canadian housing so that it is superior, I believe, to the comparable product in the United States. In one particular field Canada has excelled: in the design of 'townhouses'; and that is very much the consequence of the missionary work done through the CHDC by two outstanding architects, James Murray and Jack Klein. The credibility of the Council came from Andrew Hazeland's deep understanding of how a house can be a pleasure to live in, in all its spaces and in all its little working details.

To describe all the outreachings of all the members of the group would be far beyond the bounds of these pages, so I will confine myself to some affairs in which I was particularly involved: in setting up an urban research council, in trying to stimulate public discussion of the social

policies of housing, and in the preparation of legislative proposals which
were, in a sense, my last will and testament to CMHC. But, first, I must
briefly explain what I wrote in *Cities in the Suburbs,* published in 1962,
because this was a statement of philosophy that helped me very much
in all that I did thereafter.

The opportunity to think out and write down this philosophy came
about by accident. I have already mentioned the accident: how I stumbled into an impossible situation in taking over the information functions
of CMHC and then retreated to lick my wounds. Isolated in this retreat
for several months I tried to write down a general prescription for the
growth of big cities, in response to the universal dissatisfaction that had
been so well expressed in Gertrude Stein's famous comment about Los
Angeles: 'There is no There there.' In Canada and in all North America,
cities had grown by sprawling out into formless suburban acreages of
housing which were the product of the enormous success of National
Housing Act mortgage-financing and of CMHC in Canada, and the corresponding operations in the United States. In *Cities in the Suburbs* I tried
to give a description in nontechnical language of a growth process by
which large mother cities could give birth to new offspring communities,
each having its own heart or town centre, complete with all the essential
elements and institutions of community life. Whether the new communities were tucked in tight around the mother city, or set out in a chain
along a main transportation route, or more widely separated as satellite
towns, was not an issue, it seemed to me, as important as the social
completeness of each new biological offspring of an urban society. If the
heart of each new community were clearly determined, then all the other
pieces of a living society would fall into place; this would be a creative
act, like making a new person with all the limbs stuck on in the right
places. The unplanned suburbs are like human monsters. In a rational
community design, housing for certain kinds of people would cluster
close around the centre (higher density housing for the people most
dependent on public services and public transportation) while low-den-
sity family housing would spread further out into the natural landscape.
In *Cities in the Suburbs* I tried to define which elements of community
life should constitute the town centre and how this would provide a
starting point for organizing a full social mix in each new offspring
community, so as to avoid having ghettos of middle-class blandness in
the suburbs and ghettos of poverty remaining in the central city. It was
a great satisfaction to me to have a few months in retreat so that I could
quietly put these ideas in order and argue out the logic of them. (Since

the book has now sold more than 10,000 copies, I now know that a good many others have followed the same sequence of thought.)

For some time our group had discussed the question of whether CMHC, an agency primarily concerned with the financing of housing, was really a suitable body for funding urban research. Though the Advisory Group managed the research funds available through the National Housing Act, all money allocations had to have the approval of CMHC's board of directors and, ultimately, of the minister and the Treasury Board. The directors of a mortgage corporation are naturally tuned in to the assumption that any kind of investment ought to pay off in some material form; but in this period research money had to be used imaginatively to stimulate the inquisitiveness of a new generation in a new field of scholarship. We had to expect some disappointments in making grants to unknown young professors in the new universities, and it was always difficult to admit this hazard when asking for the approval of the board of directors. As an example, we wanted to explore the complaints and attitudes of public-housing tenants in a large Maritime city; we knew of the discontent but it was hard to put one's finger on the precise improvements that ought to be made in the next round of urban renewal and housing. Discussions with an enterprising social scientist in a nearby university led to the suggestion that a good place to search for explanations of the discontent would be in the taverns in the town, where the phlegmatic Maritimer is most articulate and lucid. So it was agreed that the social scientist would go underground, become an accepted member of the tavern clientèle, and reappear when he had got to the heart of the matter, perhaps in three or four months. A few months went by and then a year and then two years without any news that our professor had surfaced. He finally reappeared some years later, on the staff of another university in another part of Canada, by which time his information was not only confused but quite irrelevant.

The idea of a separate and distinct urban research institution had appeared in two other quarters. The Canadian Federation of Mayors and Municipalities (CFMM), for many years under the management of George Mooney (my partner in the early housing movement of the 1930s), had felt the need for a flow of new knowledge and new ideas that would help in formulating the social, economic, and planning policies of cities. The Federation was itself engaged in research in a small way, particularly for delivering its annual message to the federal cabinet, but there was no systematic process and no central clearing-house where anyone could discover who had already researched what. The idea of a new centre for

urban research also came into view as one of the recommendations of the
Committee of Inquiry into the Design of the Residential Environment.
This study had been conducted by three distinguished architects: Peter
Dobush (Montreal), John Parkin (Toronto), and C.E. Pratt (Vancou-
ver), with Alan Armstrong as organizing secretary; it was in itself an
outreach of the Advisory Group, propounded in a speech written for
Stewart Bates to give to the Royal Architectural Institute of Canada, and
it was financed with funds from CMHC.

So the proposal for an urban research institution had been waiting in
the wings for a year or two when, in January 1961, I returned to the
Advisory Group from a kind of sabbatical year, with an appetite for a
new enterprise. A large part of the next year I spent in close companionship with Peter Dobush who had been the chairman of the Inquiry into
the Design of the Residential Environment, and with Eric Beecroft who
was then the Ottawa representative of the Canadian Federation of Mayors and Municipalities. It would be difficult to imagine two more tireless
partners, as we ploughed our way through the successive organizational
stages that led, a year later, to the inaugural meeting of the Canadian
Council on Urban and Regional Research (CCURR). The nub of the
problem was to design an institutional structure that would embody the
three main interests. the private developers, those engaged in urban
management at all levels of government, and the research community of
both academics and professional consultants. These three parties in urban affairs are traditionally suspicious of one another and, as we gathered
the forces around us, the arguments were long and passionate in round
after round of committee discussions. On the final day of conception I
particularly recall the strident voice of David Slater, then of Queen's
University, cutting through the pandemonium of debate. We emerged
with a formula for a council of sixty, prescribing the representation of
academics, governments, and private business. But what really assured
the success of our efforts was the goodwill of Paul Ylvisaker, on the staff
of the Ford Foundation, who gave us good advice from the sidelines and
secured us an initial grant of $500,000 on the condition that the govern-
ment of Canada would support the council to an equal extent. To pro-
nounce a blessing at the birthday banquet, we invited Robert Weaver,
then head of the US Department of Housing and Urban Development
(HUD) and the first black man to serve in an American cabinet.

The immediate effect of establishing the new research council was to
increase greatly the number of people personally involved in examining
urban problems. During the next few years, with Armstrong as staff

director of CCURR, much new talent was uncovered and a start was made on a catalogue of all serious work done in this field. This was a turning point in gaining coherence and respectability for the study of cities which are, after all, the characteristic feature of contemporary civilization. Without this build-up I doubt whether it would have been possible to find staff for the new Ministry of Urban Affairs a few years later. Now, a decade later, the research money disbursed annually by CCURR has risen from $100,000 to $250,000; and I note that CMHC now, annually, awards 125 graduate fellowships for urban studies, an expansion from the eight fellowships that I was able to initiate in 1950.

Of course, doing urban research doesn't, in itself, solve any problems at all or make cities any better to live in. The purpose of research is to find out the whole spectrum of choices that we have in organizing the environment around our chosen way of life. How an urban society makes these choices and acts upon them depends upon its capacity to take action within the unwieldy machinery of democratic government. And the choices ultimately depend upon society's philosophy of life and its sense of social justice.

The second outreaching I will describe came from my continuing concern that there ought to be much more public discussion about housing so that policies really would develop out of a philosophy of life and out of a sense of social justice, rather than out of political opportunism and out of the pressures of the mortgage market. What makes the subject of housing so sensitive is that, in spite of all the technological advances and all the manipulation of financing, it is still not possible to satisfy the housing needs of about one-third of the population without some fairly large redistribution of the public's money; to satisfy reasonable expectations for a good way of life, either incomes or housing costs have to be subsidized. How best to do this is what discussions of 'housing policy' are all about. Amongst those who need help, who should have the priorities and how are their needs to be filled? Should the poor, the underprivileged, the most seriously disadvantaged always have the first priorities even though they make the heaviest demands upon the available subsidy funds? Or should the available money be spread wider among a class of people who are nearly able to look after themselves? What does your religion and your sense of justice tell you about this choice? Unfortunately Canada has not been very successful in developing public discussion of this subject; unlike the United States and Britain we have not had a strong national organization to speak for those in serious housing need. There have been lobbies for house-builders and developers, for money-lenders, and for upholding the sanctity of home-ownership. But there has not been a lobby for overcoming the social inequities of housing. Consequently housing debates in Parliament and in provincial legislatures have been lamentably weak.

Looking across the country in the sixties, one could see the few isolated figures of those who would always stand up and speak for public housing. Perhaps first amongst these was Dr Albert Rose, now head of the Toronto School of Social Work, who, like his predecessors in that position, Dr E.J. Urwick and Dr Harry Cassidy, was an intelligent and well-informed national spokesman for public housing; he served on the Board of the Metropolitan Toronto Housing Authority and on the Ontario Housing Corporation and was continually in demand as a speaker with his well-reasoned addresses. In Montreal was the grandfather of the cause, George Mooney, manager of the Federation of Mayors and Municipalities, whose patriarchal style and persuasive authority enabled him to draft briefs in support of public housing which unsuspecting mayors would read to the federal cabinet without perceiving just what the words meant. Out on the west coast was the lean and ascetic figure of Peter Stratton, ready to die like a Christian martyr for any of the humanitarian causes he espoused; he would arrive unobtrusively at committee meetings, sit in the back row without taking off his old raincoat, state his position in a quick low voice, and be off again to some unrevealed destination. There was an air of mystery about Peter Stratton's appearances which somehow made a committee feel more confident because he had passed by. In counting the faithful I must also include Frank Dearlove, the embattled manager of Regent Park North; Paul Ringer who knew the rough and tumble of life in public housing and could talk about it like a professional footballer; Peter Burns who left CMHC to become the director of community renewal for the city of Ottawa and always made an impressive contribution with his quiet professional air. And from within the family of CMHC, none spoke with more strength and effectiveness than Fred Coll and Homer Borland, two very articulate public servants. But, however dedicated these isolated spokesmen might be, they were at a disadvantage without some kind of organized force around them.

It was Pat Brady, formerly director of the Metropolitan Toronto Housing Authority and at that time second-in-command of the Ontario Housing Corporation, who first suggested that it was time to gather the isolated spokesmen into a national forum to discuss social housing policy. Over a year or two we discussed this idea in hotel corridors and a correspondence developed between Brady, Harold Clark, and myself. One possibility was to build upon the existing association of Ontario's housing authorities who were bidden each year to a conference to discuss managerial problems and to receive honeyed words of commendation from Stanley Randall, the provincial minister who had appointed them to their positions. Since this was the largest regular rally of people connected with public housing, the suggestion had some merit, if the conference could be opened to a coast-to-coast membership and entitled to discuss policy questions as well as housekeeping matters. Another suggestion was that, historically, the right to convene a national housing conference really belonged to the surviving heirs of the last national housing conference that had taken place in Toronto in 1939. In 1947 the surviving heirs, who were George Mooney and myself, together with Harold Clark as chairman of the Toronto Citizens' Association, had agreed to pass the baton to the Community Planning Association of Canada, rather than try to sustain two national bodies with rather similar interests. It had been understood that, if the CPAC did not prove to be a true champion of public housing, the succession would, as it were, revert. As the outcome of all these discussions, the Canadian Welfare Council assumed responsibility for convening a national housing conference, by an arrangement made in 1966 with Reuben Baetz, the director of the Council. CMHC provided grants to support the preparatory phases and the conference took place in October 1968. We were fortunate in finding Michael Wheeler, then a social affairs officer at the United Nations, to act as organizing secretary of the conference, a task he concluded as editor of the proceedings published under the title *The Right to Housing* (Harvest House, 1969).

The expression 'the right to housing' came spontaneously out of the conference discussions and reflected a great shift of social evolution that had taken place during the thirty years since the previous 1938 conference. The chairman of that earlier event was the white-haired and well-polished lieutenant governor, Dr Herbert Bruce, who thought of himself, I'm sure, as a paternalistic figure, motivated by 'noblesse oblige'. All of us who were there had been brought up to have an instinctive sympathy for the under-dog. But it would never have occurred to anyone to invite any of the poor to the meeting, and the chairman would certainly have been shocked if they had claimed any right to be there. But under Harold Clark's chairmanship in 1968 there was no doubt that the poor did have a right to be there and to claim as part of their rights of citizenship not only a decent place in which to live in their own country, but some choice and some share in the making of decisions and policies about their housing.

This was a big change in the social and political climate within my lifetime, and perhaps I have had a small part in bringing it about.

My last will and testament, when I departed from my life within CMHC, was wrapped up in the Advisory Group's package of proposals for extending the National Housing Act. (The testament had a strange subsequent history to be related in another chapter.) The package of legislative proposals was put together in the following way. Not long after Herb Hignett became president of CMHC, in succession to Stewart Bates, he asked the Advisory Group to make proposals for bringing the National Housing Act up to date with contemporary circumstances. Hignett was a popular choice as president because he had joined the corporation at the very outset in 1946, he knew everyone, and he had a quiet, methodical, friendly style. So our group embarked on the task Hignett had given us, in our own quiet, methodical, friendly style: on 10 May 1965 we set out on a two-month journey that took us across the country from east to west, stopping for a few days in every major city. We had arranged in advance to meet about two hundred people who had worked on housing and urban development and knew the virtues and the limitations of the National Housing Act. In each stopping-place we had a comfortable arm-chaired sitting room where we could talk with one person at a time, sometimes for a whole morning or afternoon and sometimes for no more than an hour. It's a simple and unsophisticated technique, depending upon a free and friendly atmosphere and on keeping the initiative in a probing and exploring dialogue. The absence of any formalities makes it possible to search quickly for the subjects on which a person has creative and deeply felt views, with little time wasted on secondary subjects that are not fruitful. Out of these personal conversations we accumulated an inventory book full of suggestions, ideas, new directions, complaints, idealistic notions, and comments on every aspect of the Housing Act. Then we had the task of sorting out and distilling all this material into a coherent statement of proposals. In the following years there were a number of other attempts to make a coherent statement of housing policies, including the Hellyer Report of 1969, the Lithwick study of 1970, and the Dennis Report of 1972. They each had their merits, their prejudices, and their obfuscations. But I think that the method we used drew most effectively on the collective intelligence of a great number of people across Canada and distilled the meaning of all this into the most positive conclusions.

Our package of proposals, completed in November 1965, dealt with three principal topics: the suburban expansion of metropolitan regions, the problems of those parts of Canada that don't have much urban growth, and a general shift of intergovernmental policy so as to direct a larger proportion of public funds towards the housing of lower-income groups. There was nothing very unusual in what we had to suggest on the second and third topics; the continuing efforts to spread the benefits of an affluent society. But we did open up two radical proposals for dealing with the growth of metropolitan areas, trying to get to the real heart of the difficulties caused by private land specultation, by the social resistance to putting housing for people of modest income in the new suburban areas, and by the problems of transportation linkage throughout growing urban regions. We proposed that the National Housing Act should provide for collaboration with provinces and the big metropolitan cities so that the process of urban growth could take the form of the successive creation of properly planned new communities, each one large enough to contain a variety of housing, rented and owned, built by both private and public enterprise, with each new community having its own town centre with commercial and community services, schools, open spaces, and so on. We suggested that provinces and metropolitan cities should set up corporate agencies to act as the developers of these new communities. The federal government would provide long-term loans for assembling land and the debt would be discharged out of the proceeds of land sales. The advance planning of each community would make it possible to hold sites for housing people of modest income near to shops and transit and open spaces. And through the advance acquisition of land, the eventual increase in the market price caused by the growth of the community would accrue to the community itself rather than to the private speculator, and so help to meet the costs of public housing and other public features.

None of these concepts was, in fact, new: the general theory of new town development had been much discussed throughout the twentieth century in many parts of the world and I had myself already written on this theme (in *Cities in the Suburbs*). What was new in the Advisory Group's proposal of 1965, was that Canada's National Housing Act should now be extended to provide financial arrangements to initiate actions along these lines, so that there might be a beginning in the discovery of some peculiarly Canadian way of reaching this ideal.

In the 1965 package of recommendations the Advisory Group also dealt with the subject of 'transportation corridors'. We reported:

The availability of wide corridors or ribbons of land, within which to channel increasing volumes of traffic, will make it possible to enlarge these volumes in future years and to introduce additional and new forms of transit without damage to adjacent properties. Adequate transportation space, like parkways, can be assets to the environment, rather than disamenities. The early determination of open spaces and transportation routes would also help to expedite the residential process within a network of main travel routes.

The idea of a 'transportation corridor' had been in my mind for a long time, ever since my early interest in the two landscapes, green and black, and a growing realization that Ebenezer Howard's original classic concept, of an encircling greenbelt as the setting for satellite garden-cities, was no longer relevant to the modern metropolitan city. When, in 1939, I had planted the trees along the Queen Elizabeth Way and then seen them gradually destroyed for the rising tide of traffic through the next thirty years, I had realized that there was a need for a much bolder realization of a landscape corridor. And in 1963 I had taken part in developing an actual design of a landscape corridor, as a member of the advisory committee to the 'Metropolitan Toronto and Region Transportation Study' (MTARTS) that was set up by the Ontario government to examine the whole sprawling urban region along the shores of Lake Ontario from Oshawa to Hamilton. (The proposals that came from this committee are the origin of the 'parkway belt' that is now a key feature of the plans for the future growth of the Toronto-centred region.)

Within the package of proposals that the Advisory Group presented to the management of CMHC in November 1965, I had a special interest in two items: the proposals for new communities and for transportation corridors. My thoughts on these subjects came out of my own life and out of my own way of looking at the landscape and understanding the social environment. These ideas were precious to me. This is a difficulty for a person who lives by clinging to idealisms and who chooses to work within the public service: the outcome of all one's work depends on people who haven't been through the same experiences and who are interested in only a mild and tepid way. I might be able to explain myself and win my cause within the company of CMHC. But in the final analysis, the fate of these proposals would depend upon the understanding of a minister who would have to make explanations to the cabinet and in Parliament. The minister then responsible for CMHC was John Nicholson, also the Postmaster General. I had been introduced to him once or twice and, on the one occasion when I had travelled on a government aeroplane with him, I couldn't help noticing that he spent the whole time studying a book of newspaper clippings about his public appearances.

I felt fairly confident that the Advisory Group's proposals would, in the slow course of political time, be brought into public view because they clearly dealt with three of the greatest obstructions in the growth of cities: the terrible cost of land caused by private speculation, the difficulties of housing people of modest income in the middle-class suburbs, and the whole complex issue of transportation within built-up urban regions. Sure enough, the time did come and it was John Nicholson who had to present the proposals. After an intervening chapter I will relate the rather strange way in which this occurred.

13
Down-Under
and
Up-Over

Canada was almost incomprehensible before we knew it from the air. Now we travel through the sky and look down upon the land stretched out below, its landmarks as familiar as the home town. You get to know the look of each city from the air; how you wheel into Winnipeg in a great curve around the city; how you slide down across the St Lawrence and the Seaway into Dorval airport; how the tree-tops look below your wings as you approach Halifax, and how on the descent into Vancouver the sea is wrinkled behind the long ships coming out of the Fraser River. As you fly over wilderness expanses you look for small traces of settlements in the woods. The straight cut of a transmission line across forests and rock and lake is like a scratch on the surface of the globe. With sinuous curves a railway winds its lonely route around lakes and through valleys. You get a glimpse of cars creeping like small insects around the corners of highways. Then the plane flies out over open cleared land where survey-ors have long ago established the scale and pattern of human settlement.

Most dramatic of these transitions to be seen on a west-bound flight is where the intricate random texture of the Canadian Shield suddenly is replaced by the square regularities of Manitoba, the farmer's patch-work quilt in squares of black earth, fresh green, or harvest colours. On the other edges of the Canadian Shield, Ontario and Quebec each have their distinctive patterns which explain so much past history. The tidy hundred-acre farms of the English settlement system are aligned in a network of concession roads 1¼ miles apart; it is a pattern rather easily subdivided to form the framework of the vast regional city which now stretches around the whole western arc of Lake Ontario. This is the pattern that I see from the air, whether I am looking down on the suburbia of Scarborough, Missisauga, and Peel with their coral reefs of house-roofs and sky-blue swimming pools or whether I am over the rich agricultural land between Waterloo and London.

Very different is the pattern of Quebec with its long narrow farm strips fronting on a country road lined with houses and barns to form a long stretched-out parish community. Often the back-ends of these farm strips are still in the edge of the woods, a resource of fuel and pulp-wood. And sometimes the strip pattern fronts on a winding stream that was once a canoe route. It was a good pattern for a small-scale habitant way of life, but there could not have been a more awkward legacy for the old rural Quebec to pass on to the new urban Quebec; these long narrow strips don't convert easily into land for city streets and subdivisions.

Most Canadian cities began on some kind of waterfront: on a river, a lake, or sea harbour. They pulled their boats up on the shore and the settlement straggled out along the water's edge. After a time, the first houses were replaced by warehouses and waterfront industries. The city centre developed at the heart of the settlement and gradually moved up the hill behind the waterfront. The first suburbs grew up behind this centre, as the woods were cleared and back roads were built. Now, more than a century after the original settlements, there is much concern about these obsolete areas of cities:

1 The primitive waterfront itself. Here, amid the chaos of old ironclad industries and warehouses, there are buildings of great historic interest and character. Halifax, Quebec, Montreal, Toronto, and Vancouver are all trying to save this part of their heritage.

2 The core of the city. There is great commercial competition to occupy the magnetic centre of concentration: Place Ville-Marie in Montreal, Scotia Square in Halifax, and wherever this may prove to be in Toronto, as the hearts of cities shift and solidify and take new shape.

3 The old inner suburbs. Here the houses are now in their vintage years, from fifty to a hundred years old. All the questions about their rejuvenation and re-use, for the poor, for the middle-class, the rich, are still unresolved.

I have walked up and down all the old harbour streets of St John's, Newfoundland, and in the north end of Halifax; the painted wooden houses are packed tight together and, along the sidewalk, the doorsteps are worn smooth and rounded by seamen's boots and by generations of wives and children and cats who have sat there waiting for the boats to come in out of the fog. There have been big changes in these last few years. In St John's, at the foot of the hill, is the new city hall with its imperial staircase, its big-city architecture, and handsome décor which is rather forbidding to the adult generation of old St John's; but at the top of the hill the young generation of Newfoundlanders spread themselves possessively in the new cultural Centre. I have also walked along every old street of Saint John, NB, and wondered how it would ever be possible to make any plain-sailing out of this wistful city so hopelessly entangled with its many waterfronts and reversing tides. I have known the Atlantic cities in their heroic efforts to dig themselves out of the past, sorting out what is still useful in the legacy of picturesque old houses and civic architecture, applying the imported techniques of urban renewal and public housing and inserting some of the culture of big cities, the theatres and the universities, so as to offer a new quality of life to the next generation.

I have visited the Western cities to marvel at their phenomenal growth and vitality, as they unfolded into the great spaces around them; Edmonton, Calgary, and Saskatoon have each discovered their peculiar combinations of private enterprise and public control for arranging their new sprawling neighbourhoods. But they are alike in that distinctive western characteristic: the wide-eaved suburban ranch houses with garish stripes of colour to relieve the bare landscape without a tree in sight. To fly over the towering ranges of the mountains and land safely in Vancouver has never failed to seem like an adventure. The next morning when you stroll along Georgia Street, the people have a certain charisma: they are handsome, expensively dressed, and self-satisfied. The local Canadians cannot be distinguished from the Americans who drive up from Seattle, San Francisco, and Los Angeles; they all seem more languid, more self-possessed, and casual than the serious hardworking eastern Canadian or the lean wind-bitten refugee from the prairies. After the first impressions of envy for the charismatic people and the magnificent mountain scenery of Vancouver, the 'amour-propre' of the Easterner is restored when he discovers that Vancouver is, in fact, an ugly and undisciplined city that has consumed its available land in a wasteful way and is now threatened with all kinds of difficulties. Perhaps it is the only city in Canada for which a no-growth policy really seems appropriate.

Midway between east and west, Winnipeg is unlike any other city and has been through an uncomfortable period during the forty years that I have known it. I have known the city, partly because I married into a Winnipeg family and have loved people who live there, and partly through having been there so many times for purposes connected with

Winnipeg's discomforts. It has been a divided place with a social and economic élite amongst whom there is a great bond of loyalty (the bond of Winnipeggers is matched only by the loyalties of Haligonians) and its many ethnic groups who also have their loyalties: Ukrainian, French, Métis, Oriental, Icelandic, and others. Perhaps there is no other city where the expression 'the other side of the tracks' has such real meaning. While Winnipeg was the gateway to the West and the flow of immigrants passed through the CPR station, many immigrant families stayed to live beside the tracks and many others returned here in a backwash of dissatisfied settlers. After the immigrant era the social élite and the ethnic groups had to settle down and live together; it is not surprising that Winnipeg has been the scene of so many attempts to work out a viable form of metropolitan government, to fit around its inherent social diversity. My many visits to Winnipeg were mostly concerned with the long succession of studies and plans for providing decent housing and a better way of life for the people who live near the railway tracks. In looking after their own people Winnipeggers have needed a great deal more coaxing than Haligonians.

Southern Ontario is my home territory and I know its highways and its cities from the Ottawa Valley to the Niagara escarpment and on to the Detroit border. Throughout my years with CMHC I had a ringside seat to view the growth and change of the cities and to see the best and the worst of their housing and planning activities. In the sixties I was fortunate in being invited to take part in a planning study that will leave its imprint for all time upon the landscape of Southern Ontario; that was the first comprehensive study of the whole Toronto-centred region. The study, commonly known as Mootarts (MTARTS), was a combined operation of four provincial departments and Metropolitan Toronto and arose out of the shattering experience of building the 401 freeway across the northern edge of Toronto only to discover that on completion it was already inadequate to carry the traffic and the number of lanes had to be multiplied immediately and at enormous expense. It became apparent that it was meaningless to design a transportation system without first setting out the future pattern of communities to be served by the system. Consequently a Regional Development Advisory Group was set up, on which I joined Hans Blumenfeld, Leonard Gertler, and Albert Rose, with a departmental staff of community planners. Out of our study came the proposal for the parkway belt to provide an east-west corridor of open space, wide enough to contain a variety of transportation systems that might evolve from future needs and future technologies. We sug-

gested several locations for the corridor and for the future communities
on either side of it.

The province of Quebec is only just across the Ottawa river from where I live; the infinite forest to the north of us is as much our hinterland as the farms of southern Ontario. The woods and the lakes and the ski-slopes of the Gatineau hills are an intimate part of our family habitat. No other city in the world is within half-an-hour's drive of such a beautiful landscape playground where one can walk for miles in the autumn woods, ski along the winter trails, and plunge into the clearest lake-water in the summer. But the cities of Quebec have not been part of my life and the social and political philosophy that has guided their growth is often obscure to me. All the world has admired the 'hauteur' of Mayor Drapeau who stimulated the central growth of Montreal; it was indeed exciting to see Place Ville Marie rising into the sky where for so many years there had been just a hole in the ground. This was 'haute architecture' to match Drapeau's taste for 'haute cuisine' and 'haute musique'. The new city centre has been a successful monument to the big corporations which inhabit it. But as a social policy for leading a resurgent Quebec into a new age of economic democracy I can't believe that this was a very wise direction to take. Far too little has been done to rescue low-income Montrealers from the old waterfront slums and not nearly enough attention has been given to the quality of community design in the new middle-class suburbs. Expo 67 gave a tremendous stimulation to the quality of design in the rest of Canada, but it didn't do much for the environment of life in Montreal.

Now that we are able to encompass and comprehend the entirety of Canada, by flying over it and by driving across it on the Trans-Canada highway, we have also become more interested in making comparisons. When we cross the border into the United States, we notice the subtle differences in people's behaviour and appearance, in the look of their cities and farms, and the different character of their regional topographies. And, vice versa, that is why Americans visit Canada and are usually quick to notice the different flavour of our life and our landscape. Because we only have one neighbouring country, there is no other comparison immediately available, to help us sharpen our perceptions of what we are really like and what kind of a place we live in. Europeans have a far wider range of comparisons; the English and Germans have always been the greatest travellers, seeking out and enjoying the flavours of other countries. But making comparisons between Canada and the United States has its limitations, partly because, as people, we are so alike and partly because we know one another so well that the subtle differences of flavour have somewhat lost their distinguishable bouquet. It was for this reason that, in 1967, I was so delighted to be able to visit another country whose people have so much in common with Canadians but who live at the other end of the earth. Australia.

I went to Australia in June 1967 to help in setting up the Australian Institute of Urban Studies. The rapid growth of metropolitan cities has been a worldwide phenomenon and, during the sixties, centres of urban studies were established in several parts of the world. Harvard and MIT had set up a joint centre in 1959 and on the Pacific coast another centre was established on the Berkeley campus, both of them with the support of the Ford Foundation. In London there was the Centre for Environmental Studies, and there was a discussion about the possibility of Ford Foundation support for centres in Japan and in Australia. But at this stage the Ford Foundation became deeply committed to the domestic urban problems of the United States and was not willing to extend its funds into other countries. But the Foundation was prepared to help by paying the travel costs of a Canadian to go to Australia to explain our approach and experience in setting up the Canadian Council on Urban and Regional Research; it was regarded as a good model because it was not the monopoly of a single university and provided a framework for participation by all universities and governments in the country and by all sectors of the research community. Peter Dobush, the chairman of CCURR, was not well at the time and I was more than willing to undertake the task.

Like most Canadians I was only dimly aware of the principal points of comparison between Canada and Australia. There is Australia's equable climate, so that one can play tennis all the year round; and there is Australia's homogeneous population, all mispronouncing vowels in the same charming way. Less well known is the fact that, although Australia has only half the population of Canada, her two principal cities, Sydney and Melbourne, are both rather larger than their Canadian counterparts, Montreal and Toronto. We have heard that Perth is a kind of Shangri-La on the West coast of Australia, as far removed from the big eastern cities as Vancouver, our Shangri-La, is removed both geographically and spiritually from Toronto and Montreal. But it is less easy to grasp the significant difference: that Australia has no cities at all in the middle—nothing to correspond with Winnipeg, Regina, Saskatoon, Calgary and Edmonton. In Australia this has been a subject of concern, that there are not enough cities on which to base all the growth of population that they hope to have in the future, to fill some of their vast empty spaces. Australians are, of course, very conscious of these spaces; but not, I think, in the same way that Canadians are aware of living on the edge of an immense northern wilderness. Our wilderness is more threatening and overwhelms our spirits, as Margaret Atwood has pointed out, with apprehensions about survival. These differences of mood and attitude are a fascinating aspect of a visit to Australia. One soon realizes that, though the language is the same, Australians are in so many ways distinguishable from Canadians and Americans and English people; environment certainly does have distinct effects upon people and one tries to catch the nuances of this.

I arrived in Australia in June, and perhaps my whole internal system was programmed to expect a Canadian summer temperature. In Australia it was the onset of winter when they are programmed to expect chilly rooms in which you would want to wear a heavy tweed jacket. I was uncomfortable, immediately got a cold, and wanted to go straight back home. I was puzzled by a device on the frame of my bedroom door which turned on an electric heating unit if I closed the door. It seemed to be a 'non sequitur': what has the closing of a door got to do with turning on the heat? The irrationality of the connection was strangely upsetting. Was it perhaps something to do with being in the southern hemisphere, upside down?

I think it was the sensation of being chilled inside a house that first gave me the feeling of 'déjà vu' that pursued me throughout my Australian visit. It was a distant memory of English schoolrooms. The chilblains on the fingers, the draught in the hall, that took me back into the past. Everywhere I went in Australia made me feel that I had been there before. People I met I seemed to have met before. 'Yes, Professor Robertson, and how are *you*?' (I must have met him before, he seems so familiar.) The architect with the kind face and utopian ideas; the Scottish engineer with the square jaw and the sceptical, pragmatic views; the city alderman with his deep and sincere concern about sewers; surely I know all these people. I like them because I understand them. I almost seem to know them well enough to tease them the very first day I meet them. I'm sorry that tomorrow I have to go on to the next city on my itinerary–and I'll never see any of them again in all my life. 'Déjà vu' is wistful. I like Australians very much and seem to get along with them easily.

The small group of enthusiasts who were engaged in founding the Australian Institute of Urban Studies had arranged that within about four weeks I would visit Canberra, the federal capital, and also the capital city of each state–Melbourne, Sydney, Brisbane, Hobart, Adelaide, and finally Perth on my westbound homeward journey through Athens and London. With a day or two in each place, I would call on the premier of the state and the mayor of the city, have a seminar with an academic group on each university campus, meet a group of businessmen downtown, and dine with a group of planners and architects. And in Canberra I was to deliver a keynote speech at the founding conference of the new institute. It was all arranged with the utmost efficiency and I soon perceived that the real significance of my tour was not so much to exchange information about urban studies as to create a kind of public image that would help the sponsors solicit funds from the governments of states, from city councils, and from big business. Australians do this sort of thing in a much more methodical way than Canadians do, preferring the formal frontal attack to our more devious ways of raising money.

The first city on my itinerary was Sydney and, after having met some of my sponsors for lunch, I found myself in a lofty, cathedral-like Gothic-Revival salon in the city hall where some kind of reception was in progress; there were drinks and a crowd of rather formally attired citizens, all male. I was sipping a scotch-and-soda when a hush came over the assembly, the lord mayor cleared his throat, introduced me to the audience, presented me with a pair of cuff-links bearing the arms of the city, and I breathlessly realized that this had all been set up for me to perform, and that on the credibility of what I now said might depend the whole future of the Australian Institute of Urban Studies. Urban research isn't a very easy subject to work your way into in the first paragraph of an impromptu speech, but in 1967 one could always get some momentum with a reference to Canada's Centennial and Expo 67. After I had been through the experience of a 'civic reception' in several cities I began to feel more like the Duke of Edinburgh and, by the time I reached Perth, which has a very beautiful modern city hall with a sumptuous reception suite at the roof-garden level, I could take this strange Australian custom in my stride. The impression that I got from this round of city hall ceremonies was that Australians regard municipal and urban affairs with much greater respect and solemnity than Canadians do; and perhaps this is understandable because the size of their cities in relation with their total population makes lord mayors a dominant feature in Australian life. And it also helped me to understand that in all their affairs Australians have a great liking for formality and do it very

well. This sense of style is a contrast to the Canadian manner of 'joshing',
refusing to take formality seriously, and seeking friendship with the good-humoured poke.

Having migrated from one part of the British Commonwealth to another, I had often wondered what life would have been like, and how I might have become a different kind of person, if I had taken a different route at the important cross-roads. In Australia are the children, grand-children, and great-grandchildren of my mother's brother William and when I met them it was fascinating to recognize behind the Australian voice and posture, some familiar features and mannerisms: the shapes of the nose and the jaw that persist through generations, and something recognizable about the humour and the way of looking at things. I had often been told that my first cousin Eddie and I were alike in appearance and manner. I went to stay with another cousin, Peter, on his cattle and sheep station, a day's drive from Sydney, behind a range of wooded hills; he lives at the centre of a great rolling expanse of grassland enclosed by a horizon of hills, a pastoral place of great beauty that made me feel that an eye for the landscape runs in the family. But Peter was unmistakably Australian in his lean outback way.

What made my stay in Australia particularly enjoyable was that, after each sortie to the cities, I was able to return to Melbourne and stay with my sister-in-law Marjorie Smart, who is principal of St Hilda's College in Melbourne University. Marjorie is the fifth of Dr C.W. Gordon's six daughters, she had known all my family and friends over a long span of time, and through her Anne and I met one another and were married. So there is a close bond of affection, we had a great deal to say to one another, and my pleasure in being with Marjorie was unmistakable. When I arrived at her beautiful little house, attached to the college, I was immediately aware that her companion, Gus, was not equally pleased to see me. When we drove down to her cottage by the sea, the next weekend, he was very insistent upon sitting in the front seat beside Marjorie, sitting up rather straight and stiff, sniffing the fresh air, with me in the back seat behind. And on the very last night, just as I was leaving to fly to Perth and I was wearing my best suit just back from the cleaners, Gus lifted his leg and soaked my trouser leg. He was a very participatory dog.

Because I was kept so busy travelling and talking I didn't have enough opportunity to see Australian cities in any detail. But inevitably I was often asked the question: 'As a Canadian, what strikes you about our cities?' In a speech that I made at the end of my tour, I tried to answer this question, suggesting that Australia had an advantage over Canada, in the fact that so many who settled in Australia were urban people who had seen and known big cities. I said:

Canadians were not originally city people; most of them came from the little fishing harbours of northern France, from the hills and villages of Scotland, and from the agricultural interior of Europe and the Ukraine. We gradually evolved into an urban people and this has taken us rather by surprise and as a matter of excitement. What impresses me very much about Australia is the assumption from the outset that there were going to be big cities. In the nineteenth century you built handsome wide streets, your early public buildings and your houses have an air of classic assurance about them, and I think your contemporary architecture has inherited this look of authority. As an urban people you were accustomed to a stratified society and you are good at doing things with an air of serious formality and ceremonial, in a way that doesn't come naturally to Canadians. I find this impressive and the word 'handsome' keeps coming to mind as I admire Australian people and their cities.

Then I went on to say that Canadians seemed to be much more willing than Australians to experiment and reconsider the whole structure of city government. Canada had carried out some important changes in metropolitan and regional government of a quite revolutionary kind. But Australians didn't seem to be so adaptable and were more inclined to patch up old systems with complicated co-ordinating devices and planning authorities. In this respect, perhaps because urbanization was newer to us, Canada seemed to have a spirit of freedom and flexibility.

I was tremendously impressed by Canberra, the federal capital of Australia, not only because it is a city created with imagination and great enterprise, but also because it is in a landscape that was also, literally, created by man. At the founding conference of the Australian Institute of Urban Studies in Canberra I said: 'Building cities is far the most difficult, complex, and majestic thing that men do. In this we come nearest in scale to what God does in creating the landscape, the stars, the hills, and the forests'.

From my visit to Australia I returned to Canada in the high summer of 1967, the centennial year, the year of splendid pride in Expo, the year of national ecstasy. There were many visits to Expo 67 that summer, but the best of all was when my whole family went to stay in Habitat, the remarkable experiment in housing design which was the most imaginative and controversial feature of Expo. On an upper level of the great

townscape of houses-in-the-sky, one of the houses had been furnished for
the use of senior people connected with CMHC. Stepping out on to our
garden-terrace we were high up on the bank of houses, looking down on
the lower terraces, gay with their sunshades, awnings, and flower boxes.
At night time we looked across the water to the illuminated towers of
the new Montreal that had grown so dramatically in the previous decade.
And, below us, ships were tied up along the quay, amongst them a
French naval vessel, one of the vanguard of the fleet that brought General de Gaulle to deliver his shocking cry: 'Vive le Québec libre!'

Moshe Safdie had conceived and designed Habitat. Only a few years
earlier, as an architectural student at McGill in 1959, he had been selected to go on the first in a series of student tours sponsored by CMHC.
We hoped that the new generation of architects would discover for
themselves that the architecture of housing is the pinnacle of their art.
So each year, one student of special talents was selected from each school
of architecture in Canada, to make a five-week tour of North America,
to visit many cities, to see the work of their contemporaries with their
own eyes and then, within this talented group of new friends, to discuss
what they had seen. This proved to be an extraordinary experience for
many who were chosen, year after year, and none was more gifted and
few have reacted more positively than the young Israeli, Moshe Safdie.
In his book entitled *Beyond Habitat* (Tundra Books, 1970) Safdie has
recalled:

> I had set out on this trip with preconceived ideas, feeling suburbia was bad–
> after all, the Mediterranean cities were my background. But my conclusion was
> new: I felt we had to find new forms of housing that would re-create, in a
> high-density environment, the relationships and the amenities of the house and
> the village. I remember coming back to Ottawa and saying so in our formal
> presentation; and I remember Humphrey Carver . . . replying that it couldn't be
> done, that families belong on the ground, they belong in low density. At that
> point I said, 'Well, I'm going to try and do it.' I decided to abandon my plan
> to do a parliament building in Jerusalem for my thesis and instead do a housing
> system.

How a young man with a prophetic vision, an unknown and inexperienced architect, managed to persuade the government of his country
to build a fifty-million-dollar housing experiment, is a fairy story that
ought to be retold through the centuries. The story has a fabulous quality
not because the decision was fantastic, absurd, or inexplicable–but because the decision was so absolutely right. In his book, Moshe Safdie

identifies Ian Maclennan as the man who first carried the proposal through a series of 'go, no-go' situations. 'If this is built,' said Ian, 'it will set housing in Canada fifteen to twenty years ahead.'

The importance of Safdie's Habitat idea was that it dealt with the comprehensive question of how man can live an urban life within a green landscape. His idea has to be considered alongside le Corbusier's 'Unité d'habitation' and Clarence Stein's concept of a greenbelt town. Le Corbusier's idea was to encase the whole life of a village-size community within a single great concrete hive and lift this structure off the ground on vertical supports called 'pilotis'. The surrounding green landscape of rolling contours and woodlands would not be interrupted and would flow, as it were, right under the habitation structure which would be like a gigantic Henry Moore sculpture placed out in the fields. This is a thrilling and lyrical image. Clarence Stein's idea was a further refinement of what had been done by Raymond Unwin and the other Garden City designers; Stein introduced the clustering of habitations around internal green spaces so that the green landscape was integral within the modelling of the townscape.

In Safdie's Habitat the preformed boxes of dwelling units are banked one on top of another, in an intricate and elegant three-dimensional pattern, so as to form a great shelving hillside which itself becomes a landscape form. The roof of each unit is the garden terrace of the unit above, the whole man-made construction having the proportions of a pyramid standing up from the surrounding plain. This also is a poetic image and fulfils Safdie's undertaking to provide *For Everyone a Garden* (the title of his most recent book).

There are, I think, some serious limitations to Safdie's idea which makes it a less satisfying model than either le Corbusier's or Clarence Stein's. It's true that it provides 'for everyone a garden', but one must add 'for nobody a tree'–and gardens without full-grown trees are unnatural and incomplete. Also the positive and sunny side of the terraced bank of houses-and-gardens unfortunately has a negative side too: the backside and underside which is shaded from sunlight and under the shadow of the whole cavernous structure, thus creating a sterile and unnatural ground surface. Also, let it be said, the wonderful geometrical intricacy of Safdie's design lacks the gentle humanity and sculptural simplicity of what le Corbusier and Clarence Stein showed us; it is too much a product of the computer. But in spite of these points of criticism, Habitat has to be acknowledged in history for its bold handling of the whole complex problem of man's life in the landscape. It was an intellectual climax to a decade of cultural expansion in Canada. The rest of the world took notice that Expo 67 was not just a good show staged by a country vulgarly rich in resources. We had dared to confront a fundamental problem of urban civilization.

For millions of Canadians, Expo 67 was an extraordinary and uplifting environmental experience. We walked through the place, literally, with tears in our eyes; it was so beautiful and we were so proud that it was ours. But now, a few years later, the magic of it has faded and it is almost impossible to reconstruct how we felt about it and why. The simple explanation is, I suppose, that Canadians had had a deep longing to create something that was unquestionably great and beautiful and civilized. Somehow this had always eluded our grasp and our attainment. We had entered a vast land, we had survived, and we had built large cities. And yet we had only just scraped through and nothing we had built ever seemed to have an air of grace, to the manner born. We had made a living and admired modesty and plain things. But the ultimate mastery of the arts, of music and painting and architecture and gardens and civilized cities, was left behind in Europe. We were just Americans without even the money to do things some other Americans can do.

And then suddenly—we entered the gates of Expo and none of this was true. There was an authority to the way it was done that removed any doubt that this was the real thing. People came from all over the world and they recognized the authority of it, too. This is the simple explanation of our emotions and happiness. It's great to know that you've finally made it.

14
The Turbulence

Prime Minister Pearson invited the premiers of all the provinces to attend a conference on housing and urban affairs, to take place on 11 and 12 December 1967. As the date approached it became clear that CMHC's legislative proposals were to be the key piece in the conference agenda, though a number of other government departments were drawn into the agenda discussions, to provide papers on urban transportation, pollution, welfare, and the like. And of course the Department of Finance was listening in and looking over our shoulders. Jack Hodgson, who was then the principal person on the Prime Minister's staff (he had been director of CMHC's Development Division at the beginning of the Stewart Bates period), was in charge of the agenda arrangements and through November we spent many hours with him at the long table in the CMHC board room, editing each page of the proposals so that they would be as understandable as possible to the provincial premiers. The focus of attention was to be on the subjects contained in the Advisory Group's recommendations of 1965, namely: the suburban expansion of metropolitan regions (including the proposals for new communities and for transportation corridors), the problems of those regions that do not have much urban growth and economic development, and a general shift of intergovernmental policy so as to direct a larger proportion of public funds towards housing middle-and lower-income groups. The subject of urban renewal was not prominent on the agenda because, it was explained, a great deal of effort had recently been put into this at the time of the 1964 amendments to the Housing Act; good progress was being made and the on-going process should not be disturbed.

While these proposals were being polished up, a proposition of quite

a different kind was introduced into the preparatory discussions, at the
suggestion, so we understood, of the Prime Minister himself. This was
the idea of setting up an intergovernmental 'urban council'. Since CMHC
staff had continually lived with the difficulties of getting effective collaboration with provincial and municipal authorities, the concept was a
familiar one; but we were very doubtful of any success in offering it to
the assembled provincial premiers and feared it would divert attention
from discussion of the more specific legislative proposals. So there was
some foreboding about Mr Pearson's intentions. Furthermore, confidence in the success of the conference was seriously undermined when
a senior official of the Department of Finance managed to delay cabinet
approval of the conference papers to such an extent that the legislative
proposals could not be sent out to the provincial premiers in advance of
the meeting. The rather lordly attitude of the Department of Finance had
always been an aggravation to Central Mortgage and Housing Corporation.

The day finally arrived for the very first top-level Canadian conference
on housing and urban affairs. It was 11 December, a week after I had
finally retired after nearly twenty years with CMHC; but, as a courtesy,
I was admitted to the large high-ceilinged conference chamber in the
West Block on Parliament Hill. The room had been dolled up as a kind
of movie-set for the televised series of constitutional conferences, in a
decorator's style quite inconsistent with the admirable Gothic-Revival
exterior. (Sir Brian Dunfield, who was there with the Newfoundland
delegation, referred to the style as 'Venetian manqué'.) I was able to sit
among the TV cameras facing the half-circle of tables. Mr Pearson was
at the centre and beside him sat John Nicholson who, as minister responsible for housing, would have to deliver the statement on our legislative
proposals. On the other side of the Prime Minister was Paul Hellyer,
Minister of Transport, and the federal government group was flanked by
John Robarts on their right, Quebec's Daniel Johnson on their left and
so on down the hierarchy of provinces, to give Joey Smallwood the free
end-position from which, at federal provincial conferences, he habitually
delivered his cunning, witty, and sentimental descriptions of life in Newfoundland. I awaited expectantly for the presentation of proposals on
which I had expended so much labour and love during the final few years
of my career in the public service.

The official record of the conference does not reveal the chaos of what
actually happened. Mr Pearson had at that time acquired a reputation
of being accident-prone and, with his delicious sense of humour, I'm sure

he must have felt that some kind of accident was almost inevitable, with John Nicholson on one side of him and Paul Hellyer on the other, one so inadvertent and the other so eager and intent.

Mr Pearson led off with a quite long introduction about the growth of cities in Canada, quoting from the reports of the Economic Council of Canada and concluded with some emotional references to Expo 67 as the place where Canada had finally come of age and won her spurs as a great urban nation. 'Sir Wilfred Laurier's dream for Canada may yet be realized if, in the twentieth century remaining to us, we meet the challenge for Canadian greatness in our urban growth . . . the opportunity is ours at this conference to face this challenge together as Canadians . . . ' Just before the concluding rhetoric, Pearson put a good deal of emphasis on his proposal for setting up an urban council, making it sound like a respectable counterpart of the Economic Council, with the provinces sharing the costs of a central staff and regional offices. After Mr Pearson's introduction most of that first day was taken by the premiers, each making a formal statement, to display on the television screens of the nation their most endearing style and territorial imperatives, like so many exotic birds displaying their plumage in some kind of sexual dance.

The next morning Mr Pearson returned to the conference with his usual geniality rather subdued, explaining that he had been scared by the events of the night before when his minority government had narrowly escaped defeat in the House of Commons. He was, understandably, a little distrait. He then opened up the principal conference subject, urban development, but, thinking perhaps that the long speeches of the previous day had been too formal and boring, and something more relaxed was required, he didn't invite John Nicholson to make the key statement of the legislative proposals. He simply invited a spontaneous discussion. The talk moved quickly and inevitably into the subject of public land-assembly and, with horror and amazement, I heard Nicholson denying any thought of federal government involvement in this, except for purposes of public housing. What could he mean? What about the new communities program and the transportation corridors? Had Nicholson not even read the papers from which he was expected to deliver the key statement?

At 11 o'clock that morning someone belatedly distributed the paper which explained the proposed legislation and, glancing at this as they sat around the conference table, the premiers began to realize that something was seriously amiss. After a few oblique references to the embarrassment, Mr Pearson sought a way out by inviting Paul Hellyer to make a statement on transportation. Hellyer, then Minister of Transport, was never unwilling to be seen on television and was already aware of the political excitement ahead; for by this time it was clear that Mike Pearson's retirement was imminent and there would be a leadership convention in a few months. Hellyer made an emphatic speech on the importance of urban transport which gave John Robarts an opening to tell *him* all about the GO train in the Toronto region. Then other federal ministers, John Drury and Jean-Luc Pepin, unwisely followed suit, wanting to lecture the provincial premiers about themselves and their urban interests; and the premiers became increasingly restive.

After the morning's confusion Pearson, the old baseball pro, was obviously reluctant to put John Nicholson up to bat, doubting that he would be able to retrieve the situation. But by mid-afternoon this obviously had to be done and Nicholson ad-libbed his way through the carefully written paper, supplemented with a number of misinterpretations. And finally, coming to the end of the agenda, Pearson himself had to explain more fully his proposal for an intergovernmental council. The premiers quite expectedly didn't like the idea, partly because any provincial premier looks with suspicion on an arrangement that favours quiet negotiated arrangements rather than more melodramatic political confrontations. But at this stage in the conference, the weakness of the federal representation was so obvious that it seemed unkind to labour the matter. Mr Robarts quietly sought refuge in the opinion that such a council would be too expensive, which seemed an absurd opinion to come from such an affluent quarter, with Mr Robarts looking like a handsome and well-fed master-of-foxhounds. And Mr Daniel Johnson, always a perfect gentleman, after a long and kindly comment, said (so the transcript reads), 'If it will help you, sir, to make a decision—you can be very quiet and you have not displeased anybody if you don't go along with the Council as it is proposed in your document.' To which Mr Pearson replied, 'Thank you very much for your offer to help me out again. We can now go on to the next subject. What is the next subject?'

It was ironical that my hopes and expectations were dashed by a person whom I have liked and admired enormously, Mike Pearson; and since that December day I have often thought about the explanation of this. As chairman of a meeting it had been Pearson's special skill that he could create a relaxed atmosphere by throwing away the formalities—and even the agenda—and so reaching out to the real people and the real human issues behind the façade. By doing this he had saved the day in many an international confrontation and won fame for himself and for Canada. When the first volume of his autobiography appeared in 1972, the reviewers noted he had been so good at this because of a rare quality, that Mike the public person and Mike the private person were one and the same: friendly, perceptive, unshakably patient and brimming with humour. This was a gift of genius that made him so pre-eminently successful in the role of a negotiator, trying to reconcile conflicting positions. But was it, in fact, a relevant style for a prime minister seeking support for a specific new direction of urban policy? That required a more positive style of exposition. I am bound to conclude that in failing to give confident guidance to a reorientation of policy, Pearson acted with a good-natured innocence that was the beginning of about five years of stumbling confusion in housing and urban affairs. I think perhaps Pearson's interest in the idea of an urban council arose out of his international experience. He perceived the provinces as independent bodies which could be brought within an institutional framework for discussion, a kind of United Nations within Canada. The urban subject was strange territory to him and perhaps the whole episode becomes more understandable if one sees it this way.

Though the December 1967 conference was, I think, generally regarded as a disaster, in fact the officials of all the provinces and the federal government continued to meet in discussion of the legislative proposals and during 1968 complete agreement was reached on the whole package. The fact that these follow-up discussions had taken place and that agreement had been reached was never made public, perhaps because this process was going on during the period of turning over the leadership of the Liberal government from Mr Pearson to the incoming Prime Minister, Pierre Elliott Trudeau. But the discussions and the agreements were certainly known to Mr Trudeau's new Minister for Housing who chose to ignore them. That minister was the Honourable Paul Hellyer.

Paul Hellyer had been very interested in the idea of building new cities; I remember him giving an impassioned speech on this subject in the banquet room of the Royal York Hotel in Toronto. I think it was a subject that appealed to his romantic and prophetic imagination. For this reason I thought it was very strange that he did not rather eagerly put his hand on the CMHC legislative proposals; the New Communities Program and the emphasis on regional planning were conceived in the same imaginative spirit. If he had accepted the momentum of ideas on which we, in CMHC, had been working for a number of years, there would have

been much more rapid progress in housing and urban affairs through the
next period and Paul Hellyer's own political fortunes might have been very different. But Hellyer wouldn't open this book and, turning his back on his prospective friends within CMHC, he started off on his own in July 1968, with the task force on housing and urban development authorized by the Trudeau cabinet and with Hellyer himself as the leader.

The members of the task force were Dr Doris Boyle (who had been head of the social science Department of St Francis Xavier University, Antigonish), Dr Pierre Dansereau (a distinguished ecologist at the University of Montreal), Peter Carter (a mortgage investment expert on the staff of the Royal Bank of Canada), Robert Campeau (the highly successful Ottawa housebuilder and developer), C.E. Pratt (Vancouver architect), and Dr James Gillies (urban economist of York University and in later years a Conservative member of Parliament). Under the energetic leadership of Hellyer, the task force toured urban Canada between September and December 1968 and their report was published in January 1969. Among the literature of housing, the report is a strange document in at least two respects: the photographic illustrations are not of housing subjects but of members of the task force in various cities with the sun shining on the handsome head of Paul Hellyer. It is also rather revealing that the minister's name appears on the opening page but, to find the names of the report's other authors, one has to turn to an appendix at the end. Respect for other people's feelings did not seem to be one of Paul Hellyer's outstanding virtues.

Fred Coll of CMHC, one of the first members of the Advisory Group, travelled with Hellyer's task force, to help them and advise them. At one point as the cavalcade swept through Ottawa, Coll invited me to come to the Chateau Laurier to meet Dr Doris Boyle and Dr Pierre Dansereau so that I could give them a little glimpse into the stream of thinking that had flowed through CMHC during the previous years. But I had hardly sat down in Dr Dansereau's hotel bedroom before there was a summons from their leader, Hellyer, to move on again. I don't think I am very easily hurt, but I must admit to a twinge of regret that I could contribute nothing to a cause in which I had been interested all my life. But Paul Hellyer was anxious to protect his task force from contamination by those who had passed along this road before.

The immediate outcome of the task force's report was that Hellyer put a stop-order on public housing and urban renewal because he found them distasteful. The report was scorching in its condemnation of public housing. 'Public housing is, in a sense, an "imported" concept in Canada

... [it] drew its real strength from the policies of Franklin Delano Roosevelt during the depression years in the United States ... then a decade later, following the veterans's housing programme, it came to Canada'. The task force commissioned Martin Goldfarb Consultants Limited to make a study; Goldfarb, they said, denounced 'the rent-geared-to-income system as one which elevates "successful cheating to a symbol of success".' He reported that teenagers were looked at with a jaundiced eye while children in large public housing projects were left to play without any supervision or direction in a confined area. He suggested that the problems of living in public housing were 'akin to those experienced by some Indians who are on reserves.' The task force recommended that the federal government initiate a study into the economic, social, and psychological issues of public housing and that 'until such a study is completed and assessed, no new large projects should be undertaken'. With this sweeping indictment Hellyer stopped the machinery, resigned from the cabinet on 23 April 1969, and left the stage with a roll of thunder and a flash of lightning. I was invited to comment on this event after the CBC national news the next morning, and said:

In Mr Trudeau's cabinet, Mr Hellyer assumed the role of minister responsible for housing, with the unusual qualification that earlier in life he had been a house-builder. He was successful and he built very good houses. He is also, I believe, an imaginative and enterprising person.

But unfortunately he committed two or three political errors–and those of us who had been watching his course with fascination could not see how he could survive.

His first political error was that, in seeking new lines of housing policy, he could not resist the temptation to be the chairman of his own task force. As author of the task force's report, he became committed to policy ideas before he had obtained the agreement of his own cabinet colleagues. If the cabinet could not immediately adopt some of the task force proposals they were, by implication, repudiating their own colleague Paul Hellyer. Mr Hellyer has no one but himself to blame, that he worked himself into this awkward position (unless one can believe the suggestion that Mr Trudeau allowed him to hang himself).

The second political error was that, in gathering views about housing policy, Mr Hellyer pointedly didn't ask the advice of his own staff people in the government's housing agency, CMHC. Nor did he speak to the housing administrators in the provincial governments. His explanation of this was: that Mr Trudeau had enunciated the admirable political doctrine that policy ought to be made by cabinet ministers and not by bureaucrats. But I doubt that Mr Trudeau really meant that a minister should not find out as much as possible from his professionals before choosing his own policy position. But Mr Hellyer, as a former housebuilder, was perhaps too proud to do this. And he denied himself this advice to his own peril.

People who were more up to date than Mr Hellyer in their knowledge of housing and big city problems were quick to see that the task force report contained some serious errors of judgment, was not at all advanced in its views, and had not, indeed, picked up some significant new ideas already familiar to those in CMHC and elsewhere. It was certainly not a very sophisticated statement of objectives.

Mr Hellyer has said that he really parted company with Mr Trudeau over the philosophy of Canada as a country with ten nearly autonomous provinces and a weak central government. He has suggested that Mr Trudeau is still at heart a university professor attached to a nice political theory, but an unworkable one.

Mr Hellyer had genuinely hoped to deal with the problems of housing and the cities from a position of strength in a strong federal government. He was deeply attached to the heroic gesture of founding a new city, a splendid utopia. But surely, in this it was Mr Hellyer who was being unrealistic. The problems of cities and housing are the problems of regions and communities; and if Canada had entered these decades of immense urbanization without a structure of provincial governments–well, we would have had to invent them.

Finally, there is a tragic aspect of Mr Hellyer's short tenure of office in housing, which must be a danger signal to his successor. Mr Hellyer could not conceal his strong personal prejudices against public housing as a means of helping poor families. His prejudices slowed down the whole difficult process of getting more housing for poor people. Thousands of them have suffered as a consequence. And this is a sad record to have to chalk up against the Trudeau government, which is supposed to be dedicated to the Just Society.

Paul Hellyer's abrupt performance was quite a shock. A senior member of a federal cabinet had staked his reputation in the field of housing and urban affairs–and lost. But the issue was not at all clear: the momentum of the machinery had been stopped but no new directions had been offered except a rather messianic recommendation to build a 'new city'. There was, however, one recommendation of the task force which was now clearly overdue: the establishment of a new Ministry of Urban Affairs to give all these confusing problems a proper status in the business of the nation. It fell to Robert Andras to be the first Minister of Urban Affairs and he was welcomed with great relief as a man of reason and calm common sense who was going to work hard at the job. No one of this calibre had been on the housing scene since Robert Winters in the pre-Diefenbaker years. It is greatly to Andras' credit that besides displaying the abilities of a practical working politician in a confusing period, he was willing to bring into play two people with high academic qualifications for the intellectual task of thinking a way through the enormously complicated network of urban problems. The first of these was Harvey Lithwick, economics professor of Carleton University and, following him, Peter Oberlander who became the first under-secretary (deputy minister) of the ministry. Peter, who had joined the staff of CMHC with me in 1948 and had then founded the school of town and regional planning at the University of British Columbia, had in the meantime played a role in Vancouver as chairman of the School Board and chairman of the Planning Board.

Lithwick was a recognized scholar of the urban scene and had been a beneficiary of both CMHC and CCURR grants in support of his work. His report entitled *Urban Canada, Problems and Prospects* was completed less than a year after Hellyer's resignation and was far the most sophisticated interpretation of Canada's urban problems that had yet appeared. For the first time it brought together into a unified argument the many threads and themes of the whole subject, showing the relationship between the problems of poverty, economic growth, land development, transportation, bureaucratic controls, politics, and citizen aspirations. Out of this tangled network Lithwick arrived at quite logical conclusions. But unfortunately his analysis was expressed in such difficult language that much of its value was lost. It was rather as if one was reading a professional economist's validation of the propositions of Jesus Christ.

Reduced to their simplest terms, Lithwick's conclusions were:

1 / If cities are left to grow spontaneously, as they are now doing, many beautiful and satisfactory things will certainly happen. But also a lot of ugly and crushing things will happen. There are now a good many indications that we have reached a stage where the bad things are going to overtake the good things. (The green landscape is getting greener, but the black one is getting blacker.)

2 / The cancelling out of the benefits of our urban civilization by the disbenefits (the costs and the environmental pollution) does not need to happen. It can be prevented if the public is able to recognize that the problem really exists and if society can discover the right combination of actions to prevent it happening. In other words we have the choice to 'design' the future, rather than let it drift.

3 / Lithwick didn't claim to be able to prescribe the correct design solution or 'urban policy'. But he suggested that this may well be a policy for developing new communities as integral parts of existing urban regions (as distinct from separate 'new towns') with linking transportation corridors. He explained that, through public acquisition of the land for new communities, the incremental value could accrue to the public rather than be dissipated in private profit. He noted that this concept is not new, but its application has usually not been very successful because of the failure to integrate it fully into the whole urban system and its growth process. And he observed that the most successful application of the idea had been the Vallingby-Stockholm development in Sweden which seemed to be very relevant to Canada because so many of our cities are also 'linear' in shape.

4 / Finally Lithwick expressed the view that the implementation of such an urban policy could not happen without the use of a national urban council, to draw together all the complex inputs and relationships of the three levels of government. This was essentially what Prime Minister Pearson had tried to explain to the assembled provincial premiers in December 1967. Harvey Lithwick resigned from the Ministry of Urban Affairs when he saw that this last recommendation was not going to be accepted by the federal and provincial governments.

In February 1973, new amendments to the National Housing Act were finally introduced; they provided for financing a New Communities program and for the acquisition of transportation corridors and for a new version of urban renewal in the name of Neighbourhood Improvement. So the original version of the testament written by the Advisory Group in 1965, which had been put into an authorized version for the 1967 conference and then into Lithwick's revised version in 1970, finally reached the statute books in 1973.

But in the meanwhile Canada had been through an extraordinary turbulence of social evolution which must in many ways affect the whole future of how urban policies are conceived and carried out. Those were the years when university campuses were rocked by rebellious youth, when 'the poor' first claimed a place at the table where their welfare was being discussed, when people in cities began to question the judgments of planners and to challenge the accepted criteria of progress. In Ottawa it was a period of strenuous confusion. Urban researchers multiplied like minnows, task forces took off in many different directions, the new Ministry of Urban Affairs and CMHC were confused in their mutual relationships, and there were power thrusts and counterthrusts. Perhaps this was all to the good in enlarging the number of people who were trying to understand the problems of cities, but it wasn't very productive.

The chaos of Pearson's urban conference and the subsequent melodramatic behaviour of Paul Hellyer were manifestations of the turbulence, as were the battles on the university campuses and the protest movements in the inner cities. The turbulence in Canada was also, of course, part of a worldwide stirring of minority groups and the social expression of a new generation born and raised in the permissive years after the Second World War. In the United States the turbulence is particularly associated with Viet Nam and with the surge of black power; but in Canada the turbulence had its own indigenous characteristics and effects. One of the effects was certainly to undermine the capacities of existing institutions and programs for building cities. Private developers of the middle-class suburbs had always been a target for some popular derision, but now public housing programs for low-income people also came to be regarded as 'alien' because they seemed to reflect a patronizing attitude towards the poor. Private developers, the advocates of public housing, and CMHC found themselves strangely linked together as a joint establishment to be looked at with suspicion and mistrust. And, in search of new directions, the protesters–the students, the activists, and the spokesmen for the poor–sought refuge in what came to be called 'the third sector': the co-operatives, the non-profit programs and the rehabilitation of old houses near the centres of cities. This was at least a way of avoiding the stigma of both the bourgeois suburbs and the ghettos of public housing. How these attitudes are going to affect the progress of events after the era of turbulence, we do not yet know.

An engaging aspect of the turbulence has been the use of costume to express a person's liberation from orthodoxy and his participation in the scenario of the ballet. (Blue jeans, of course, eventually became a uniform and so lost their point.) I have always felt that the opening scene of this theatrical phase of history was the appearance of Pierre Elliott Trudeau at the Liberal party's leadership convention in July 1968–Trudeau the harlequin with a carnation in his mouth, Trudeau who married a flower-child and had two children, each born on a Christmas Day. The favourite costumes have been in the folk/wilderness genre, suggesting an utter rejection of the square-cropped world of the business executive and his suburbia. At the meetings of a committee I have attended from time to time to discuss Canadian housing policies, one member of the committee, a university professor, wears an old blue sweater and always looks as if

he had just come ashore after rowing an open boat across the Atlantic,
with his long hair, matted beard, and eyebrows windswept and ice-
coated. He takes the view that CMHC, like all government bureaucracies,
is by definition incompetent, lacks insight, and is beastly to him personally. (Does he really believe this, or does he say it partly to tease me?)
He is deeply committed to the do-it-yourself co-operative 'rehab' process
with its heroic small-scale exercises in neighbourhood activism. I think
this is what the costume signifies: rowing a small boat across the Atlantic.
I am to understand that he has rejected the practical possibility that an
agency of the democratic state could work for the people. I think he is
serious about this because he is a sincere man and I like to see his
pale-blue eyes sparkle when he speaks with such indignation about the
Central Mortgage and Housing Corporation.

After I retired from CMHC in 1967 I did not have any further role in
the public affairs of housing. But I did have an unexpected opportunity
to see what was going on in Canada because I was invited to undertake
three tasks, each of which took me on an expedition from coast to coast,
exploring some of the social undercurrents and manifestations of a
changing society. The first of these tasks was concerned with the way in
which the present stresses and turbulences are occurring and how social
policies and programs might be designed to be constructive or 'developmental' rather than simply charitable. This task was part of the process
of converting the former Canadian Welfare Council into the Canadian
Council on Social Development. As chairman of a reorganization committee in 1968 I travelled from city to city and talked to people in every
variety of social service, trying to discover their common interests in
social policies affecting family life, the old and the young, the poor and
the alienated, the dependent and the disoriented. In its new form the
Canadian Council has tried to look at the dynamics of a whole society
and to move away from the limited attitudes of charity and welfare.

My second expedition was concerned with a more professional subject:
the kind of people who are working in urban planning across Canada,
the legitimacy of their qualifications to call themselves planners, and to
work in this role. This task was undertaken for the Town Planning
Institute of Canada (of which I had been president in 1964) and I was
in company with Harry Lash, at that time moving from Montreal's
planning staff to be director of planning in Vancouver. On our long
expedition we found some whose competence was confined to the bylaws
and bureaucratic mechanics of city planning, some who were more at
home with the idealisms and larger implications of planning, and others

who were specialists in transportation or housing or the law. How catholic should the planning profession be?

The third of these expeditions was a most delightful task undertaken in 1970, as a joint project of the Massey Foundation and the Canada Council. The purpose was to select about a dozen outstanding examples of contemporary places in Canadian cities which somehow expressed and fulfilled the aspirations of people. The formal expression was 'excellence in the urban environment' or, in the current cliché, 'people-places'. I was chairman of the jury team which travelled across the country, the other members of the group being Michel Barcelo (town-planner, Montreal), Sidney Buckwold (at that time mayor of Saskatoon and now a senator), Gérald Fortin (sociologist, Quebec), and Doris Shadbolt (curator of the Vancouver Art Gallery). Some of the places we saw were local products of the 1967 centennial and, like Expo 67, were climactic achievements of great beauty and distinction. I think our happiest moment of discovery was in arriving in Trois Rivières, Quebec. In our report I wrote:

The outstanding example of a central place is the new heart of Trois Rivières, Quebec. The old square was there before, with the handsome cathedral along one side. Now on the other side of the square are the principal public features of a modern community: a beautiful and expressive city hall, a cultural centre with library, theatre and art gallery and an interesting link into the city's main street of shops and restaurants . . . the active life of the city now flows through these community places and out into the central square. The whole composition has made such an attractive and theatrical place, with its courtyards and sculpture and fountains, that this is where everyone likes to go. Surely something excellent has happened when the young people of a town enjoy sitting on the steps of the city hall, feeling that this is *their* place? If you want to see excellence in the design of the urban environment, this is it.

These three expeditions across the length and breadth of Canada gave me an unusual bird's-eye view of the whole scene. I had a detached and panoramic view partly because I was no longer an actor in the play. I could enjoy my view of this very restless period and I could look back over the events of the quarter of a century since I had joined CMHC. It seemed to me that there had been three successive phases.

First was the period of *Innocence and Authority.* In the years immediately after the war, the strong authority of CMHC, under the personal management of David Mansur, had created the Canadian housing industry which shaped the new suburbs of family housing. This had been the

assignment given to Mansur by the postwar government and he had
carried it out with great competence and authority.

Then there followed a decade of *Expanding Horizons* from 1955 to 1967, in which the concepts of a new urban Canada began to ferment in people's minds. The frontiers of housing policy were broadened to encompass the separate needs of the student generation and of old people: and a new wave of intellectuals and professionals began to perceive the whole city as a social and physical milieu affecting the lives of people. Expo 67 was the climax of this period, an exultation that revealed a new self-assurance and competence of Canadians to design their own urban environment.

Then came the *Turbulence*. Perhaps it was an inevitable consequence of the intellectual activity of the previous period, acting upon the receptive minds of a new generation. It was certainly a boiling-over that has changed the nature of Canadian society though we do not yet know how this is going to affect the man-made environment.

What I have seen happening during this period of twenty-five years has been one cycle in an evolutionary process. At first, the depression and the war and pressing demands of suburban growth all tended to diminish the democratic system and favoured authoritative forms of management; this was the situation when I entered CMHC. In the next phase I was a minor actor, as chairman of CMHC's Advisory Group, in a period of intellectual fermentation when policy directions were mostly conceived by a new intellectual-professional élite who were the first to understand the new circumstances of regional urbanization; leadership did not come from political quarters. Then came the turbulence, a resurgent challenge to restore the democratic process in some new and appropriate form. It is understandable that the early thrusts of this challenge would take the form of community organizations that rejected the established organs of the state and preferred to substitute home-made mini-states in the form of co-operatives and communes and little enclaves of rehabilitation that can only serve little bits of the whole population. These have been spontaneous responses to the problem, highly self-conscious, and deliberately small in scale; but they do not provide realistic solutions to the problems of big cities which are so enormous in scale and whose problems cannot be confronted in such isolation. It is true that anarchy has some uses, but in the long broad haul it's simply no use being isolated, alienated, and separated from the state and rejecting the organs of a democratic society. Somehow the new urban society must itself take over the organs of the state and make them work. This is what the reform movements in our large cities have already started to do and have experienced the initial difficulties of escaping from their subservience to the alienated small-scale protest groups from which they originated. The further stages of this evolutionary process will be fascinating to watch.

Having worked for so long in CMHC which is one piece of Canada's whole city-building apparatus, I am naturally most interested in the future of this piece, and in how it could become truly a part of the democratic process. From time to time there have been upheavals and reorganizations which have generally been intended to make CMHC's local branch offices more directly responsive to circumstances in each community. There is an anomaly to the whole idea that the Ottawa head office of a federal government agency, or that a federal minister, could possibly exercise sound judgments about local situations; and in fact the federal constitution was designed to avoid such a thing being attempted. From this one could argue that there is need for a central body to co-ordinate services and funds for city-building and which is a 'central' (not 'federal') part of the local community apparatus, rather than being an agency of the federal government. The logic of that point of view could lead to an interesting reshaping of a central body for working out urban policies and programs that could arise from genuine community participation in the democratic process.

Or one could argue just the opposite way: to urge that CMHC and the Ministry of Urban Affairs should quickly be brought into a single entity, as an organ of the federal state. The image of CMHC, one might say, as a kind of independent insurance company managed by its president, is a relic of the last period of authority and innocence and should have been changed a long time ago. Within a democratic system there is no place for a bureaucracy that is not part of the responsive thread that links citizens, through their elected representatives, to the machinery that formulates urban policies and carries out public programs.

The future of Canadian cities will depend a good deal upon the choice between these two logical directions of change.

Part Three

is about the place where I have lived
for many years, in the capital of Canada
and about its meaning
to other people.

It's about returning, later in life,
to a new love for the natural landscape
the lake, the river, and the sea
and how they have to be protected
for everyone's enjoyment.

And, finally, it's about the family
of which I am a part
and which has made me
the way I am.

p. 196   The aesthetics of waterfalls is a rather esoteric subject. The International Joint Commission set up a board to consider whether the American Falls at Niagara would look better if the accumulation of fallen rocks (the 'talus') was removed. The pictures are photos of the model on which we worked. Which appearance do you prefer?

197   The reedy shore of a lake or stream is a fragile place, to be cherished and conserved. The only artifact that doesn't seem out of place is a canoe; within its fishy shape one can slip quietly into the natural universe of birds and plants and creatures that live in the water.

198   This is the Atlantic shore of Nova Scotia. Here, in Peter's photo, are my wife and children, my grandchildren, some cousins and friends. On the mile-long sandy beach in the background they ride the waves and stretch in the sun.

199   The ocean deposits great stone sculptures on the shore. Their surfaces are tilted at subtle angles to one another and their millstone edges have the rough burr of sea-life upon them. I try to put some of this character into a water-colour sketch.

200   Before my grandfather Benjamin Carver took his family to live under the grey skies of Manchester, they lived in a house called the Palace in Gibraltar. Here is an old drawing of the house and garden which my grandmother Emily yearned for so longingly. And above, in the studio of a Gibraltar photographer, Benjamin is obviously enjoying the effect of his debonair pose.

201   My mother's family, the Creswells, lived in the little Spanish village of Campamento, on the Bay of Gibraltar. My mother returned here many times in her life and loved to sit in the sun and sketch. This is her water-colour of the Spanish hills and the farm where young bulls were bred for the bullfights in Cordova and Seville.

15
Living in the
Capital

During the war I had spent long periods of time in Ottawa on military duty, and one Sunday morning I walked out along Sussex Drive beside the Ottawa River and discovered, for the first time, the path that leads down through the Rockeries where daffodils grow wild and bunchy in the long grass in the spring. It was a sunny day and I was feeling very homesick for my family in Toronto and was altogether in a reflective mood. At the end of the Rockeries path I found a cluster of pleasant houses under some magnificent elms and, in the distance, the shimmering surface of a small lake visible through the trees. I thought it was a beautiful place and wished this was where I lived. The woods, the quiet Sunday morning houses, and the water beyond somehow reminded me of an English village in the Cotswolds that I had first discovered on another Sunday morning many years ago and to which I had returned many times because there was something about the place that haunted me. The Cotswold village was in the basin of a gentle valley, where the road goes through a water-splash and there are ducks placidly floating on the water.

When I moved to Ottawa in 1948, just Peter and I bereft, we first lived in a rented house on Acacia Avenue with a housekeeper and a dog to comfort us. We had swapped houses with the Plumptres when Wynne Plumptre went to Toronto as editor of the weekly magazine *Saturday Night*. In a few months the time came to move out, and in this perplexing and lonely phase of my life I came within two weeks of the deadline without having been able to decide what steps to take. The day finally came when I could procrastinate no longer. So I looked in the evening paper, noticed the street address of a house for sale and took the dog for a walk. To my astonishment, the house was near to the foot of the Rockeries path and looked across the shimmering surface of MacKay Lake. By lunchtime the next day I had arranged to buy the house, and that is where I have lived ever since. Perhaps there is some ancient environmental imperative that draws us to certain places, like the instinct that draws salmon up their ancestral river or the compulsion of migrating birds to return by the same flyway to the same pond year after year.

Two years after making this move, Anne and I were married and we enlarged the house to make room for our new family. One evening, about ten years later, we were at a gathering at Joyce Wrong's house in Ottawa and, at opposite ends of a crowded room, simultaneously found ourselves in conversation with a couple who said they knew some Carvers in England and–how very odd–their names were also Anne and Humphrey. That summer our whole family was going on a trip to England and we thought it would be interesting to see where the other Anne and Humphrey lived, so we found out the address from the friends we had met at Joyce Wrong's party. At one point in our summer travels we were in Cirencester, on the edge of the Cotswolds, and realized that we were not very far from the place. In the evening, with a map, we found our way into an exquisite Cotswold valley, dipped down a little country road and found that it turned towards a cluster of stone buildings around a place where the pebbly road goes through a shallow ford, with ducks floating placidly on the water. It was one of the most beautiful places I have ever seen. In the stone-walled yard of the house by the ford a man was washing his car and, by the house, his wife was tying up the roses.

'Are you Humphrey and Anne Carver?'

'We are Humphrey and Anne Carver'.

'I have always known that Humphrey and Anne Carver live in a place like this.'

I have now lived in this house in Ottawa for twenty-five years, and it is full of family history. By this kitchen window I stood one morning and experienced a strange new sensation. I had been so accustomed to the presence in my life of one child, dependent on me–and now there was another one tugging at my heart. That day of Debby's birth, Peter, then sixteen years old, was at home in bed with a touch of flu and, seeking intuitively to reassure him of my continued devotion, I cooked him a particularly good dinner before rushing off to the hospital to see Anne and the baby. I did him a steak and then with some genius, I thought,

heated up a pudding which he always liked, and took it up to him. Peter
sat up in bed and looked at it appraisingly. 'What, no sauce!' he said
indignantly. Anne said that she could hear me laughing as I ran down
the hospital corridor to her. It is wonderful when children lay their
claims upon us, particularly when their expectations are beyond our
capacity. My frequent failures are referred to kindly in our family as
'Daddy's errors'. That is love.

Since my wife, among her many other wonderful qualities, is an extraordinary and magnificent cook, a good many of the memories enshrined in our house are connected with food. When the girls were still little
and came back at midday from school, skipping down Prospect hill,
there were often other footsteps. Tim Stowell, aged four, appeared one
day with his legendary question: 'Mrs Carver, what's for dessert?' Peter's
friends also became aware that there were good things to be found here;
from several blocks away Murray Hogben was able to sniff the aroma
of Anne's mincepies and would arrive while we were still eating and sit
at the end of the table with hungry eyes. Love and marriage and good
food go together. And as the years have passed the gatherings have got
larger and the food, if that were possible, become more sumptuous.
There are now more than a dozen of our immediate family living in
Ottawa and the table is often full. And on special occasions such as my
brother-in-law King Gordon's seventieth birthday and my own two
years later, we have sat down forty souls to dinner. Not to mention the
uncountable numbers of invited and uninvited guests who flow in and out
of the house all night when our daughters Debby and Jenny are reported
to be at home.

To say that I have 'left my footprints' on this familiar neighbourhood
might be a figurative expression, but in this place it is literally true, for
it is a great place for walking. We walk here because it is a pleasant
landscape that has never lost its woodland character, as it was when
there were just a few summer cottages scattered through the Rockcliffe
woods. There are no curbs or sidewalks and the houses, over a period
of about a hundred years, have been built one by one, tucked in between
the trees and shaded by the high canopy of the elms. People walk in
family groups on Sundays, they walk their dogs in the early morning or
evening, or they walk in lonely cogitation when they have a problem to
solve. For walking is the best aid to creative thought. In recent years one
of our local walkers has been John G. Diefenbaker; he goes by, sometimes in the halflight of dawn when the milk-truck is making its rounds,
and I see him concocting some provocative and witty intervention for

tomorrow's debate in the House, trying out the flavour of the words with his lips and chuckling to himself over the ingenuity of the phrases. And the morning after the 1972 general election when Robert Stanfield seemed to have toppled Prime Minister Trudeau's government but the outcome still hung in the balance, I saw the dark-coated figure of Stanfield, with longer strides than usual, unable to sit still at home while fates determined his destiny, working off his nervous energy with a walk.

I walk with our English setter Alfred who, so my family say, bears a remarkable resemblance to Mr Stanfield, with his sad, honest face like one of Thurber's dogs. Alfred has lost his hearing and become a bit elderly in his ways, so when the younger dogs bounce around him he tries politely to quicken his pace but then reverts to his accustomed style, trotting along behind me and sniffing around every tree. The other day he suddenly came upon a friend, took a sniff, and sat down as if stunned. 'Wow!' As I disappeared around the next corner he was still sitting there motionless with a silly half-smile on his face. It's a pleasant place to walk, mostly because of the landscape and the views across the river, but also because interesting people and dogs live around here.

One of the places on a walk is what we called the Village Green when we made this little park in Centennial Year. It was a few acres of rough unused land at the middle of the village near the school, with a beautiful group of acacias on one side and the ground strewn with enormous glacial boulders, many of them four or five feet long, like fallen monoliths. In Centennial Year every municipality in Canada was invited to undertake a community project with some government financial aid. This was our project and a lot of people took part in making it. We set the boulders in a kind of druids' circle. With a bulldozer this was easier than it had been for the builders of Stonehenge or Carnac; Andrew Hazeland and I placed every stone and in the middle put the two finest sculptural specimens, one a tall one and the other we called 'Henry' because it had the shape of a Henry Moore piece. The benches and the trees that were planted bear the names of families living in the village and the flowers were put in by Mary Lea Platt and Peggy Heeney. We hoped all this would still be here when the next centennial comes around.

If I walk a little further I can look down on the big river and get an even longer sense of history. 'This is the oldest trans-Canada throughway,' reads a sign erected by the National Capital Commission, 'the canoe route by the Ottawa River, Lake Nipissing, Lake Superior and Lake Winnipeg and the Churchill River to Lake Athabaska and the Rockies. Past this point travelled many explorers from Brûlé, Champlain and la Vérendrye to Mackenzie, Thompson and Fraser ... The fur traders from the early 'coureurs des bois' to the later brigades in big Montreal canoes paddling to and from the 'pays d'en haut' made this river their highway.' This is history of a legendary and heroic age.

When Champlain moved up and down the river more than three centuries ago, he passed through the great forest of white pine cut down in the nineteenth century to build the ships which sailed the oceans of the world in the imperial age of Queen Victoria. It was another heroic period in the history of the river as the birthplace of the nation. My father-in-law Charles Gordon (Ralph Connor) was born in 1860 in Glengarry County, forty miles downstream. In *The Man from Glengarry* he tells about the lusty life in the woods and on the river, the intermingling of French Canadians, the Irish, and the Highland Scottish of his own Glengarry people.

Driven from homes in the land of their fathers, they had set themselves with indomitable faith and courage to hew from the solid forest homes for themselves and their children, that none might take from them. These pioneers were bound together by ties of blood, but also by bonds stronger than those of blood. Their loneliness, their triumphs, their sorrows, born of their common life-long conflict with the forest and its fierce beasts, knit them in bonds close and enduring. The sons born to them and reared in the heart of the pine forests grew up to witness that heroic struggle with stern nature and to take their part in it. And mighty men they were. Their life bred in them hardiness of frame, alertness of sense, readiness of resource, endurance, suberb self-reliance, a courage that grew with peril, and withal a certain wildness which at times deepened into ferocity. By their fathers the forest was dreaded and hated, but the sons, with rifles in hand, trod its pathless stretches without fear, and with their broad-axes they took toll of their ancient foe.

A number of families made fortunes out of the great forest of the Ottawa valley and built themselves handsome roomy houses on the Rockcliffe height of land overlooking the river. In the course of time almost all these houses, being too large for any private family to maintain, have now become embassy residences. Around the outside edge of the village are the embassies of Israel, Switzerland, Austria, Spain, Japan, Sweden, the United States, the Soviet Union, and Denmark, with many others nearby; the diplomatic representatives of twenty-seven countries live in the village. There is no other place in a Canadian city where the big houses and gardens of a previous generation have remained so well-kept and immune from redevelopment.

The most substantial of all the early houses was Thomas MacKay's regency-style stone house built in 1838, which he named Rideau Hall. Over the years it was transformed and enlarged to fulfil the expectations of the exiled nobility who served as governors general; the final touch that gave it a truly royal flavour was the entrance façade that you now see as you approach the house, with a broad pediment containing the royal coat of arms. This was added in 1913. Somehow Rideau Hall has never quite lost its Victorian and Edwardian flavour, the flutter of an expatriate English family, the ladies in big floppy hats and long skirts patting tennis balls and having tea before dressing for dinner. Nowadays in summertime the tourists are encouraged to see the 'changing of the guard' ceremony at the Rideau Hall gateway; the band arrives in a bus, there is much marching and countermarching and two red-coated lads are left to strut in front of their sentry boxes. The whole thing has a musical-comedy effect: a chorus of young ladies with tennis rackets will surely appear through the gate and rescue the melancholy sentries.

At the present stage in our national evolution, the original symbolism of Rideau Hall is no longer relevant and some thought might be given to changing the image. It was originally an enclosed and protected place for an expatriate family, where they could live a private life, entertain generously, and implant some of their own culture into a wilderness country. That was the lifestyle of Lord Monck, Lord Lisgar, the Earl of Dufferin, the Marquess of Lorne, and Princess Louise. It was all a long time ago, but somehow the symbols–the formidable iron fence that surrounds the park, the lodge at the gateway, the royal arms–still persist in conveying the élitist message: 'Keep out. This is the sanctuary. Do not speak. Do not enter'.

From the gateway of Rideau Hall, with the prime minister's residence just across the street, the two-mile route to Parliament Hill begins along Sussex Drive, past the French Embassy, over the Rideau River bridges, past the new External Affairs headquarters and Earnscliffe, originally the home of Sir John A Macdonald, first prime minister of confederated Canada, and so up to Wellington Street, by 'Confusion Square' and the National Arts Centre to 'The Hill'. It's a route that is rich in historic associations and interesting architecture and, because of its place in the national capital, this is surely the most important street in Canada.

Though the symbolism of Rideau Hall has rather lost its relevance, at the other end of the processional route up to the Hill, the group of Parliamentary buildings has gained authority and beauty with the years. It has been said that this is the finest Gothic-Revival composition in the

world and that its silhouette of towers and pinnacles and spires is unmatched for its romantic quality. As public architecture has become
more impersonal and colourless we have come to respect and enjoy the
idiosyncracies of Victorian design, the willingness of an architect and his
client to be absurd. Nowadays there isn't a touch of playfulness in the
façades of government buildings. (But an absurdity has sometimes been
added by a piece of sculpture in front of the building.)

Some of the buildings on Parliament Hill are now only a shade less
venerable than the Houses of Parliament at Westminster, which were
built only twenty years earlier. There is no doubt that the Westminster
buildings are finer architecture; they were largely designed by Pugin who
was the acknowledged master of the Gothic-Revival style and the whole
composition has a unity of form and detail. The Ottawa buildings were
designed by several people, but the Gothic style lends itself to this kind
of variation and counterpoint. The centre block, as we see it today, with
the graceful shaft of the Peace Tower and the tall copper-green roofs, was
redesigned by John Pearson in 1918 after a fire had destroyed much of
Thomas Fuller's original building of 1865, which had been a rather
dumpy-looking affair with a quite grotesque tower. The library building
on the river side, however, survives from the 1865 building and when its
crowning turret is illuminated at night is a bold and lovely Gothic
construction.

The East Block contains the prime minister's office and the cabinet
chamber and is the inner sanctuary of state; here the sovereignty of
Canada is enshrined. The building was the work of the architectural firm
of Stent & Laver and is a genuine Victorian oddity with its towers
blossoming out into ironwork on the roof; the building somehow has just
the right old-fashioned archival air. At the front of the building stands
the statue of Laurier looking proud and patrician; and rather oddly
placed just outside the windows of the cabinet room is a sinister statue
of Mackenzie King looking like a mafia chieftain, ready to shoot from
the hip. I remember the day that Mackenzie King's funeral passed by
along Wellington Street and the entrance to the East Block had been
draped with black and purple cloth; he would have enjoyed the eerie
solemnity of it.

The West Block on the Hill is built around a graceful and lofty tower
of Flemish style designed by T.S. Scott in the seventies; it gives a touch
of elegance to the whole composition. On the fourth side of the space
enclosed by these buildings, and across the road on Wellington Street,
are two quite modest buildings in polite Renaissance style; one is the

American embassy and the other the Rideau Club. It's hard to avoid the feeling that there are watchful eyes behind the windows of these two élite institutions. So it's reassuring to be invited to lunch at the Rideau Club and to discover that, in fact, the same familiar members of the Ottawa establishment are still there, innocently sipping their martinis and having their oysters on the half-shell.

Enclosed by these buildings on Parliament Hill is a great lawn, a handsome public place nobly proportioned for great occasions, to contain large crowds gathered in celebration of an historic national day or to acclaim some visiting royalty or great statesman. Across this space a paved walk, about fifty feet wide, leads to the steps at the foot of the Peace Tower and the main entrance to the Parliament buildings. I was there one summer day at the time of a recent Commonwealth Conference; a crowd was lined up on both sides of the broad walk; Elizabeth II accompanied by Prime Minister Pierre Trudeau walked and talked with the people on one side, and on the other side Prince Philip teased the boys and girls in the crowd as he strolled with Margaret Trudeau, her smiling luminous beauty under a wide-brimmed garden-party hat. But usually this wide space is comparatively empty and dwarfs the few figures on the broad walk and the steps. Some hurry along purposefully on the nation's business: an MP, perhaps, hoping that his words will read well in Hansard; a couple of civil service mandarins plotting a political strategy; a few subdued-looking secretaries and messengers; also usually a few visitors lingering here to taste the sensation of being at the heart of their country: an old warrior, a few students from distant regions of Canada, and one or two from small towns and remote constituencies. For each of them it is a comtemplative moment, trying to perceive himself and the context of his life.

I never walk on Parliament Hill myself without enjoying this kind of reflection, thinking about my own migration to Canada more than four decades ago, what kind of a place this has turned out to be and what I have done in those forty years. My part in the nation's affairs has been very modest indeed, just a middle person's input; and yet, in this central place, I can understand the relationship between the big historic events and the little bits that I have taken part in. I try to find words of appreciation for the country I chose to live in, expressing my gratitude for its qualities. These are private thoughts and it's difficult to build words around the abstractions.

What has appealed to me so much about Canada? I search for an expression. Perhaps 'the accessible society' would do–meaning that

Canada has been, for me, a place where I have been able to pursue the ideas that have interested me and, in doing this, I have found people who have shared these interests and been my friends. I have not been confined within a social structure with fixed positions of class, income, and intellect. I have been myself and done what I wanted to do. I have known Canada in a process of evolution, in a period of great migrations, through a great era in the building of cities and in an age of freshly evolving philosophies about people and their environment. Since I came here the population has doubled, from around ten million to over twenty million. Altogether it has been a wonderful period and I am glad to have taken part in it. Though what I have done will have no place in history books, yet I have had a nodding acquaintance with many who have been at the centre of history-making. Unlike the visitors on the Hill–the old warrior, the students, and the small-town constituents–I have known the East Block, not just as an old-fashioned Gothic monument, but as a place where the affairs of Canada have been directed by people I have known as neighbours and admired as friends. That is one of the pleasures of living in a country that is comparatively small in its social dimensions. And that is one of the pleasures of living in a capital city where one can actually know some of the leading actors in the drama. That is what I mean by an 'accessible society'.

There is another quality about Canada that I have enjoyed. I will call it 'the compassionate society', though that may seem too pretentious a term. Because the vast spaces and stern climate made it impossible for people to survive in this land without the aid and support of one another, the essential attitudes of public policy have always had to be compassionate. Confederation was built upon recognition of the disparities that had to be overcome, the recources that had to be redistributed, the communications that had to be subsidized, between one region and another and between the layers of society. As a microcosm of human society, Canadians discovered from the outset that politics based on power are inevitably destructive and the only ultimate test of public policy is its compassion. When it was my job to recommend social policies for housing and city-building, in spite of any difficulties of communication and political inertia, there was never any doubt about the ultimate respect for the compassionate motive, when this was made clear.

Only an immigrant to a country can fully understand this kind of comparative evaluation, which is the consequence of having made a choice. As a young man, I knew England and felt the inaccessibility of a society with such rigidities of social class and all the hangovers of feudalism that are so difficult to describe. Not until I came to Canada did I really begin to be a person in my own right; I realize that stronger people have been able to break their way through those English fences, but too many have accepted the middle-class enclosures. For comparison, I have also known the United States quite well, seeing it as a gigantic society, overwhelming in its power and complexity and inner contradictions of good and evil, so that the real centres of authority and direction are almost impossible to discover and only people of almost ruthless aggressiveness can win their way to positions of influence. I am sure that I would not have had a sense of fulfilment as an American. And supposing by some toss of the coin, more than forty years ago, I had taken a boat to Australia? I greatly respected and liked what I found there, in a short visit; but I think that Canada is a far more interesting place in which to live because of its greater social complexity and diversity, compared with the more simple and homogeneous dimensions of Australia. I have also recently been in South Africa and in Rhodesia, where my brother Maurice has lived and where I have many other relatives. Africa is a beautiful land and I can understand their deep attachment to its earth and to its climate; I also appreciate their intuition that it is right to be there, helping to strengthen the spirit of compassion that has been so dreadfully abused in the treatment of black people. Countries without problems are not necessarily the best places to live in.

These are the reflections of an immigrant in the capital of his chosen land, validating a choice made long ago. The native-born Canadian, on the other hand, comes here to discover something new about the real nature of his own country; he hopes to find that the capital is not just a political headquarters but is the one place where the whole is seen to be greater than its parts. Here one should be able to see how it all fits together. But when I observe the visitors on the Hill–the old warrior, the students, and the small-town constituents–I sense their disappointment in finding that the capital is somehow so inarticulate. I know about this because I have lived here a long time and have tried to explain the place to so many visitors. We drive admiringly along the handsome parkways, comment on the history and the charm of the Rideau Canal built in the 1820s, praise the tulips presented by Queen Juliana of the Netherlands and the 'bikeways' introduced by the admirable Douglas Fullerton, recently chairman of the National Capital Commission. Ottawa indeed has charisma in its handsome landscape setting; but this is a surface decoration and it is difficult to convey to the visitors an understanding of what

really goes on here. I have wondered whether the National Capital
Commission has focused its efforts on the wrong things, on the decorations rather than on the essential elements.

There are, of course, many things that could be done to make this a more illuminating place, where Canadians could find out more about their country. I have my favourite ideas and I will mention three of them which I will call: 'Canada the Great Estate', 'Canada the Society of Societies', and 'Canada's Place in the World'. And there is the question of symbols.

First of all, about Canada the Great Estate. It's right that the central focus of attention should be on Parliament because this is the expression of our sovereign right to manage our own affairs. But the fact is that nowadays it is not the process of legislating in the House of Commons that most interests Canadians, but rather the actual business of managing the great estate from coast to coast, of which we are the twenty million owners and shareholders. These are our cities and rivers and mountains and resources in the earth and in the waters. This is the landscape we inhabit and which we try to look after. When I worked in CMHC I always felt that on the ground floor of the building there should be a large hall where people could have a view of how we are managing the growth and renewal of our cities and our housing. The urban ministry and CMHC are deeply involved in what happens in every community and the public should be able to comprehend and compare the results. And consider, for instance, the Department of the Environment which is now housed in a tower on the Quebec side of the Ottawa River. The tall building is a landmark, but there is no way of knowing what goes on behind its expressionless windows. The people inside are dealing with the creatures in the three oceans on our coasts. They watch the winds that are building up ice-formations in the Great Lakes and they care for the forests at the headwaters of the little streams that flow into the great rivers of Canada. These continental views transcend local and provincial affairs and profoundly affect the lives of Canadians. But no one is invited to enter and discover the scope of these management responsibilities; and the same could be said about dozens of other federal government buildings in the capital. They are closed to the public and, in the vestibule, a commissionaire is posted to see you don't come in. You are, however, permitted to stand *outside* the front door and admire a monumental sculpture of obscure meaning; every new government building has one of these in order to fulfil the Department of Public Work's obligation to spend a percentage of building cost on works of art. If the ground floor of every departmental building was a kind of Expo, to display and explain some part of the management of our great estate, the capital would be a much more interesting and communicative place. The public is permitted to enter the Parliament Buildings, to sit in the gallery and watch the legislators perform; I think the shareholders are just as interested in how their estate is being managed.

What I mean by Canada a Society of Societies is that the real fabric of Canadian life is the whole pervasive network of non-governmental organizations (what are now called NGO s) which bind us together through our personal interests and provide everyone with a chance to take a part in the life of the country. People discover themselves and express themselves by joining some kind of association, society, club, institution, or group through a personal interest as a consumer or as a worker or a professional, or through an interest in the arts, in business or in sports, and so on. This web of human relationships originates in the grassroots and has its summit in the capital of the country. As a manifestation of the democratic process in a free country, these associations are in many ways even more important than the political electoral system; this is where the process really starts. This is the reality of citizen participation. The national representations of this network are scattered all through the central area of the capital. Some of them are in the back ends of run-down Victorian houses with no more than one man and a part-time secretary, a wooden filing cabinet, and some second-hand chairs for the directors' quarterly meetings. Others occupy whole floors of modern office-towers with batteries of secretaries and xerox machines, a library, a board room, and the paraphernalia of status symbols. I have been involved in the formation of several national organizations to do with social affairs, and I have learned the great need for more effective collaborations within this whole network. So I have had utopian dreams about a splendid campus within the national capital, rather like a university campus, with conference halls and meeting-rooms of various sizes and shapes, dining-rooms and club-rooms for the 'faculty' and a permanent staff and apparatus to serve the joint needs of a whole host of useful national organizations that would not then have to use so much of their limited funds in duplicating similar requirements. Parliament Hill is the campus for political and governmental Ottawa. Another campus could be designed around the needs of that vast network of Canadian social organization, an equally important aspect of a democratic society. Is this too utopian a dream?

One of the functions of the national capital should be to reveal Canada's Place in the World. This is the point of contact with the rest of the world through which the two-way relationships flow, an interchange through which we seek our place as a trading nation, as a nation sometimes able to mediate between great powers, and as a nation that seeks special relationships with the younger developing nations. No aspect of our existence as an independent country could be more important than this, and yet this whole process is virtually invisible to the visitors on the Hill–the old warrior, the students, and the small-town constituents– though Ottawa is a diplomatic centre and quite a cosmopolitan place. Until 1973 there was not even a building that one could point to as the centre of External Affairs; its personnel were secreted in the East Block and scattered in a dozen down-town office buildings. Now there is at least the massive pile of the Lester B. Pearson building on Sussex Drive, between the Hill and Rideau Hall. But the presence in Ottawa of a large international diplomatic community would hardly be noted, except for the number of cars on the streets with red diplomatic licence plates. The invisibility of 'international' Ottawa lends some substance to the popular impression that ambassadors and high commissioners spend their entire time entertaining one another at cocktail parties in their Rockcliffe Park residences. 'I say, have another one, won't you? But don't tell me anything you ought not to tell me about, you know, what!'

Though there may be some advantages in conducting international affairs with a low profile, yet it would be very helpful to Canadians to be able to appreciate the importance and the scope of our international relationships, to find that here is a window that looks out upon other people in other parts of the world, in friendship and in sharing some of the resources of our great estate. I have had a utopian dream about this, too, and have visualized an international place within this city, another kind of Expo, where in microcosm one could see Canada's place in the world, the things we each possess, for giving and for receiving.

These are at least three functions of the capital which have not yet, I think, been satisfactorily worked into the design of the place for everyone to see and understand the management of our great estate, to see the way individuals are active in the organized life of the nation, and to get an impression of our place in the world. As an expression of what Canada is really like today, the capital is now rather out of date and too much of a monument to the earlier age of innocence and authority. It is not that one would want to destroy the statues of our political heroes and the monuments to our past history, but simply that there is a need to reflect the mood and style of a more wide-open and participatory generation.

(In 1970 I was invited to be chairman of a group in Ottawa who had taken as their title: 'A Capital for Canadians'. I was grateful for the opportunity to discuss some of my favourite ideas on this theme, including what I have written above. But to my great chagrin I eventually found that the group was really only interested in the preservation of old buildings in Ottawa. I am fond of old buildings too, and I grew up a great reader of John Ruskin who was largely responsible for the sentimental flavour of the Victorian style. I am also an ardent admirer of the Preraphaelite painters. But I don't think that the preservation of Victoriana is likely to be a galvanizing force in the future of this national capital.)

What about symbols? A capital city is expected to enshrine the concepts on which the state is based, to give a spiritual and moral authority to national endeavours. In a ceremony on Parliament Hill in the centennial year 1967, Prime Minister Pearson, after a few moments of difficulty with a torch, illuminated the Eternal Flame. The flame represents some kind of mystique though no one knows what the mystification is about. The summer tourist in the capital who seeks to penetrate the mystery is offered a symbolic display on the great lawn of Parliament Hill in the form of marching figures of red-coated guardsmen (they aren't really guardsmen at all, but specially recruited university students, and they have a British look to them–certainly not French Canadian) who are then taken off in a bus to the gates of Rideau Hall which is the nearest approximation we have to a national shrine. But the message is obscure. There are references to certain historical associations with the British Crown and if you timidly go through the park gates and up the drive to the Hall you may sign a book in the lobby and then, if you are lucky, you may receive an invitation to a garden party. As you go back along the drive you may notice that some of the trees have markers to explain that they were planted by visiting kings and queens, and there is the tree planted by President Kennedy who displayed his spadesmanship with such vigour that he cricked his back and was never quite the same again. In the summer, also, you may catch a glimpse of an awfully British game of cricket being played in the Rideau Hall grounds. There are no royal deer in the park, but there are some royal Windsor swans in the Rideau River nearby. Does all this seem very irrelevant and incongruous and remote from the Canada that I have known and loved? There is nothing here to express or symbolize or enshrine the high purposes and lofty aims in the life of an individual or in the life of a nation. There is nothing here to match the Lincoln Memorial in Washington within which are inscribed the marvellous words of Abraham Lincoln in the Gettysburg address and at his second inaugural, expressing the compassion of the state as a creation both human and divine. I have been in Washington many times and stood beside black and white Americans, young and old, reading these inscriptions with tears in their eyes; I envy them this feeling for their country, as I might that of the English for their royals.

Perhaps one can get a hint of what is missing here from recalling what our Canadian-born governors general have added to the image. Vincent Massey, a patrician, saw the state, I think, as the fountainhead of our civilization, the great patron of the nation's culture. The Vaniers, man and wife, added another dimension with their emphasis on family life and their saintly compassion for those who remain like children all their lives; the Vaniers surely represent Canada's welcome to people of all races and creeds. I'm not sure what dimensions were added by Roland Michener. He was a 'jogger' in an age that admired the uniqueness and perversity of human personality; so the message I get from Michener has to do with a man's respect for his own person, his health of body, and sanity of mind. Perhaps this also represents a rejection of the 'great patron' concept of the state: the state is just a lot of ordinary people, jogging along, doing their best in life—and don't let's pretend that the men at the top are really any different and any less vulnerable than you and me.

It would be good to see a complete rethinking of the presence of the governor general in Rideau Hall, starting with questions like: 'What are the concepts and principles over which the symbolic head of our state presides? What are the special things in our heritage, to make us love, honour, and obey our country?' The capital of a country is an empty place unless these concepts and principles are somehow manifest; though these may be abstractions and mysteries yet they must provide the focus of all the ceremonials and pageantry and expressions of respect for the state over which some chosen one of us must preside. Something is needed here, more luminous and intelligible than the charade of mock guardsmen strutting at the gates of Rideau Hall and the vague prospect of being invited to a garden party. There ought to be something here about the great land which is the environment of our national life, some reminder of the sense of brotherhood that brings us together in a confederation of many people and races, something about the compassion with which we share the good things of life and the fruits of our piece of the earth. Some may say that all these are self-evident and well-known matters. Of course they are. And it is the art and the purpose of the capital to give fresh interpretation and vivid expression to the aims in life that make this a good place in which to be alive.

16
Edge of the Wilderness

In the later years of life one naturally turns to look out upon the surrounding landscape. The working part of a professional life takes place in offices, city streets, airports, hotel conference-rooms, and other crowded places. After working in town, dealing with short-term, closed-in things, one instinctively heads for the country, for the long views, and the quiet contemplative rhythms of the natural world. This is a sequence in life as instinctive as sex or breathing in and breathing out; it's hard to explain something which is so much part of one's own nature.

What does it mean, to say that the shadows on the hills, the colour and smell of the woods, and the sparkle on the surface of the sea are wonderful and beautiful? What is the connection between the actual information received through the eyes, about the sky and the earth and the water, and the lyrical emotional response? Is this appreciation of beauty somehow connected with an intellectual comprehension that we are part of the ecological chain of life, on the earth, in the sky, and within the water? In the later years of life one has leisure just to enjoy the scene and one also becomes more curious about these connections which are so inexplicable.

Since I retired from a working job, I have returned to my earlier interest in the natural landscape, a theme that I put aside, in a professional sense, after my first few years in Canada when I moved into Toronto so as to become more closely involved in the affairs of housing and the cities. I have now come back to this subject in a period of great public concern about the threat to the natural environment caused by the swarming growth of the population and by the careless behaviour of urban people. We now know that our continued enjoyment of the land-

scape and the wilderness around us is going to depend upon our own
willingness to accept disciplines. We all have rights to a share of this
enjoyment, but these rights can only be effective within a framework of
law–the laws that protect the earth and what grows upon the crust of
the earth, the laws that protect the lakes and rivers and oceans and all
the living things in the waters. In the last few years I have had three
personal experiences which are, perhaps, worth recounting, because they
illustrate that this connection between the law and the enjoyment of the
environment occurs not only at the scale of national and international
affairs, but is also something that affects my personal enjoyment of my
surroundings, every hour of the day.

THE LAKE

I have now lived beside MacKay Lake for twenty-five years and treasured my good fortune in looking out upon this little fragment of the
natural world, now almost surrounded by a large city. It is smaller than
Thoreau's Walden Pond, which he described as 'a clear and deep green
well, half a mile long and a mile and three quarters in circumference, and
contains about sixty-one and a half acres: a perennial spring in the midst
of pine and oak woods'. MacKay Lake is only a quarter of a mile long
and three quarters of a mile in circumference, with an area of about
twenty acres. But it is our Walden Pond. There are fish in its deep water
and its shores are alive with creatures in the water, on the land and in
the air. From the windows of our house I look out upon the surface of
the lake as it responds to the changing winds and lights and moods and
seasons.

The west side of the lake is at the foot of the steep bank or rock cliff
that gives this village its name; here the water is twenty-five feet deep.
From this cleft the lake bottom rises gradually so that the eastern shore
is soft and wet and marshy and, under the reeds and waterside plants,
it would be hard to say where the water ends and the land begins. It is
this kind of aquatic-terrestrial margin that has the richest and most
fascinating ecological character, containing the whole inter-related web
of life; birds, insects, animals, and plants all depending upon one another's existence. Whether an appreciation of this fertile water's edge is
an aesthetic response to its colour and form and texture–or whether we
respond through an instinctive urge to protect and enjoy its ecological
integrity–is a mystery. Whatever the explanation of one's feelings may
be, those who live near the lake have known that this was a treasure we

all shared and enjoyed. And this enjoyment could be translated, we assumed, into material values; the environment was an asset that enhanced the value of our properties. There are only about forty houses from which the lake is actually visible but it is seen every day by all who live within the same neighbourhood.

It is now eight years since the morning when, with a sense of horror, we first saw a succession of dumptrucks enter upon this scene and deposit their loads right on top of this delicate marshy shore. The first to notice this event and express their alarm were my nearby neighbours, the Tolmies. Our first impression was that there must be some mistake. Why would anyone want to damage the very scene around which we had all congregated? But over the succeeding years we have witnessed a continuing procession of dumptrucks enter the view, tip their contents on the soft ground, slap their steel tailgates noisily, and waddle off to fetch more loads of fill. The wet, reedy shore of the lake has been submerged and crushed under a six-feet depth of miscellaneous material and our spirits have been crushed by our inability either to soften the heart of the person responsible for this devastation or to find any legal method for restraining him.

I suppose it could be said that this is a highly sophisticated neighbourhood. What other Canadian community contains such a large proportion of people with great experience in the higher echelons of public affairs, the law, and the professions? And yet we have seemed to be guileless and innocent in dealing with a problem of environmental protection, a subject now regarded as pre-eminently important to civilized societies.

The essence of the problem was that the owner of the strip of land along the eastern shore of the lake had previously developed and sold the residential properties behind this strip, encouraging the purchasers to believe that, between them and the lake, was a 'reserve' that would forever protect the water's edge environment. That anyone would really set about to bury this natural landscape under six feet of fill was so inconceivable that only one purchaser had obtained a covenant in his deed to protect him against any such eventuality. However, the shore of the lake was private property and the owner exercised the privilege of changing his mind when it was convenient for him to do so. He now proceeded to convert the edge of the lake into building sites. How this reversal could be prevented simply baffled the neighbourhood. The householders around the lake gathered together in consternation and hired a lawyer. The reeve and council of the village obtained legal advice. There was protest and lamentation. The aggravation had a social and political effect, as must happen when a community awakes to the realization that it has been too easy-going and good-natured in its expectations. The households around the lake gathered a larger support and formed the Rockcliffe Park Conservation Association which nominated candidates for the next municipal election, a revolutionary step for a community that had traditionally arranged who would be members of the council by acclamation.

The interested parties finally confronted one another in 1972 when the chairman of the local conservation association persuaded the provincial government of Ontario to invoke the powers of the Environmental Protection Act, to stop further damage being done to the margins of MacKay Lake. This was a new piece of legislation that had only been enacted in 1971, in response to the public concern for the pollution of rivers and lakes and the deterioration of the atmosphere that is breathed by people in cities. The authors of the Act had not visualized a situation like the damage done on the margin of MacKay Lake which was now to be put under the control of a departmental official called 'the Director of the Waste Management Branch of the Ministry of the Environment'. It was not at all clear how this official would be able to direct the owner in restoring the edge of the lake to a reasonable condition, but this became clearer when the case came before the Environmental Appeal Board which spelled out more specifically what was to be done: that the filled land was to be 'landscaped and planted in harmony with the surroundings, and that the remaining areas of the perimeter of the lake be permitted to remain in their natural state or revert thereto'; and that plans for doing this were to be submitted for the approval of the ministry 'three months from the date of the Order' and that this landscaping would have to be done within six months of the approval. In making this order the Appeal Board, under the chairmanship of Mr Irwin W. Pasternak, also commented:

There is no doubt that the handling of the environment is going to require a great many more legal innovations to shape and integrate forums and regulatory bodies into our newfound environmental concerns . . . the development of this legislation has reached a small plateau in the entire problem relating to our environment . . . it is the Board's opinion that the Government has the right by legislation to control the use of private lands so as not to be detrimental to the environment. Chopping trees on one's land is an example. It is perfectly proper provided it does not harm the environment to the detriment of the public, and that is the purpose of the Act under which this Board has been constituted. If a private land-owner should clear his entire property of trees and such property is so large so as to affect the ecology of plant life, then I think the Government can stop him by this legislation.'

Mr Pasternak's Board defended 'this small plateau' courageously. But it was to be expected that the case would be appealed still further, as this is provided in the Environmental Protection Act. And the case then went to the county court, before Judge Peter MacDonald in the Carleton County Courthouse on Daly Street in Ottawa.

At the table before the judge are half-a-dozen lawyers in their black waistcoats and gowns. In defence of a man's rights to bulldoze trees, smother aquatic plants, and otherwise injure the ecological balance of his own property, is the appellant's counsel whom we have already come to admire for his air of wounded innocence. In these wild accusations against his clients, he asks for fair play: 'Your Honour, my difficulty is . . . ' On the other side, in defence of the environment, are the lawyers for the village, for the Conservation Association, for Pollution Probe, for the National Capital Commission, and for the Ministry of the Environment. The rituals of the law are so old-fashioned that it's hard to believe that the aesthetics of the environment–such a contemporary abstraction– could have a fair hearing. The law is a serious hair-splitting business. The clerk of the court calls for us to rise for the entry of the judge and there is a hush as his private door is opened slowly by the judge's usher, a lean and elderly white-haired man in a black eighteenth-century costume. The appellant, the real-estate developer, is sitting in the back row, behind us; in order, perhaps, to enhance his moral status in the eyes of the judge he has brought, to sit beside him, a distinguished and impeccable Ottawa citizen, a former cabinet minister. But the effect is rather lost when a court official tells him not to put his arm on the back of the seat, to sit up straight. There is nothing very aesthetic about the whole scene, except the colour of the satin facings on the judge's gown: the colour of lilac blossom. The judge is a robust, practical, intelligent person who pays great attention to the precise meanings of words. He quickly displays his doubts that the Environmental Protection Act was intended to have anything to do with aesthetic matters. He is amazed at the suggestion that a man might not be permitted to cut down a tree on his own property–what more fundamental right could there be in a country where trees had to be cut down to make space for settlers and where the forest had to be cleared for building cities? The judge does not seem to take kindly to the suggestion made by the ministry's counsel: that we are

indeed in a new age and new law may actually contradict precedents.
What will the judge make of Mr Pasternak's phrase: 'this legislation has reached a small plateau'?

At first it seems strange and absurd that the determination of what I look at across our Walden Pond, at breakfast-time each morning, should become a matter of judicial decision. Aesthetic questions are fragile and delicate flowers that seem to wither in the cold and solemn light of the law. It seems like nonsense to defend my romantic appreciation of that little lake. But as I sit in the county court, listening to this discussion about the meanings of words, I know that it is a matter of morality that is being debated, both in the court and in the legislature where environmental law is enacted. The little lake is only a left-over fragment of the wilderness, a vestigial thing surviving in our midst, too small to be of any significance in the struggle for man's survival in his damaged environment. But we are surely right to think of it as beautiful and sacred, because of what it represents.

Sitting in the county court, the judge listens to the lawyers in their black gowns as they dispute small points of law. The judge retires to his chambers to ponder his decision. More transcripts are called for. More tapes. Months pass by. We wait anxiously. It is now almost two years since the dumping was stopped. Two springs have passed by and the weeds have tried gallantly to clothe the ugly obscenity of the dumping. Then comes the news. Quick–the envelope. The judge has found in favour of the appellant, with costs. It is a victory for the dumptrucks and bulldozers. Alas, our lovely Walden Pond!

THE RIVER

I have also been involved in an environmental conflict on a much more majestic scale, at Niagara Falls, a place that I have known at the two extremities of my working life. When I came to Canada in 1930 my first job in the office of Wilson, Bunnell and Borgstrom was to do some landscape planning there; and by a curious symmetry forty years later, my last working assignment has taken me back there as a member of board appointed by the International Joint Commission.

Niagara Falls is the classic example of man's capacity to smother and tarnish the very places he most admires. It's a place of majestic beauty and also a scene of humiliating follies. It's a prodigy to be spoken of in superlatives: the biggest, the ugliest, the most extraordinary. About ten million tourists visit the falls every year, a number exceeded only, I believe, by the number of people who visit Westminster Abbey. Both places have qualities of the sublime and the ridiculous, the sacred and profane. They both evoke thoughts about eternity, about life and death, and about the smallness of one's own life in the awesome scale of time. Westminster Abbey has too many white marble monuments to dead heroes, and Niagara Falls has too many waxworks exhibits in the style of Tussaud's Chamber of Horrors, specializing in assassinations and tortures. I have often wondered whether this preoccupation with the macabre at Niagara originates in introspective thoughts about a suicide leap into the plunging chasm of the falls: being alive and, in a few seconds, being dead.

In 1967 I was appointed to a board to study the American Falls. The invitation came from Arnold Heeney, an old friend, who was then chairman of the International Joint Commission. Perhaps my name came to mind because, that same year I had been the initiator of Rockcliffe Park's centennial project, the little community park where we had gathered together the circle of glacial boulders. This wasn't much of a qualification compared with the vast experience of my US counterpart on this IJC board, Garrett Eckbo, head of the Berkeley School of Landscape Architecture and a senior partner in a San Francisco firm of landscape architects. But I was known to have a special interest in boulders.

The reason for setting up the American Falls Board was that, in recent years, some quite large pieces of the cliff had broken away and been added to the great pile of rocks, called the 'talus', which lies at the foot of the falls; in 1933 there had been a big rockfall right in the middle and in 1954 a large slice of the cliff on one side had collapsed. The accumulation of rock had gradually diminished the vertical height of the waterfall. It was a bit of a tease to suggest, as some newspapermen did, that the American Falls was on its way to becoming just a pile of broken rock, while the Horseshoe (or Canadian) Falls maintained its majestic appearance. But the tease was enough to alert the US Corps of Engineers to start investigating the rock structure, to discover the likelihood of even more disastrous rockfalls. It has to be understood that the American Falls differ from the Horseshoe Falls in one very important respect: there is such an enormous volume of water pouring over the Horseshoe Falls that, as rocks break off the crestline there, the fallen rock is simply scoured out of a gigantic pot-hole and washed down the gorge, like the flushing of a huge toilet-bowl. Only one-tenth of the Niagara water flows over the American Falls, and this is not enought to have a scouring effect, so the fallen rock simply accumulates in a pile.

The Board to which I was appointed was confronted with the fascinating aesthetic questions: Would the American Falls 'look better' if the
talus rock were removed? Would it be a good idea to reinforce the cliff
so that no more rock would fall? Is there anything else that might be done
to conserve and enhance the beauty of the falls? One might well doubt
the feasibility of dealing with aesthetic questions through a committee,
particularly one based on engineering skills–and an international committee at that. In addition to Garrett Eckbo and me, the board consisted
of two joint-chairmen (following the pattern of all IJC operations), both
of them engineers; one was the incumbent regional commanding officer
of the US Corps of Engineers and, on the Canadian side, a senior official
of the federal Department of the Environment. The work-force for the
board's study was supplied by the US Corps of Engineers and by the
Department of the Environment.

It's not an easy thing to evaluate the artistic merits of a landscape and
there are even fewer criteria for making aesthetic judgments about a
waterscape or 'fallscape'. Some people have natural good judgment in
matters of taste; some don't. For instance, my mother and several of my
aunts were ladies of considerable artistic talent who appreciated all the
beauties of the world around them and did extremely competent watercolours that were hung on the walls of all the family drawing-rooms.
After a picinic they would sit down with sketchpads, watercolours, and
brushes to record and improve upon the scenery. I see them sitting on
the grass, each with an arm outstretched towards the landscape, one eye
closed and the head on one side. If they had been asked the aesthetic
questions about Niagara Falls, I think they would each have been able
to give a pretty good answer after, perhaps, half-an-hour of deep thought
with the head on one side. But if you are appointed to a board of the
International Joint Commission or you are on the staff of the US Corps
of Engineers, a great deal more is expected of you. And I came to
appreciate this. I also began to acquire a sense of urgency about a
situation that had been evolving for quite a long time. In the gradual
process of erosion by which the Niagara River has carved the great
gorge, the talus at the foot of the American Falls began to accumulate
somewhat later than the birth of Jesus Christ but definitely before the
time of William the Conqueror, and the position of the Horseshoe Falls,
at the head of the gorge, has moved appreciably but not significantly
since the time of Champlain. Even the most unlikely subjects can be
reduced to an orderly procedure and we were soon caught up by the
systematic competence of the US Corps of Engineers. Now and then the

US joint-chairman, a general, or his chief of staff, a colonel, would be off to Viet Nam and a new face would appear at the board table; but the system carried us along in accordance with the flow chart for money-spending and engineering work. Enormous quantities of paper began to accumulate in my study, at home, and had to be stacked in cartons picked up from the supermarket. Mail frequently arrived on a Sunday by special delivery and thus I had an incongruous sense of urgency.

In order to find out the real state of the rock structure and the talus pile, it was decided to 'de-water' the American Falls, an action which seemed to have a kind of biblical panache. It was easier than de-watering the Red Sea for the Israelites, requiring only a 600-feet dam across the American Falls channel. The official report of the board notes that 'practical closure was made on 12 June 1969, at 10:30 hours' and when the cofferdam was removed six months later 'the actual breaching of the structure took place at 10:43 a.m. on 25 November'. The cost of damming this part of the river was $445,412, but in effect it cost nothing because the American and Canadian hydro-electric power authorities paid for the use of the water that would otherwise have gone over the American Falls. This investigation revealed the whole pattern of deep fissures and cleavages in the rock and where the next succession of breaks would probably occur along the crestline of the falls, some evidently being quite imminent. It was concluded that engineering technology was quite competent to reinforce the rock structure and restrain this natural process of geological evolution. It was also concluded that it was technically feasible to remove all or part of the talus pile. So the aesthetic questions had to be answered. Should one interrupt the processes of geological evolution and change the face of nature, to make a waterfall 'look better'?

It was not enough to form an aesthetic opinion about the falls by making sketches and by putting one's head on one side to visualize what it would look like, if . . . So a large working model was built for us in the hydraulic laboratories of the Ontario Hydro-Electric Power Commission at Islington, in the suburbs of Toronto. In this model the American Falls were about 22 feet wide and 4 feet high and we were able to paddle around in high rubber boots and arrange the pile of talus rocks and appreciate a great variety of water-sculpture effects. From these experiments, there was no doubt in our minds that the most spectacular and beautiful effects occurred when practically all the talus was removed and the falls plunged their full height and then cascaded down the shelving bedrock into the river. Working on the model, setting the rock-arrangement then turning on the water and the lights so as to take photographs, was rather like making a stage-set and, as we looked at one of these arrangements, Garrett Eckbo with his romantic imagination said: 'It looks like the Temple of Osiris', and somehow the name stuck.

I'm sure that we were right in our judgment that, by removing the accumulation of talus, it would be possible to heighten the dramatic effect of the American Falls. And it could be argued that this would not be an intrusion upon the natural processes of change; in fact the process of erosion might actually be accelerated, if the buttressing effect of the talus-pile were removed, and there would be all the excitement of viewing further rock-falls.

But there was an air of unreality and absurdity about this intense preoccupation with the American Falls as they proceed through the centuries on their majestic course of geological evolution, retreating up the river at the dignified pace of a few yards in a century. Even as we looked at the falls, the man-made part of the scene was deteriorating. The freeways from Buffalo, New York, Toronto, Hamilton, Detroit, and Cleveland were bringing more and more cars into the Niagara parks so that there was no place to put them without hastily tearing up more grass and cutting down more trees. Just outside the boundaries of the parks, real-estate developers were threatening to erect high buildings to make a wall around the scene where there had been an open horizon. Already there were several long-stemmed towers with revolving restaurants perched in the sky and now there was to be a new kind of monster –the 'rotel', a lofty cylinder that would revolve so that every guest bedroom would have its turn at viewing the falls. This was a new manifestation of the macabre and the obscene at Niagara, with its displays of the bullet-proof cars of dead dictators and gangsters, the relics of assassinations, and the wax-work simulations of death and horror, surrounded by the faint aroma of burning fat from the pans of hot-dogs and french-fries, as it might be incense in some satanic cult. On the American side of the river, Niagara Falls, NY, had already crumbled into a slum and been razed to the ground and, on the Canadian side, behind the neat flower-beds in the parks and up Nanny Goat Hill, was nothing better than a honky-tonk strip.

Niagara is a grotesque comment on human nature. It's difficult to understand why places of extraordinary beauty seem to attract this corruption and decay. What has happened at Niagara is certainly interesting as an extreme and prodigious example of both the care and the abuse of the natural environment.

Our report to the International Joint Commission concluded that the full enjoyment of Niagara does not really depend upon the particular appearance of the falls themselves; the interplay of water and rocks in one form or another will continue to be magnificent. The enjoyments and the frustrations of the place depend upon the whole environmental setting, and this is in a state of emergency. We suggested that Niagara might be made into an international place so that the two nations together might protect the scene from abuses on both sides. We suggested that the falls should be regarded as the most dramatic feature of the whole continental water system of the Great Lakes and their tributary rivers, which are the basis of human and natural life and the sustenance of the great cities from Chicago to Montreal. The urban pollution that threatens the enjoyment of the falls is a symbol of the pollution that threatens all the waters of the Great Lakes–a threat that is the particular concern of the International Joint Commission.

THE SEA

Since Anne and I were married in 1951 we have spent our summer holidays in Nova Scotia. At first we were at Petite Rivière in Lunenburg County, staying in one of Rhoda and Malcolm Macleod's delightful cottages called 'Ship Ahoy', right on the edge of the sea. Here our two small children learned to clamber on the rocks, scramble on the seaweed, and move with the tide up and down the beach. Everything was on a childhood scale and to go half-a-mile to Rhoda's canteen for an ice-cream was an adventure. And the greatest adventure was to go up Dublin Shore to La Have where, in Himmelman's store, lobsters clawed stupidly at one another in the tank; and here another friendly Himmelman still plies the small car-ferry across the La Have River. It is a benign seaside place.

Then, in later years, we spent our summer holidays further from the edge of the sea, at Struan, the cottage built in 1902 by Anne's grandfather, William Robertson of Halifax. This is at the point where the waters of Bloody Creek run into the Clyde; on these two streams generations of the family have paddled their canoes far up into the interior wilderness of Nova Scotia and brought back tall tales of the fish in the brown water and the exciting navigation down through the rapids. This great wilderness of forest and barrens and silent lakes has a firm hold upon the imagination and heart of my wife and of her sister, Mary Puxley; as children they were led through it by Carl and Elmer Atwood who grew up there by the Clyde and could find their way through the trackless forest because this was their natural habitat. Carl's daughter, the poet Margaret Atwood, has expressed the strange ambivalence of fear and love for the wilderness. But I betray my English origin, and like Mrs Susannah Moodie in her part of the Ontario forest, I know that I am an alien in this strange, silent, haunting place; I could never feel about it the way Anne and Mary do, who knew it fondly as children.

So we looked for a place by the sea, because it is the sea that has a hold on my imagination and childhood memories: the rhythmic pulse of the waves, the infinity of horizon, the taste of saltwater, the spray blowing on the rocks, the fresh pattern of tide on the beach. And in the course of time we found the place where I am writing these words, by the Atlantic shore not far from the southern end of Nova Scotia. Here long forest-covered headlands stand out to sea, with deep bays in between them. I am looking across one of these bays, a distance of about three miles to the shore of the next headland that stretches out to the final reefs marked by an offshore lighthouse. When the Atlantic fog clears off and the sun sparkles on the surface of the water, you can see the Atlantic swell breaking and leaping into the air on these ocean reefs a few miles away, on Little Hope and Lesser Hope. But the ends of these headlands, more often than not, are shrouded in white sea mist and the foghorn speaks in low warning voice.

Here on the lee shore of our headland, the forest has been cleared to make a few green acres of rolling pasture, there is an old boat-landing, and up on the hill there is a cluster of four houses and their supporting barns. And, what is most important for us, there is more than a mile of wide sand beach between this headland itself and a projecting rocky point. At the back of the beach are grassy dunes and behind these a clean freshwater lake. There are dozens of such beaches along this coast of Nova Scotia, characteristically on the lee side of a headland where the tides deposit the fine sand that is continually being milled by the waves pounding on the land. These beaches have bland domestic names like Sandy Bay or Sandy Cove, giving a homely touch to the otherwise austere wilderness coast of forests and barrens and rocks.

For more than a century these four houses had been occupied by the families of fishermen, Scottish people of skill and enterprise and good education. They moved only a few years ago to a nearby harbour where the new highway, the truck route around the province, touches the head of the bay and so they can more easily market their catch of cod, haddock, and lobsters. When the indigenous fishermen's families were just going to move out, we came upon the place more or less by accident and, together with three other new families, we moved in. We were city people who had never known one another before, but we quickly discovered a great affinity that grew out of our love for this beautiful place. Inspired by our good fortune we had acted quickly and taken possession of this ocean-shore paradise without trying to foresee all the implications. It is understandable that an environment that had been adapted over a long period of time to the special way of life of those who had lived there, cultivating the land and the sea, could not immediately fit the lives of the immigrants from the city. I remember very well that the first summer we were there, in 1970, I suffered a kind of environmental shock and actually visited a doctor in Liverpool who prescribed a pill to quieten my agitation and make me sleep more soundly. There were things that bothered me about the situation.

The first thing that rather overwhelmed me was my city man's instinct to tidy things up. There was an extraordinary accumulation of artifacts strewn in and around the barns and the sheds down on the shore where the fishermen had made their lobster traps, painted their buoys, and mended their nets. There were old motors and winches, abandoned farm implements, anchors, fish lures of many different kinds, odds and ends of boats and building material, yokes for oxen, and incredibly miscellaneous items of rope, twine, netting, and unidentifiable marine gear. Since about 1830, when the first settler family had pulled a boat out of the water by the Wharf Rock and made a clearing in the woods, their state of civilization had advanced steadily decade by decade; as they invented, discovered, and adapted new tools and materials, they had simply dropped each discarded item where they stood. They were excellent mechanics, leading an active life, and they were not prepared to waste time clearing up the deposit of their successive cultures. So I was confronted by a kind of archaeological task and found myself absurdly trying to sort out all this muddle, classifying and arranging bits of wood by size and hanging coils of rope on rows of nails. That is what my education had taught me to do.

The next thing that puzzled me was more essential to our enjoyment of the place. Our houses were set in a few acres of rolling green fields, a clearing that had been carved out of the surrounding forest, a little domestic oasis in the encompassing wilderness. The open views of the sea and the charm of this little cluster of houses on the hillside depended entirely on this open meadowland with its expanse of grass and the host of wildflowers along the fenceline path between the four houses. This open space had been made and had been maintained by our predecessors for practical and productive use; on part of it cattle and sheep had grazed and part of it had been mown for hay. But already, on some of the land that had not been used recently, the alders had begun to grow in and spruce seedlings had begun to appear along the edge of the woods. The surrounding wilderness is very much alive. It looks in, it moves in, it submerges.

In fact some of the past intrusions of man upon this scene have been obliterated like incidents almost as insignificant as footprints on the beach below high-tide line. Within the memory of the local fishermen, we are told, there was a road which is now submerged by the sea; the beach has shifted back a few hundred yards. This road used to serve another little outlying group of families behind the rocky point, at the far end of the beach. Here in the dark mystery of the forest that has closed in upon the clearing they made is a little cemetery recording the lives and deaths of those whose voices were once heard in this now silent place. Some of the men were lost at sea and, amongst the hewn stones with old-fashioned Victorian names, are some sad little fragments of rock to mark the graves of infants who didn't survive in this far place, surrounded by the misty wilderness and the sea.

In this part of Nova Scotia, along the edges of the wilderness, there are quite a few of these remnants of settlements that did not survive. A depression in the ground and a pile of stones are all that remain of a house long since burned down. Some flat stones carried the sill of a barn. For two or three generations there was an opening for human life and then the dominating forces of nature closed in again, the people and their ambitions forgotten.

Well, I think for the present we have warded off the problem. The land around the house is clean and tidy, the hay off the meadows provides feed for Gladys whose milk we enjoy in the summer, lambs are born at Eastertime in the field just in front of the house, and the edge of the forest is held at bay. But the ecological, aesthetic, and landscape problem still remains. How can such a property be converted from a productive use to a pleasure use, with its open spaces intact? What grasses, plants, and ground-cover should be growing in these spaces and what kind of mechanical equipment could be used to cultivate and protect the land? The beauty of the scene is, of course, in the contrast between the sweetly disciplined space of the human settlement and the wild ungoverned forest around it.

Not long after we settled in, a more formidable problem appeared: the vulnerability of the beach. The beach had no productive value for the previous fishing community, but for us this edge of the sea is the greatest treasure of all. There is a path through the woods down to the beach and, as you emerge on to the shore where the blue irises flower so magnificently in June and July, there is usually a row of shoes on the sand by the dune grasses. There are pairs of large male shoes, some sandals, and some very small shoes. We take off our shoes when we reach the shore to enjoy the freedom, the cool touch of the saltwater; and perhaps there is a bit of respect for holy ground. The row of shoes is also a kind of accounting system: you can tell who has started out along the shore. No words can describe the pleasure we have in this place which changes subtly in the mood of each day, with the state of the tide and the wind and the sun and the fog. We seem to enjoy it just as the birds do: the contemplative gulls who stand broodily at the far end of the beach by the little river we call the Rubicon, the terns who wheel around the cove with much talk and then plunge suddenly into the water, the sandpipers who scamper up and down the wet sand at the edge of the wave-wash. This is the interface of land and water, full of creatures in both elements, the margin between the organic and the inorganic creation. Those are my children and grandchildren scampering and floundering in the waves. Peter seems to have a special power for summoning our friendly seal to appear, sticking his neck haughtily out of the water to observe us all. Debby and Jenny called him 'Lloyd', but as we have come to know him better he has been raised to the title of Lloyd Privy Seal. By the stream there are early morning deer tracks and in the freshwater pool behind the cove is an imprint of small Jocelyn's bottom where she sat placidly amongst the tadpoles. On the offshore rocks called The Ledges, which throw the surf into the air in a storm, stands a company of tall-necked cormorants watching the approaches to the shore, now and then one of them taking off on a long scouting expedition with his broad wings skimming the wave-tops. And there, in the clearing on the headland, are our own houses looking out on this wonderful scene.

After we had bought the houses and the cleared land on the hill, a considerable stretch of the beach still remained in the hands of the real-estate syndicate who had acted as middlemen between us and the previous fishermen owners. This was a group of three Nova Scotian businessmen who had seen the opportunity for a quick profit in buying from the out-migrating fishermen and selling to the in-migrating city people, the 'foreigners'. One Saturday afternoon, one of this syndicate arrived on the beach with his family and a large camping trailer. The teen-agers raced their motor-bicycle and the jeep up and down the immaculate stretch of hard sand, scattering our small grandchildren and the brooding gulls; and after the weekend, the imprint of this sinister visit was left on the dune grasses and on our minds. We learned that it was indeed the intention of the syndicate to divide the length of the beach into cottage lots, for this was the cream of the profit in the real-estate turnover. We had been innocent in supposing that local businessmen would have any sense of concern for this beautiful part of their province.

We invited the syndicate to come and join us in conference and they arrived one morning, three Nova Scotians who had prospered from the resources of their province; one in lumbering, one in real estate, and the youngest of the three a builder in the Annapolis Valley. There were three pairs of us 'foreigners', husbands and wives. We gathered in front of our house where you look out across the bay and along the whole sweep of the beach. Instinctively we sat down in a circle around a large flat rock that heaves out of the ground there, and somehow the meeting had a kind of ancient solemnity, as if we were making history. (In fact the situation reminded me of an illustration by C.W. Jefferys in a pictorial history of Canada: 'Champlain lands on the shore and holds parley with the Indian leaders'.) Once or twice during the discussions the three members of the syndicate would withdraw to the other side of the house to discuss a point and then return to make a statement. We were trying to discover some common ground between ourselves, as environmentalists, and the profit motive of the syndicate. It would be a foolish thing, we argued, to build cottages on the beach because this would destroy the principal treasure of this whole place, its spiritual quality, and its dollar value. At all costs the beach should be conserved in its immaculate and natural state. People who want to live nearby and enjoy the beach should build houses in a clearing up the hill where water can be taken from wells and the effluent absorbed into the ground and where there is a good road. Cars should not come near the beach which is a place to be walked upon respectfully. The tidal beaches of our country are not private property; they should be conserved for everyone's enjoyment.

We argued long and passionately for some tolerant middle position. But without success. No solution appeared and the 'foreigners' had to club together to pay the price for protecting this beautiful piece of Nova Scotia's heritage. I use the word 'foreigner' here ironically, because this is the word that has been employed in reference to the sale of maritime seashore property to a new generation of immigrants. In truth, it is the native Maritimer who has turned his back on his own land, and others have adopted it, with love and admiration.

234   The seashore is where the wilderness of the ocean meets the wilderness of the land. Sitting in a circle on the grass, like Champlain meeting in conclave with the Indians, we tried to answer the questions: 'Whose territory is this? Who is to possess it, with the right to destroy it for his own profit? Who is to protect it and care for it?'

17
Epilogue

People who write autobiographies traditionally tell about their parents in the first chapter because that seems to be the obvious place in the sequence. But the truth is that only in the later years of life does a view of one's parents come clearly into focus. While parents are still alive it is not possible to have a detached point of view because one is still instinctively preoccupied with the process of separation and of discovering one's own individuality. It is only after they have gone that one begins to perceive the whole shape of their lives, in an objective way. And it is only when the shape of one's own life approaches completion that one becomes really inquisitive, in seeking comparisons with the life-experience of the previous generation. I know that everything I have done, all my reactions and responses, has originated in my own nature that came to me out of the genetic stream of family life in which I am but a passing episode. As individuals we are each unique mixtures of an inheritance. And each of us is exposed to a special sequence of environmental situations of a geographical, social, and economic kind. Why do I act the way I do? What impulses do I receive in the echo-chamber of my mind? Why am I both conservative and radical, both timid and brash, both stupid and imaginative? Who am I and how did I get that way? I can say without exaggeration that in recent years hardly a day has passed without some thoughts of my father and mother and brothers, as I have sought to understand myself and all the events of life that I look back upon.

I'm not interested in the lives of my parents for dynastic reasons or because they were important or respectable or extraordinary in any way. But, in them, I see myself confronted by situations in life, cherishing

236 ambitions, fearing failures, loving and remembering. The situations that they faced and the environment they lived in were quite different from what I have experienced; but I can recognize in them the very same kind of responses and reactions that are in my own nature. And that's what makes them interesting to me now, more than they have ever before.

My mother and father both died during the last war, both a little more than eighty years old. I had last seen them in 1938. They are buried in Harborne in the village churchyard that they knew so well, with the bells ringing the old changes in the tower. The inscription on the stone records that their first-born, Daphne, died in infancy and is buried here. And beside them, too, is Ada Watkin. Ada had come to our family to help look after the children when I was born and she was just a girl. She became part of the family and devotedly looked after my mother and my father through their final loneliness, and survived them by ten years. In the churchyard, too, on the brow of the hill where you can see a long way over the rolling green landscape to Clent and Tom Knocker's Wood, is the stone cross on which is my brother Christian's name, with the names of all the others who knew this place and didn't come back to it from the first Great War.

The monuments and the placid English scene suggest a lovely, quiet stability of social history. And the people who walked along the path from the lychgate to the church doors, who remembered my father and mother as highly respected members of the church and the village community, would corroborate this tranquil impression. Was not Mr Carver a churchwarden, the chairman of the church schools, the treasurer of the local golf club, the patron of the cricket club, an honoured commander of the local special constabulary, a kind, polite and dutiful citizen? Did not my mother regularly come to the early morning communion service, did she not visit the sick, belong to the ladies' book club called 'Calliope', and have an extraordinary talent for communicating with people of all kinds, an intellectual without a trace of snobbishness? And yet the truth is that neither of them really belonged to this environment at all and they lived out their lives as strangers in this place, and it tore them apart. To the outside world neither of them ever revealed the anguish in which they lived. Ada told me that in his later years, when my father went into the bathroom every morning to shave, she would hear him saying to himself, over and over again, slowly and vehemently, 'Damn. Damn. Damn.' He looked on his life and what he had done, with dreadful regrets.

My father and mother were both born in Gibraltar, where the Carvers and Creswells had known one another over several generations. Because of the complementary qualities in their natures, Carvers and Creswells seem to fascinate one another and there are at least half-a-dozen marriages between the two families. The convexities of the one seem to fit into the concavities of the other. The Carvers are possessive and conservative; they are worriers and it has been noted that in their later years they are subject to a kind of morbid melancholy. The Creswells, on the other hand, are light-hearted, witty, adventurous, and sociable; they don't get old in mind. So a combination of these qualities seems likely to fulfil the expected mutuality of a happy marriage, one set of qualities sustaining the other. But there is also the difficulty that one of the partners may not be able to travel the same road as the other, and that can be disastrous. I think that is what happened to my parents. The qualities that my father so much admired in my mother, her lovely effervescent self-confidence, simply became unattainable to him and these very virtues became irritants.

The earthly qualities of the Carvers have an environmental origin. For some generations the Carvers had lived at Ingarsby, not very far from Leicester; it is famous fox-hunting country and the hunting memoirs of the Quorn in the 1870s and 1880s record that the hunt often met at Ingarsby, the old stone farmhouse, and hunted over my great-grandfather's fields and fences, and that 'Carver's Spinney' was a landmark for many a sporting run. (In the summer of 1970 I went with my family to look at this ancestral house but was told, at the gateway, that the present occupant, a Mrs Gemmell, was exhausted from appraising puppies who were candidates for next season's pack of hounds for the Quorn, and a visit would not be convenient.) There is a traditional association between hunting and sherry, and early in the nineteenth century some of the Carvers had settled in Lisbon and in Gibraltar, to do business in Morocco and in Jerez. At about the same time, in the 1840s, Edmund Creswell (known in our family as 'Exodus Edmund') had been appointed inspector of post offices in the Mediterranean, stationed in Gibraltar. In an unusual civil service succession, this position had then passed on to his son, a second Edmund, and then, in an ever more remarkable succession, the appointment passed to his eldest daughter, my Aunt Maggie. So Carver and Creswell children grew up together at Gibraltar.

When my father and mother were born in the early 1860s, Benjamin Carver and his six children lived in a beautiful but not very large Spanish house called the Palace, and the Creswells, with a dozen lively children, lived over the post office. It was a high Victorian period, the British Navy sailed the oceans of the world, and most of them called at Gib on the way back and forth. There was a military band in the Alameda Gardens, there were balls on the illuminated decks of the fleet, and there were large picnic parties up into the cork woods beyond San Roque, the girls riding on donkeys and falling off with appropriate hilarity and dramatic effect. There was always the interesting possibility of being captured by brigands as one went deeper into the Spanish hills and there was the certain knowledge that all native Spaniards and Gibraltarians were smugglers. (When I visited my Aunt Maggie in the 1920s, she lived in the little village of Campamento across the bay from Gibraltar; her gardener was known as Alejandro the Honest Smuggler, and it was a common occurrence for my aunt to go to San Roque to bail him out.) Altogether it must have been a glorious place to live, in Victorian days. And that, in spirit, is where my mother lived for the rest of her life.

The Carver business prospered and shifted its attention from buying port and sherry for the hunt, to exporting cotton goods to Morocco, and finally was transformed into Carver Brothers Limited, buying raw cotton in Egypt and importing it to the Lancashire mills. So my grandfather Benjamin as senior partner in the family firm, had to take his family out of the Mediterranean sun, out of the Spanish garden of the Palace, and the family moved to a rather solemn and dreary mansion in the suburbs of Manchester. This happened when my father Frank, the third of six children, was seven years old.

My grandmother Emily's reaction to this abrupt change of environment is recorded in a long and intimate correspondence with her dear friend Marianne Paterson in Gibraltar; the letters, which are in my possession, are infinitely touching in her yearning for the friendship and warmth of Gibraltar and a reluctance to admit how much the fog of Manchester subdued her spirits. But she faded away and just before she died at the age of thirty-eight she wrote to Marianne:

There never was such a backward Spring. It makes me long for the Rock. I have been so very unwell and weak and I sit and think about the dear home there and long for all of you. I have no near neighbours and do not make friends easily and all my old friends are too far away.

She died in July and, two years later, Benjamin wrote, in a letter to Marianne:

Last Sunday the 28th. was a sad day for me. We all visited the grave after morning service. It seemed incredible that I had lived for two whole years without my darling Emily–but then I considered there were two years less to be without her. The children are all blooming and make up a happy party just now, as we have my sister Martha and three of her belongings staying with us, so we make up just a dozen at table.

But I think that my grandfather Benjamin was a silent figure at the table. Martha, by the way, was married to Tom Creswell and I like to think that her children supplied some of the Creswell effervescence to lift the mood of the bereaved family.

But if it was a shock for Benjamin, wrapping him in a melancholy that partly cut him off from his children, it was certainly a disaster for nine-year-old Frank (my father), a shy, quiet boy, desperately needing affection, too easily discouraged, interested in books, and, like so many introspective children, finding solace in the affection of the dogs and the horses in the stableyard. Amongst my family memorabilia is a school report on Frank at the age of sixteen, written by Dr Guy, the headmaster of Forest School, on 19 March 1877, with all the kindly perception of an old-fashioned schoolmaster: 'Has worked very well. Euclid especially good. Sometimes disheartened and so loses places'.

After leaving school Frank worked for a time in Liverpool but never quite fitted into the easy-going Lancashire ways; for years afterwards he was humiliated by the recollection of an overheard comment: 'Here comes that bloody freight-clerk.' Not to be wanted was a fearful feeling. And he often suffered from a bilious stomach. So when he was twenty-one his father sent him off on a trip to Gibraltar and the Mediterranean and this did him a world of good. In Gibraltar he stayed with Marianne and was welcomed affectionately by all the Creswells at the Post Office. He was made to feel like a long-lost cousin. He visited The Palace where he had been born and felt his mother's presence in the Spanish garden; he took the Creswell girls out to two balls and altogether enjoyed a sense of importance such as he had never known before. Then he toured the Mediterranean like a young milord, found many friends and relations in Alexandria and Suez, and went on to Constantinople and visited the Crimean battlefields in the company of Major Walker of the 22nd, from whom he borrowed two pounds when he got a bit short. It was altogether a light-hearted trip and he enjoyed the people and the absurdities of Victorian travel.

s.s. Minerva at Jaffa 10th May 1883

MY DEAR FATHER, . . . I took a tramp along the Jerusalem road to-day, the first part runs thro' orange groves & Lemons & Olives & of course cactus, after that it gets into open country with a ridge of undulating hills in the distance beyond which Jerusalem lies. There are any quantity of Priests & Padres knocking around here. We have the Greatest Swell in Palestine on board, the boss of all the Churches here. Also an Archbishop from Servia–however they are as dirty in their habits as all the rest of them. It is a great trial to sit at table with some of these fellows, their object seems to be to make as much use of the knife as possible & they shovel everything down their throats with that weapon; the Russians are horrible in this particular . . . I am rather struck with the following which I find written up in the Saloon under the head of 'Internal Regulations': 'Passengers having a right to be treated like Persons of Education will no doubt conform themselves to the rules of good Society by respecting their fellow travellers & paying a due regard to the fair sex'.

I have read it over several times but can make little out of it . . . Yrs very aff'ly,
FRANK

This Mediterranean trip and the good impression Frank had made on the Gibraltar families revealed an unexpected savoir-faire and as soon as he had got back to Manchester a new and much more exciting project came up for discussion. With his evident enjoyment of travel, perhaps the shy young man would blossom and expand in the great open spaces of America. There was immediate correspondence with a family connection in the Middle West and, on 22 February 1884, Frank sent his family a telegram to say that he had arrived safely in New York and was on his way to Le Mars, Iowa. His father had given him five thousand pounds with careful instructions that what he didn't need immediately was to be invested so as to provide a basic income. As soon as he arrived in Le Mars this good news seems to have got around quickly. Only a month after arrival, Frank wrote his father:

I have decided to put some money into Kingsley. I drove over there yesterday with Chapman. It is 24 miles away & is *the* growing town of these parts. Last August there was nothing there at all & now they have Hotels, Banks, stores, Saloons & lots of dwelling houses. Oldfield the Banker there is looking out for tenants for me for stores and dwelling houses. I was very anxious to go into the Ranch but as this will not be started for some time yet I put the money into Kingsley.

I think that Frank's first euphoria of confidence in Oldfield the banker must have faded rather quickly and as the prairie grass became green in the spring, he decided to take a fling at buying stock, herding them on the open prairie and making a quick turnover in the fall.

MY DEAR FATHER, . . . I went to Waverly on Monday and got back here late on Friday evening having had about 30 hours with the cattle train. We bought 240 head for my own acct., . . . 200 being steers and the rest heifers. We got them into 5 cars on Thursday at 4.30 p.m. At 2 o'clock in the morning Weir thought the train was going to stop and jumped off. It increased its speed and he missed it so I had to look after the whole 5 cars myself. I think it was the hardest work I ever had in my life. 48 in each car was a crowd & as the poor animals kept falling down from exhaustion & want of food & water I had to keep diving through the car roofs and lugging them up again to prevent them being trampled upon. I was on the car tops all Friday except when inside. One heifer died (I may say in my arms), another died next morning. The next day they were all labelled in Chapman & Rickards yard. . . . On Sunday four of us started off with a herd of 313 head for the Big Sioux Valley about 22 miles where the cattle are to be herded all summer. We only got 7 miles that day as the cattle were so weak they could not get on. . . . This cattle shipping is cruel work but one must take the good with the bad. I hear yearlings, with Chapman & Richards' commission and other charges will stand me in 18 dollars apiece on average.

When three years had gone by and Frank had not made a fortune, I think his father became a little impatient. The two older boys, Arthur and Percy, had moved easily and confidently into the business world, Fanny had married money (Hubert Wilson was master of the Cheshire Hunt and lived in a big country house, with a butler and two lakes with swans on them), and Benjamin himself was quite a tycoon, able to go to the Riviera for the winter sunshine. Reading his *Manchester Guardian* at the club one day, with his after-luncheon glass of port, Benjamin was struck by a glowing article extolling the real-estate prospects in Florida where many English gentlemen had watched their orange groves turn into gold while they sat with their feet up on the verandah rails. He wrote to Frank that night and urged him to go down and look the situation over. In Le Mars the winter was coming on and Frank was ready for an adventure in the south. He went to Orlando, Fla., and immediately found himself accepted into a hospitable society of well-heeled young Englishmen and Philadelphians; they lent him their ponies, made him a member of the club, and obviously liked his modesty and good looks. But Frank thought the landscape of sand and pinewoods was boring and not a patch on the open prairies of the northwest and, in weekly letters to his father in Manchester, discredited the whole notion that there was any money to be made in orange groves. So in the spring he headed back to Iowa, looking forward to joining his partner and taking all their stock of cattle and their horses into new green country in the valley of the Big Sioux.

All this is recorded in the letters which my father wrote home, and which are now in my possession. But at this point the correspondence ends and a cloud of mystery hangs over the most fateful change in his life. There is a complete black-out of information. All I know is that, when he was twenty-eight years old, he was on horseback in the exhilarating environment of the midwest United States, and only a few years later he is in the suburbs of an English industrial city, going every day on his bicycle over the hill into the Black Country, to a job for which he had no apparent taste or training. What is the explanation? And how could it be that my father died without my having even asked him for the explanation? That he would have sought out and married one of the Gibraltar Creswell girls is understandable, because her natural effervescence, optimism, and sociability would have sustained him in a period of disappointment and sadness. Evidently something had gone wrong and there was an abrupt turning in the direction of his life.

To fill the information blank one looks for little scraps of evidence. That my father loved the big sky and the manly freedom of the Middle West in the 1880s I have no doubt; for when we were children, he kept in a drawer in his bedroom the wide-brimmed hat, the riding-boots and rough fur gloves, and the Colt revolver that he had carried in his holster. There was no doubt that these were the treasured insignia of his real self. Could he have abandoned his life in the United States simply because he had failed to fulfil the materialistic expectations of his father, Benjamin? There is certainly evidence of this paternal loss of confidence; the inheritance did not flow to our branch of the family. But there is a more romantic explanation that I have often thought about, arising out of a small episode that occurred in 1938, the last time that I saw my mother and father. Mary and I were on a brief visit to England with two-year-old Peter. One evening we went out to a theatre and my father had waited up to see us on our return. I went upstairs to reminisce with Ada, as I loved to do, and after about an hour went down to the sitting room and there discovered my father and Mary sitting together and talking quietly. Hand in hand. It was an altogether extraordinary and astonishing and touching thing because I had never seen my father express affection in an open way; he was so shy, reserved, and withdrawn, and he hardly knew Mary. Did Mary's middle-western voice and natural friendliness recall for him some other person he had loved? She certainly touched man, 'sometimes disheartened and loses places'.

My parents went to live in the suburbs of Birmingham, a place with which they had no previous connection of any kind. Here, in a rented redbrick house, they brought up our family of four boys on whom they bestowed all their great capacity for affection and generosity. And in this place my father retreated into a deep privacy. Though ostensibly he played his dutiful part in the community, as a churchwarden, as treasurer of the golf club, and as chairman of the parish school, yet he was a stranger to everyone he met. He did not have a single friend who ever came to our home and he never entered anyone else's house. He was respected and admired as a good citizen, but as a person he was utterly reticent and aloof. He woke every morning to castigate himself because he had somehow withdrawn from the big adventure in his life and settled for being an observer rather than an actor. The happiness he depended upon was his love for his children and a deep understanding of English literature. With one of his children on his knee, sitting in the wicker chair in front of the drawing-room fire, he read to us and shared our enjoyment in *Alice in Wonderland, King Solomon's Mines,* and all kinds of imaginative adventures. He loved all the works of Dickens and knew the characters in his books as more real people, I think, than those who lived around him in Harborne. And he had a cultivated knowledge of Shakespeare's plays and language. This was the world of imagination and introspection into which he withdrew, and those who met him walking so alone and thoughtful on the streets of Harborne could never guess what was going on in his mind as he greeted them politely but perfunctorily, and hurried on.

Of course, I recognize within my own nature much of this same reticence and withdrawal and a tendency to be too easily put off. But my life has worked out more happily than my father's because of the other genetic strains that come from my mother, from the Creswells who are like yeast to the Carver dough. My mother was a buoyant, outgoing person, with an enormous interest in other people, great skills in friendly communication, and a certain flexibility of mind.

The Creswells are adventurous, pragmatic, and witty, unlike the Carvers who are cautious, introspective, and rather calculating. One gets a little glimpse of the quick Creswell opportunism, in the picture of Edmund, my mother's father, on a boat sailing out of Tilbury in the spring of 1843; he is on his way home to Gibraltar and it is always rough going across the ocean swell in the Bay of Biscay. The lovely girl on deck is Mary Fraser of Inverness, with the wind blowing her veil and an aunt hovering in the background. Edmund is quick to make his approach and, not long after he has said goodbye to them and disembarked at Gibraltar, he follows her to Florence, confronts the aunt, and marries Mary Fraser in a whirlwind. He brought her back to live over the post office in Gibraltar where they raised a large boisterous family. In later years they lived in Campamento, the little Spanish village on the sandy shore of the bay, and from here Edmund commuted to his office on horseback, riding his English bay mare Kate that had been bred for him by the Ingarsby Carvers. A schoolboy named Ricardo used to accompany him into Gibraltar on his donkey and, after breakfast one morning, Edmund gave a slice of bread to the donkey before they started. The donkey caught Edmund's finger in his mouth and chawed it. The finger should have been amputated at once, but the decision was delayed and eventually his wife had to take him to London where a surgeon, Berkeley Hill, amputated his arm above the elbow. Apart from the loss of his hand, the unhealthy wound of the donkey's bite seemed to undermine Edmund's health and for several years he made his post office rounds of the Mediterranean accompanied by Mary, his wife, or by Maggie, his eldest daughter. Both of them were charming and affectionate and good fun so that the post office responsibilities came to be thought of as a family affair. When Edmund died in 1877, aged only sixty-four, a cable came from the General Post Office in London: 'Apply for the post for one of the family'. Everyone assumed that this must refer to one of the boys, but a letter followed the cable explaining that application was to be made for Maggie who was then only thirty years old. This was the expressed intention of the postmaster general, Lord John Manners, who was reported to be greatly in favour of gentlewomen being given independent appointments. My Aunt Maggie was head of the post office in Gibraltar and Morocco for thirty years and was awarded the Imperial Service Order. As well as Maggie and my mother, there were two other sisters in the family. Katharine married into another Gibraltar family and had seven children, one of whom was Sir Philip Mitchell, governor successively of Uganda, Fiji, and Kenya. The other sister, May, exactly fulfilled my Oxford Dictionary's definition of the word 'Quixote': 'enthusiastic visionary, pursuer of lofty but impracticable ideals, person utterly regardless of material interests in comparison with honour or devotion.' She married a rather mousy-looking German protestant missionary and spent her life, mostly riding a donkey, offering protestantism to the

Catholic peasants in the hill villages of southern Spain; it's hard to imagine that there could be a more quixotic task than that.

If Britain in the Victorian age wasn't big enough to contain all the adventurous sons who went across the seas to found a worldwide empire, the Rock of Gibraltar certainly wasn't big enough for the boisterous Creswells; the six boys in the family took off, literally, for the four corners of the earth. The oldest, Edmund, became a colonel in the Royal Engineers and built part of the infrastructure of the Indian Empire, the roads and bridges and railways. My Uncle Willie, with a nautical beard and sparkling eyes, went to sea and became Sir William Creswell, founder of the Australian navy. John, my favourite uncle, married Kitty Towgood of Gibraltar, became a doctor, and was for many years the chief medical officer in Suez. The youngest, Uncle Fred, went to South Africa as a mining engineer, and was minister of defence in a Labour government. They all had a great capacity for enjoying life and for finding a place where they could 'do their own thing' with originality and independence. They scattered but they always thought of Gibraltar as their home and through a voluminous worldwide network of correspondence, largely conducted by my mother, they always remained a close and affectionate family.

My mother was already thirty years old when she left Gibraltar and married Frank, the shy, good-looking, solemn young man who had rather mysteriously reappeared from America; and she was thirty-five by the time they settled in the suburbs of Birmingham and their first child was born and died. After the sunny, gregarious family life of Gibraltar and Campamento, where everyone knew everyone else and there was a traditional conviviality, Harborne must have seemed a pretty stuffy and impenetrable place. There were three completely separated layers of society. The first wave of rich industrialists lived in large mansions tended by maids, cooks, gardeners and chauffeurs, surrounded by park-like gardens enclosed with high wooden fences and laurel hedges; they all seemed to be either relations or near-relations of the Chamberlain family (Joseph, Austen, Neville, etc.), they all went to a unitarian church as an intellectual élite, and they had their children's portraits painted, looking very good and pure. Their industrial employees, the working poor, lived in distant slummy parts of the city, with a small fragment housed in brutal redbrick terraces near the Harborne railway station; they took in washing, so that the short commuter line into the city was known as the Laundry Line. And the middle class, everybody else who lived around us, was the sober, hard-working, conservative bulwark of

England, chained to their desks, their ledgers, and their shop counters, as their sons and daughters after them would also be unless they had the wits to escape to the colonies before it was too late. It wasn't a very hospitable social environment to be dropped into and my mother, with all her sparkling skills in conversation and all her eagerness to find friendship, was, I think, quite baffled in her efforts to discover how she might fit into these solid social layers of the English midlands. So she gradually settled for another role in life. Far from the sunny skies of Gibraltar, marooned there in the grey climate of the English suburbs, she released all her immense powers of communication into an enormous correspondence with the family network that had radiated out from Gibraltar. Day after day, hour upon hour, wrapped in rugs and jerseys and shawls she sat in her little garden-house–which revolved, to catch whatever sun might penetrate–and wrote long letters to her sisters and brothers and their wives and children and friends and to anyone who would join in this worldwide network of communication that was, for her, the web of life. Her interest in all these people in India, in Africa, in Australia, and in other remote parts of the world, was intense and real. She would have loved to visit them all in person. And from time to time, throughout her whole life, she would return to spend a few weeks in Campamento to refresh herself at the heartland of the family.

I have wondered whether Gibraltar people of that period, living at the interchange of ocean traffic routes, had some special genius for this network of communication. There were four spinster sisters, the Footes, who had lived on the Rock when the Carvers and Creswells were there and who had come to live in London, still speaking with the lilting Gibraltar accent, a little like the Welsh. They were part of my mother's family-information-network, her London agents as it were, and when anyone remotely connected with our families was going to pass through London, there, sure enough, were Louie and Alice Foote waiting for them on the platform at Euston or Waterloo or King's Cross or Victoria, and in the taxi crossing London to the other railway station the two heads would be bobbing up and down in eager receipt of the small treasures of family data which would be stored away in the memory bank and selected items released through the mails through the following days.

When I was a child, this extraordinary interest in other people's affairs was simply incomprehensible, and I would sit listening to the flow of family talk with the same kind of pleasure that there is in listening to a stream bubbling and trickling over the stones. As I got older, as a young man, I developed a quite strong distaste for all this concern about other people's private lives and felt indignant that anyone would expect to know just what I did and where I went. That is entirely my own affair, I thought, and I would prefer to make my moves in life without feeling that the whole family is breathing down my neck. It's difficult enough, God knows, to discover what one should do and where one should go in life, without this dreadful accountability to others. At a certain stage in life this is a situation that often brings a coolness between parents and their adult children if there is not a mutual respect for the privileges of independence. Finally there comes a time when one can look both ways, in one direction to catch a glimpse of one's own self in the actions and responses of one's parents and grandparents and, in the other direction, to note small echoes of one's self in one's own children and grandchildren. That must surely be the most privileged vantage point in anyone's life.

I see myself as a person in a succession of generations, carrying within me many of the same qualities that I can recognize in my parents and that I cannot help passing on to my own children and so on down the line. I don't mean that we are the prisoners of inherited characteristics or that our responses to life are predetermined; each mixture is unique, we each build upon what we are given, and no one else has the same private feelings, memories, and self-realizations. But the qualities are familiar and constantly recurring in the stream of human life through generations, centuries, and ages. The possessors of these familiar qualities are exposed to different situations and changing environments from decade to decade, century to century. The social environments, the kind of society we live in, change a great deal and so do the physical environments, the landscape and the habitats and cities we make for ourselves. But people change less. The same kind of people with their constituent elements of gregariousness or shyness, self-confidence or anxiety, natural grace or awkwardness, and all the capacities for love, adventure, imagination, and their opposites–all these qualities continue within the people who have been exposed to changing circumstances as I look back through my lifetime and as others can see further back into history. One sometimes wonders what it would have been like to live in another century. I think I would have been a very useless person in Canada during the frontier period of the nineteenth century and I would also have found nineteenth-century England very uncongenial. But I have often thought that my particular 'mix' of qualities would have made me feel quite at home in sceptical, materialistic England of the early eighteenth century, particularly if I had been involved in shaping the English landscape; and though it may seem like a contradiction, I have an affinity to the mystical fourteenth century of mediaeval England, as far as I am able to judge from a little knowledge of the architecture and artifacts of that time.

We don't have choices about what century we live in, but we do have choices about where to live and how to live and we are also able to take part in changing the social and physical environments of our lives. Most of the satisfactions in life arise out of the way we do these things, and as I look back through the pages of what I have written here, I see that this is what it is all about. To be free is to seek and find a place where you can be yourself in your own way, using your own unique combination of qualities and appreciations. To be free is to express yourself through taking some part in shaping the social and physical environment within which you live.

> This is the Key of the Kingdom:
>   in that Kingdom there is a City
>   in that City there is a Town
>   in that Town there is a Street
>   in that Street there is a Lane
>   in that Lane there is a Yard
>   in that Yard there is a House
>   in that House there is a Room
>   in that Room there is a Bed
>   on that Bed there is a Basket
> In that Basket there are some Flowers:
>
>   Flowers in a Basket
>   Basket on the Bed
>   Bed in the Room
>   Room in the House
>   House in the Yard
>   Yard in the Lane
>   Lane in the Street
>   Street in the Town
>   Town in the City
>   City in the Kingdom:
> Of the Kingdom this is the Key.

Index

This book

was designed by

ALLAN FLEMING

with the assistance of

ANTJE LINGNER

and was printed by

University of Toronto Press